SCENES FROM A RO

DAVID LANE

Scenes from a Roman Century

1924–2024

HURST & COMPANY, LONDON

First published in the United Kingdom in 2025 by
C. Hurst & Co. (Publishers) Ltd.,
New Wing, Somerset House, Strand, London, WC2R 1LA
© David Lane, 2025
All rights reserved.

Distributed in the United States, Canada and Latin America by
Oxford University Press, 198 Madison Avenue, New York, NY 10016,
United States of America.

The right of David Lane to be identified as the author of
this publication is asserted by him in accordance with the
Copyright, Designs and Patents Act, 1988.

A Cataloguing-in-Publication data record for this book
is available from the British Library.

ISBN: 9781805262930

This book is printed using paper from registered sustainable
and managed sources.

www.hurstpublishers.com

For Franca, our daughter Clara and granddaughter Cassia
Romans by adoption
and in memory of my sister Elizabeth whose last foreign journey was to Rome

CONTENTS

NOTE

Chance treated me kindly by taking me to Rome as a management consultant in April 1972. It has continued to treat me well. In summer 1974, when my future threatened a return to London, Carlo D'Ottavi, an early Roman acquaintance, suggested how this could be avoided. And when consultancy work dried up in 1977—it later resumed flowing in different forms—the *Guardian* took my first speculative article on Italian business. The *Financial Times and The Economist* followed, and the Italian banking, insurance and finance federation kept me busy as a journalist until 2022.

Manager of the Servizio Affari Generali (general affairs service) at the Cassa per il Mezzogiorno, the development fund for the south of Italy, D'Ottavi was a key figure in my introduction to Italy, to Rome and its customs, to gestures (some vulgar) and words that are best not repeated in polite company, and to the Italian bureaucracy and to matters of politicisation and clientelism. My project at the Cassa was concerned with its vast paper archives in which the contracts archive of 30,000 projects alone amounted to around six million pages, and documents dealing with the revision of prices for 6,000 projects to a further four million pages. Other archives were also voluminous. Letters from politicians urging the acceleration of payments or variations to projects occasionally cropped up in files, but presumably such pressure often went officially unrecorded.

D'Ottavi oversaw the archives and was the liaison manager for my consultancy assignment. He was a young army officer when Italy signed an armistice in September 1943 and, rather than continue serving Mussolini, had spent a year and a half in an Austrian prison camp. D'Ottavi was a representative of the Confederazione Italiana Sindacati Lavoratori (CISL, the Christian Democracy trade union federation) and his smoke-filled office—everyone seemed to smoke—was usually also filled with other trade unionists and second world war veterans on the Cassa's staff. One of the veterans, a Neapolitan captured by the British in East Africa, then spent most of the war working on a farm. Another regular was a young representative of the Unione Italiana del Lavoro (UIL, a centre-left trade union) who took me to a viewing of fascist newsreels in a 1930s building on the Via Ostiense near the San Paolo basilica. These were propaganda films showing the Duce at work.

All who met in D'Ottavi's office were derisive and contemptuous of Mussolini, his regime and the Confederazione Italiana Sindacati Nazionali Lavoratori (CISNAL), a trade union federation affiliated to the neo-fascist Movimento Sociale Italiano, whose first secretary had been a parliamentarian in Mussolini's Fascist Party. Michele Mazzoni, my father-in-law, expressed similar sentiments to those heard in D'Ottavi's office and regularly complained that the state had stolen eleven years of his life, the time he spent in uniform after being called up.

That this book has been written is thanks in good part to many friends, colleagues and acquaintances who enlightened me about Italy and Rome but, above all, to the encouragement and tolerance of my wife Franca, born a Lucana, an alumna of Naples University, an economist at the Cassa per il Mezzogiorno and a teacher of Italian to an ingenuous young Englishman.

INTRODUCTION

WORDS ABOUT ROME

Shouting Romans make the sun dance

William Shakespeare, *Coriolanus*

"*Faticosa*—exhausting." Such is Rome, summed up in a word by an architect who worked for the city administration. And that is probably how many 40- to 50-year-old professionals experience living and working in the Eternal City. Yet Rome has another side which made the stress and hassle worthwhile for the architect, again in a single word: "*Bellissima*—beautiful." And those two adjectives, exhausting and beautiful, may also be among those most frequently used to describe the city by the millions of tourists who visit each year, spending around two to three days on average to traipse, often in energy-sapping heat, along asphalt or concrete pavements, or over *sampietrini* cobbles, between dimly lit churches, shadeless archaeological sites and crowded museums, palaces and piazzas.

In describing Rome, to "exhausting" and "beautiful" I would add "neglected"—*trascurata*. And this third adjective must also spring to the minds of many tourists as they walk carefully on uneven or broken paving, or notice part-completed but abandoned roadworks and out-of-order station lifts and escalators.

1

Graffiti's urban curse has struck visibly and widely. Yet the authorities seem powerless either to stop the spread or to rectify the damage of spray-paint vandalism. Efficient garbage collection and street cleaning appear beyond the decision-making and managerial capacity of the politicians and public servants running the city and the municipal utility tasked to do the job. Daytime appearances of rats at the Colosseum and other places in the historic centre are not unusual, and tourists visiting or staying in outlying districts occasionally have the opportunity to watch as wild boars scavenge among uncollected waste overflowing from roadside bins. The accumulation of what seem several autumns of fallen leaves lies compacted with other rubbish in many gutters, blocking drains and causing floods in heavy rain. Weeds grow unchecked beside lengthy stretches of pavement. Roads throughout the city are deeply potholed, and the white stripes of pedestrian crossings worn away. As for traffic enforcement, double-parking or parking on pavements and pedestrian crossings rarely incurs penalties. Large numbers of motorists treat speed limits and pedestrian priority as optional.

Almost every day, the Rome pages of Italy's two principal national daily newspapers, *Corriere della Sera* and *la Repubblica*, carry stories about the capital's problems. Photographs and letters from readers highlight issues that have been left untackled, often over decades. In March 2022, about four months after Roberto Gualtieri, a centre-left politician, was elected mayor, *The Economist* described his job as the least enviable in Italian politics. For the weekly magazine, Rome had been visibly deteriorating for years and the city faced "such a vast range of problems that its decline seemed irreversible" when Gualtieri began his term. *The Economist* didn't offer its suggestions as to when the decline began, and it is easy to remember the distant past as being better than it really was, but, despite social tensions and political terrorism, the 1970s and the first half of the 1980s return from memory as years of good administration, first under centre-right Christian Democracy and then from 1976 to 1985, when three Communist politicians wore the mayoral *tricolori* (green-white-red) sash. The arrival in July 1985 of a five-party coalition to govern Rome reflected the complexion of national government, where deep and widespread institutionalised corruption was rotting Italian politics at its heart.

Indeed, perhaps the capital's decline began with *tangentopoli*, the bribesville scandal that exploded in 1992 in Milan, or with the entry onto the national political stage in 1994 of the populist politician Silvio Berlusconi and his Forza Italia party. Or perhaps it coincided with his return to power after parliamentary elections in April 2001, when he led a rightwing coalition that included the neo-fascist Alleanza Nazionale (AN, National Alliance) to a crushing victory over a coalition headed by Francesco Rutelli, who had resigned as Rome's mayor to stand as the left-of-centre candidate for national leader. From June 2001 to February 2008, Rutelli was followed as mayor by Walter Veltroni, a member of the Partito Comunista Italiano (PCI, Italian Communist Party) until its dissolution in 1991 and subsequently leader of two successor parties. In parliamentary elections in mid-April 2008, he too would be defeated at the hands of a rightwing coalition led by Berlusconi.

For many left-leaning Romans, the election on 28 April that year of Gianni Alemanno as mayor was the moment that Rome started to crumble. If those Romans are correct about the city's slide, the blame falls on an extreme-right politician who in the late 1980s and early 1990s headed the young people's wing of the Movimento Sociale Italiano (MSI, Italian Social Movement). The direct predecessor of AN, the MSI was set up soon after the war by supporters and members of the fascist regime and Mussolini's Salò republic, the Repubblica Sociale Italiana (RSI, Italian Social Republic) established in September 1943 at Salò, on the western shore of Lake Garda in northern Italy. On the other side, many right-leaning Romans attributed the city's decline to Rutelli, Veltroni and Ignazio Marino, a well-regarded organ-transplant surgeon who, carrying the banner of the centre-left Partito Democratico (PD, Democratic Party), ousted Alemanno in June 2013.

Other Romans might forget the political colour of the city's administration and place the beginning of the city's problems thirty to forty years before the arrival of Roberto Gualtieri, to the time when Italy's public sector finances were slipping out of control. A key measure of a nation's financial health is the ratio of public sector debt to gross domestic product, and it worsened significantly in Italy during the 1980s. Having risen from under 40 per cent at the beginning of the 1970s to almost 60 per cent in 1979, the ratio soared, arriving within a whisker of 100 per cent in 1989. By the mid 1990s public sector debt amounted to around 120 per cent of gross domestic product, the result of national management of public spending and fiscal policy being badly out of kilter. It may appear paradoxical that while the country was indulging in a seemingly uncontrolled borrowing and spending spree and was increasingly submerged by debt, the fabric and public services of its capital were worsening.

Although its cultural patrimony is not directly threatened, Rome's plight is not dissimilar to that of Venice. With a wealth of architectural and artistic treasures, Rome is a historic city that needs large amounts of money both to remedy the deterioration that time, neglect, use and misuse have wrought on the urban fabric, and then to maintain it. Yet how and where can funds be found, and which parts of the creaking city should be priorities? Shouldn't the under-privileged suburbs, where the mass of less well-off Romans live, be at the front of the queue for public spending on road maintenance, the upgrading of waste collection, and investment in public transport and in other services and

4

amenities? However, the Roman economy relies heavily on income from tourism, so the centre, the sights and the sites must be cared for. But whether resident or visitor, seeing how Rome has been allowed to decline is both maddening and saddening. Even so, despite the evident degradation and the crush brought by large numbers of tourists, many parts of Rome's historic centre remain undeniably beautiful.

* * *

That Rome's history and its huge inventory of art and architecture have been, and continue to be, the subject of an immense number of books is unsurprising. One of the bookshops of the Feltrinelli national chain enjoys an enviable central Roman location. It stands on a corner of Largo di Torre Argentina and several major historic places lie within a radius of 500 metres: the baroque churches of Sant'Andrea della Valle, the Gesù and San Luigi dei Francesi among numerous places of worship, for example, together with the Pantheon, Piazza Navona, Piazza Venezia, Palazzo Farnese, Palazzo Altieri and Palazzo Doria Pamphili. The Centro Storico of Rome is compact, the city's architectural and artistic attractions mostly within walking distance of one another. Another Feltrinelli store is close to the main Termini railway station and the hotels on streets around it and on Via Veneto.

Targeting visitors, Feltrinelli has placed a large section of books about Rome near an entrance. Those in English include general guidebooks from Lonely Planet, Rough Guide and National Geographic, while visitors seeking something specific on Rome's archaeological treasures can turn to a far weightier volume from Oxford University Press.

Feltrinelli's Rome flagship store stocks works about the Pantheon, the Colosseum, the Forum and the Seven Hills, as well as on medieval Rome and sacred Rome and possibly almost as much as one could imagine of Rome's past, people and places, and culture from ancient times to the present day. Away from the section aimed at tourists, and particularly English-speakers, several metres of shelves on Italian history also hold books about Rome. The weight of all these works about the capital would make normal shelves creak, as the desk at which I write creaks under just four massive volumes, specialist or limited editions not available at Feltrinelli's bookshop on the Largo di Torre Argentina. While these are monsters of around quarto size that would buckle a coffee table and that are best weighed on bathroom scales instead of those in the kitchen, they are also elegantly produced, well written, handsomely illustrated, and interesting but scholarly books about Rome.

Legions of specialists and experts from various professions and historians of different periods have studied, researched and then passed on their knowledge, experiences and enthusiasms through their books, and their contributions to books, about the Eternal City. Even so, sometimes there are fresh angles and unexplored paths to follow. New facts come to light. New theories are expounded. Some writers find novel ways of looking at places and their pasts. And personal experiences offer pegs for books. On return from or during their Grand Tours, some aristocratic and bourgeois travellers in the eighteenth century wrote accounts of what had caught their eyes and captured their interest. Unsurprisingly, so did writers of that period.

* * *

"Now, at last, I have arrived in the First City of the world!" Dated 1 November 1786, these words open the account of his life in Rome that, drawing on memories, diaries, sketches and letters, the German writer Johann Wolfgang von Goethe wrote several decades later. The book was translated into English by W.H. Auden and Elizabeth Mayer as *Italian Journey, 1786–1788*. Goethe had two extended stays in Rome, from the beginning of

INTRODUCTION

November 1786 to the end of February 1787 and again from July 1787 to April 1788, visiting Naples and Sicily between his periods in Rome. His lodgings were at number 18 on Via del Corso, close to Piazza del Popolo.

Just ten days after those enthusiastic first words, Goethe mentioned that he had seen a great aqueduct while walking along the Via Appia to the Tomb of Cecilia Metella. The German writer wrote of the aqueduct, "What a noble ambition it showed, to raise such a tremendous construction for the sake of supplying water to a people." Whether in huge structures like the Baths of Caracalla, which Goethe probably saw on his way out of Rome that day, the Circus of Maxentius near the tomb, and the Colosseum, which he saw in the twilight when returning to the city, and in roads like Via Appia, ancient Romans exhibited great engineering skills. Armies of slaves had allowed those skills to be turned into the archaeological sites that have interested historians and archaeologists for centuries and are high on the list of attractions for millions of people who visit Rome each year.

Yet Goethe wrote about only one of the numerous baroque fountains in the city to which the aqueducts supplied water. And the one about which he wrote would probably be one that modern tourists visit least often of the city's best known and principal fountains. Goethe began his description: "In the square in front of San Pietro in Montorio we paid our respects to the powerful current of the Acqua Paola, which flows in five streams through the gates and openings of a triumphal arch to fill an enormous basin." Goethe was part of a group that included lovers of architecture who enthused about the fountain's columns, arches, cornices and pediments, which they considered reminders of arches through which conquering heroes passed on their return to Rome.

When the German composer Felix Mendelssohn arrived in Venice on his way to Rome he began a letter with the words "Italy, at last!" During his long stay in Rome, from the beginning of November 1830 to the beginning of April 1831 and then for ten days in June that year, Mendelssohn wrote to Goethe, to whom he had been introduced by Carl Friedrich Zelter, his music professor in Berlin, to whom he also wrote. Like many educated and cultured people of his period, Mendelssohn was a conscientious letter-writer. "Imagine a little house with two windows at number 5 Piazza di Spagna, which for the whole day is lighted by the sun's warm rays; the room is on the first floor where there's a good Viennese piano; on the table are some portraits of Palestrina, Allegri etc with their scores, and a book of psalms in Latin for composing the *Non nobis*; it's there that I live," Mendelssohn wrote on 8 November 1830, in his first letter from Rome to his family in Berlin.

He found time for composing, writing at the end of November that he had been working every day on the *Hebrides Overture*. In a letter on 20 December, he told his family that it was finished. Unsurprisingly, Mendelssohn also worked on his *Italian Symphony* and had made great progress by February. He wrote that "it will be the most enjoyable piece I have ever written, especially the final movement". Inevitably, however, his letters carried more about Italian music than they did about his own and, understandably, much of what he wrote was concerned with sacred music.

From Mendelssohn's long reports on his experiences in Rome, he clearly enjoyed being there. He was happy, in better health than he had been for some time and had energy for his work. He had a sense of tranquillity and joy, combined with a serious-minded approach to his composing. He was lodged comfortably. He had a valued circle of friends and acquaintances. He liked Rome's luminosity and the spring-like weather that the city mostly offered. He experienced the Eternal City at Christmas, during Carnival and Holy Week, and at Easter, and at the death of a pope and during the lengthy conclave to elect his successor.

He found immense interest in the artistic and historical treasures that were around him.

Yet Mendelssohn was often critical. Romans had a religion in which they didn't believe, they laughed at the pope and others in authority, they cared nothing about their past. And perhaps Romans have changed little since the composer wrote those words. Indifference to the pope's death was horrible, thought Mendelssohn, who had visited Saint Peter's when the dead pope's body was lying there, and saw priests standing around the catafalque chatting and laughing. Carpenters were at work and their noise prevented hearing the words of masses that were being sung. As for music, he listened to bad music, badly sung or badly played. The idea of having his own music played in Rome should be immediately forgotten. Orchestras are worse than you could possibly imagine, Mendelssohn told his family in one of his letters. Each violinist had his own way of playing and made his own decision about when to start. As for the voices, the best singers had fled the country and those that remained added decoration like that heard in backyards, and not nearly as good. He noticed graffiti on the walls of the Vatican loggias and that the Apollo Belvedere had been defiled in large letters and with emphasis: "CRISTO!" Roman practice evident to modern visitors has historical precedent.

Although Mendelssohn made no mention in his letters of any fountain, not even Piazza di Spagna's Barcaccia boat, he wrote about places that would be priorities for visitors in the twenty-first century, places to photograph and be photographed at: Saint Peter's basilica, the "luminous" Vatican, the "terrible" Colosseum, the Campidoglio, the Pincio, the "massive" walls of the Castel Sant'Angelo and even the Antico Caffè Greco on Via dei Condotti, the street that lies directly across the Piazza di Spagna from the Spanish Steps. Of course, Mendelssohn's world was music and his months in Rome were mostly concerned with that, whereas twenty-first-century travellers are equipped with lists from internet websites and with guidebooks suggesting what they should (or even must) do and see while in the Eternal City.

* * *

This book about Rome is not meant as a guide for tourists or as a learned work to explain details of Rome's history or artistic patrimony—there are enough of these on the shelves of Feltrinelli's bookshops. Instead, the aim is to provide a portrait of the city, looking at Rome through some of the important events that happened in the period of one hundred years from 1924 to 2024, and important changes that occurred during it. The book falls into two parts, Rome during the fascist *ventennio* (twenty years) and post-war Rome from 1945 to 2024, three chapters in the first part and four in the second. The seven chapters are prompted by places in and around Rome, and by events that left impressions on me during half a century of living in the city.

When the twenty years of fascist rule began is open to debate. Some place the moment at the end of October 1922 when Mussolini's blackshirts marched on Rome. Others on 10 June 1924 when Giacomo Matteotti, a leading Socialist politician and opponent of Mussolini, was abducted in Rome and murdered, Mussolini thwarting the opposition soon after and culling conservatives from his government. For Italians, its ending depended on where they lived: in July 1943 for Sicilians, after the Allies' liberation of the island, and in September 1943 for others in the south, when Italy signed an armistice with the Allies. Liberation arrived for Romans in June 1944 and for much of the rest of country in April 1945 when nazi Germany's army in Italy was finally defeated.

A major exhibition about Matteotti—his childhood and as a young man, his political commitment at a national level, his abduction and murder, and his continuing legacy—opened at the

INTRODUCTION

city authorities' Palazzo Braschi museum on 1 March 2024. The richly documented and authoritatively curated exhibition, which alas attracted fewer visitors than it merited, closed exactly one hundred years after Mussolini's thugs eliminated the regime's most effective opponent. This book's first chapter tells the story of that tragic event. The other chapters about the *ventennio* describe events and changes in the city during those two decades: a chapter about sixteen years of peace and a chapter about four years of war. Fascism continues to hold a certain interest, although perhaps more for those who were alive during the second world war or born soon after, and maybe that explains why public attendance at the Palazzo Braschi's exhibition was less than it ought to have been.

The era of Hollywood on the Tiber, the chapter that opens the second part of the book, is truly distant. Hollywood on the Tiber began just five years after the end of the second world war, when the war's damage continued to be seen and its costs felt. By the 2020s, the war had become for most people either vague memories or no more than lines in history books. The arrival of famous American film stars with their glamour and wealth helped to create an atmosphere of optimism. The possibilities of post-war were bright. Indeed, it was during the fifties that Rome, with its growth and expansion, participated in Italy's economic miracle, the subject of the second chapter in the second part of the book. The Eternal City had long attracted visitors, but numbers surged in the 1990s and looked to surge still further during the Jubilee Holy Year of 2025. Visitors are the subject of the third chapter on post-war Rome. Mass tourism poses problems and is a challenge for cities like Rome. The Italian capital faced challenges of a very different type and truly dark nature in the 1970s. Apart from the first bombings carried out by terrorists from the extreme right of the political spectrum in 1969 and the early, non-murderous exploits of the extreme leftwing Red

11

Brigades, I lived in Rome throughout the Years of Lead when, using explosives and bullets in a strategy of destabilising tension, extremists of right and left tried to push government, parliament and the nation in their preferred directions. Newspaper headlines that made shocking reading and television news broadcasts showing film clips of scenes of death and destruction return clearly to mind. A chapter on terrorism offers a bleak picture of some of the events that bloodied Rome during a particularly ugly period of recent Italian history.

Few of the millions of foreigners who visit Rome concern themselves with Italian politics, but perhaps the rise of the extreme right to become Italy's principal party of government should have worried Italy's foreign friends more than it did. With unfortunate timing, the centenary of the March on Rome had been preceded in September 2022 by parliamentary elections in which the Fratelli d'Italia party (FdI, Brothers of Italy)—a successor to Mussolini's Fascist Party through a chain from the Italian Social Movement to the National Alliance to the Popolo della Libertà (PdL, People of Freedom)—won the biggest share of the vote by a substantial margin. Its 26 per cent vote share made the party by far the largest in the victorious rightwing coalition, while the centre-left Democratic Party, which led a progressive coalition, obtained just 19 per cent. Such a result would have been unthinkable before the entry into politics of Silvio Berlusconi, whose accommodative views of Mussolini and fascism were widely reported in September 2003. (Berlusconi was prime minister at the time.)

The FdI's leaders did not and could not deny their party's roots in Mussolini's fascism. How could they? That's where their party came from. And they did not admit that the fascist regime was fundamentally evil and criminal, thereby agitating the political centre and left, which also wanted FdI's leaders to recognise that the defeat of nazi-fascism in 1945 brought the liberation of

Italy and a return to freedom and democracy, and that Italian partisans played an important part in this. That so many of the electorate voted for the Brothers of Italy may have been a sign of forgetfulness or of ignorance of the country's twentieth-century history, or a measure of approval of and yearning for Mussolini's ways of governing. The green, white and red flame (the colours of the Italian flag), the symbol of the Brothers of Italy, had been adopted by the Italian Social Movement in 1947. For some it represented the flame on Mussolini's tomb. Tablets set into numerous walls around the city commemorate victims of nazi-fascism. Fascist symbols, fascist buildings and the Mussolini Duce obelisk at the Foro Italico sports complex recall the capital's *ventennio*. The Brothers of Italy's three-coloured flame on a sign by the entrance to the party's offices on Via della Scrofa in the centre of the city is another item in the long list of Rome's reminders of its fascist past.

PART ONE

THE FASCIST *VENTENNIO*
1924–1944

I

THE KILLING OF GIACOMO MATTEOTTI

There's not a nobler man in Rome

William Shakespeare, *Julius Caesar*

Doers of brave or noble deeds. A greatness of soul. This is the stuff of heroes, and of Giacomo Matteotti. Unceasing and fearless in opposing Benito Mussolini and his black-shirted, club-wielding followers in the early years of fascism, the young Socialist leader earned his place in Italy's pantheon of heroes. "Show me a hero and I will write you a tragedy," offered F. Scott Fitzgerald, filing the thought among epigrams in a notebook. And the story of Giacomo Matteotti was a tragic one.

A problem for Fascist Party leaders, Matteotti became a target for their thugs. Fascist gangs had beaten up a dozen Socialist parliamentarians in the twelve months that followed Mussolini's March on Rome, the paramilitary coup through which Mussolini forced or bamboozled his way to power at the end of October 1922. And attacks and intimidation continued. The success of Fascist Party candidates on 6 April 1924, in the first parliamentary elections after Mussolini seized power, was due to violence, threats and fraud, said Matteotti, when he addressed parliament's lower house on 30 May. Those who packed the right of the chamber of deputies for the legislature's opening session owed their places to the bruising, bloodshed and broken bones that Mussolini's bullies had inflicted on opposition politicians and supporters, and on the electorate, during their brutal election campaign. The conservative national slate that the Fascist Party dominated had won 65 per cent of the vote and took 374 of the lower house's 535 seats, while Matteotti's Unitary Socialist Party took 24 seats with 6 per cent.

The elections were invalid, and invalid in every constituency, because Italians had been prevented from making their own decisions about how to vote, said Matteotti. "There is an armed militia that has this fundamental and declared scope: to support the current head of fascism as the head of government," he noted. Mussolini's militia had obstructed free expression of popular and electoral will. Before polling day they had prevented the collection of signatures needed to sponsor candidates, and the campaigns of opposition candidates had been disrupted by armed gangsters. Places where meetings were being held were invaded by club-wielding fascists. A Unitary Socialist candidate in Genoa had been beaten so severely that he had to spend eight days in bed. Armed bands silenced free and public debate. "We found ourselves in the condition that sixty per cent of our candidates were unable to move freely in their constituencies," the Unitary Socialist leader told the lower house.

Fascists had collected certificates that entitled Italians to vote and given them to trusted followers for voting. Some voted up to twenty times in different names. Twenty-year-olds voted in the place of sixty-year-olds. "Those electors who dared to vote found themselves joined in voting booths by fascists charged with ensuring that voting went the required way," said Matteotti. About 90 per cent of polling stations were run by fascists, with members of opposition parties excluded. Votes were counted by

Fascist Party members. Throughout most of the country there were no guarantees to ensure clean and fair elections.

"We recognise that in some places, in a few towns, cities and provinces, there was a kind of freedom on polling day. However, this freedom was limited both geographically and temporally, to places in the public eye and heavily populated areas where people might otherwise have reacted," Matteotti noted. It was not a coincidence that the opposition received votes in such numbers as to comfortably beat the fascists in places where freedom was allowed, for cosmetic reasons. Violence occurred in these places after the elections and not before. In Milan and Genoa, where the opposition performed best, the destruction of newspapers, vandalisation of buildings, and physical violence against people were particularly marked.

Near the end of his off-the-cuff denunciation of fraud and violence, Matteotti demanded the annulment of the elections that had consolidated fascist power in parliament. Matteotti knew he would be ignored. He made his statement to tell the country and the government that the Unitary Socialist Party under his leadership would provide rigorous and intransigent opposition. Addressing the crowded, noisy ranks of fascist deputies, he told them, "Every day you say you want to re-establish the authority of the state and the law. Do so, if you still have time, otherwise you will destroy the innermost essence and moral foundations of the nation." Matteotti knew he faced danger. He had seen the violence of fascist gangs. He knew the nature of fascism. Opposition to fascism required courage.

Scowling and with arms folded, Mussolini was in the chamber for most of the hour and a half that Matteotti spoke, the speech often interrupted by jeering fascists. Mussolini feigned indifference to the Unitary Socialist leader. He occasionally opened the newspapers lying in front of him. He tapped his fingers on his desk. Mussolini was irritated and worried. According to an account given later by Mussolini's chief press officer, when Matteotti finished speaking, Mussolini suggested, "After that speech, the man should be taken out of circulation."

We know about Mussolini's oratorical skill from recordings made in the 1930s when appropriate technology was available. Matteotti's speeches went unrecorded. Piero Gobetti, a radical journalist, described the Unitary Socialist leader's voice as precise and inconspicuous. It was seemingly made for parliamentary speaking, for making specific and uncompromising accusations using data and documentation against the fascists, as he had in local government when dealing with economic and financial matters. For Gobetti, although Matteotti was one of a handful of superior types in the Italian parliament, his public speaking would never have been able to sway the mass of ordinary folk. Yet, on the page one hundred years later, Matteotti's words seem impassioned and inspirational. Perhaps that's because we know what would soon happen. Giacomo Matteotti told his party colleagues, "I've made my speech. You must now prepare my funeral eulogy." The 39-year-old lawyer had less than a fortnight to live.

For Matteotti, the way to his home, in an apartment block on Via Pisanelli, about two kilometres from Montecitorio—where the lower house of parliament sat and still sits—was along Via del Corso, the street joining Piazza Venezia to Piazza del Popolo in a line cutting through Rome's historic centre. If he left by Montecitorio's front entrance, Matteotti walked through Piazza Colonna and past Palazzo Chigi, a building that was then the colonial and foreign affairs ministry but would become the prime minister's offices in the 1960s.

In the early 1920s, when he served in parliament, the Corso was a street of cafés, meeting places for writers, intellectuals, artists and politicians. And it was a street of bookshops, and family-owned and family-run shops for the wealthy, and the offices of newspapers and periodicals. Churches such as the Gesù e Maria, San Marcello and Santi Ambrogio e Carlo, and palaces like those that once belonged to the de Carolis, Verospi, Rondinini and Doria Pamphili families remained, but radical changes in Via del Corso's commercial fabric during the second half of the twentieth century would have made it almost unrecognisable to Matteotti. By the 1980s, notes the Touring Club Italiano's guide to Rome, the historic places that gave the street its former character had almost gone, replaced mainly by clothing shops. By the 2020s, the Corso had been stripped of elegance and transformed into the kind of charmless, busy shopping street that can be found in most large western European cities.

Photographs of the Corso in the years soon after the first world war show almost as many horses with carts as cars, a few bicycles, and people walking. There was also a tramline whose extension in the early 1920s allowed Romans to travel from Piazza Venezia along backstreets such as Via della Scrofa and Via di Ripetta, across Piazza del Popolo, through the Porta del Popolo in the Aurelian Walls and along Via Flaminia to the Ponte Milvio at the Tiber in the north. Perhaps Matteotti travelled by tram when he left Montecitorio after spending the morning on 19 June 1924 in Montecitorio's library. Or perhaps he walked home, under half an hour at a good pace.

Whichever the case, several matters weighed on Matteotti's mind when he returned home that June day. Institutionalised corruption was high among them. According to Giovanni Borgognone, a professor at Turin University, corruption soared to high levels in the 1920s. In *Come nasce una dittatura* (How a dictatorship is born), his book about the death of Matteotti and the rise of Mussolini, Borgognone wrote, "The ties linking business and politics had been progressively strengthened, engaging an ever increasing number of recruits within institutions." (Similar words would be used to describe the 1980s and early 1990s, which preceded the explosion of the *tangentopoli* institutionalised corruption scandal in February 1992.)

Matteotti often focused his frequent front-page articles for *La Giustizia*, his party's daily newspaper, on what he described as the accounting fiction of public sector finances under fascist government. Perhaps incompetence played a part, but abuse of office and corruption were evident from when Mussolini first put his hands on the levers of power. Dozens of decree-laws, to increase expenditure and authorise special disbursements, including large payments to the fascist militia and to shipbuilders, and two secret foreign payments, were among those Matteotti noted during Mussolini's first year as prime minister. Matteotti described how the fascists had made the state their servant, with the fascist council deciding what the government should do rather than the cabinet. As for a fascist militia that was paid by the state, this had taken over from an impartial police force, violating the constitution, which laid down that civil and military posts were open without discrimination to all citizens. Following the money has long been the path traced by opposition politicians, investigators and journalists trying to expose dirty government, and Matteotti had honed his forensic skills during more than a decade in the politics of Rovigo province in the Po Delta, which followed his work on the council of the small commune of Fratta Polesine.

Filippo Filippelli was the editor of a fascist newspaper called *Corriere Italiano*, whose first issue was in August 1923. An initiative of Mussolini, the newspaper was published for just one year, but during its brief life under Filippelli it was at the centre of a web of graft involving captains of industry, leaders in finance and the world of business, and senior fascist figures. There was traffic in military equipment that involved bribery, and another scandal concerned oil exploration and development licences in Sicily and in the Emilia region that Mussolini signed in April 1924. According to accounts of the affair, Mussolini's brother Arnaldo was one of the beneficiaries of a substantial sweetener that Sinclair Oil, an American firm, paid to obtain the licence.

At the beginning of June 1924, Matteotti was focusing on this. Despite the withdrawal of his passport, he had been able to travel to Brussels in April and then on to London to meet Labour Party and trade union leaders and like-minded socialist activists and intellectuals. In an article for *English Life* that was published posthumously in July, Matteotti wrote that he had found evidence of the corruption behind the licence. A speech he planned to make to parliament on 11 June would have exposed this.

Matteotti on fascism

Based on research almost one hundred years after Matteotti's death and drawing on a long-forgotten document, another work helps understanding of the early years of fascism: *Un anno e mezzo di dominazione fascista* (A year and a half of fascist domination), which was published in 2020 by Pisa University Press. Having overseen the semi-clandestine publication of his investigation and documentation of the first year of fascist rule, Matteotti decided to freshen it. During the following six months he collected more evidence of how Mussolini's regime was based on violence, intimidation, corruption, abuse of power and incompetence. He had completed this new book by early June 1924. According to a letter that Filippo Turati wrote to Anna Kuliscioff, Matteotti had told Turati that he would be unable to spend the evening of 10 June with him because he planned to correct the page proofs that would transform his record of a year of fascist domination into a record of a year and a half of fascist domination. Those proofs surfaced when the library of the chamber of deputies was transferring its collection of papers and documents from the period 1848 to 1946 to the archives, and they were made available to the Fondazione Giacomo Matteotti and to Stefano Caretti, editor of the complete works of Matteotti.

Matteotti had drawn up numerous lists in his indictment of Mussolini's government. One list named almost 500 communes where democratically elected councils had been dissolved by government decree, for reasons that included "lack of local consensus towards new national political trends", "anti-national propaganda obstructing the work of the political authorities" and "anti-national political tendencies". Fascist gangs had invaded many council meetings with the aim of forcing councillors to resign. Another list showed 32 provincial councils that had gone the same way as the communes. Matteotti also scrutinised expenditure on government press offices and propaganda. The book's many tables of exchange rates, foreign trade, price levels, bankruptcies, wages, employment, taxes (national and local), import duties, inflation, labour relations, education, public services like posts and railways, and much else show that the fascists hadn't been good managers of public money and the economy.

Matteotti had collected about a hundred cuttings from fascist newspapers and statements by Mussolini threatening violence against opponents. "Maintain equipment and morale at full efficiency, ready at every moment to respond to my call for the next inexorable developments of our revolution," the Duce ordered his blackshirts. "This parade of formidable strength has a clear and solemn meaning. It's an eloquent warning to adversaries of every stripe," threatened the *Popolo d'Italia*, Mussolini's newspaper and mouthpiece. And Matteotti listed around a thousand cases where words gave way to action through beatings with clubs, arson, shootings, intimidation and damage to property owned by political opponents.

Although Mussolini had been attracted by a political movement created in December 1917 when a group of parliamentarians formed the conservative Fascio Parlamentare di Difesa Nazionale, a national defence union, if his fascist regime can be said to have a place and date of birth, this was Milan on 23 March 1919 when he met representatives of the Fasci di Combattimento (veterans' associations). Both Mussolini and

Matteotti had belonged to the Socialist Party before the first world war. They were on opposing sides when peace arrived, but while Matteotti was elected to parliament in November 1919, Mussolini's Fasci Italiani di Combattimento, which only stood in Milan, received less than 5,000 votes, less than 0.1 per cent of the total votes cast nationally, and failed to win a seat. Mussolini would do far better in elections held in May 1921, joining a national slate with the Liberal Party and Nationalist Association, and winning 37 seats for the Fasci Italiani di Combattimento and a place in parliament for himself.

In his biography of Mussolini, Richard Bosworth wrote, "The Fascist rise to power had been scarred by up to 2000 deaths." And Matteotti's record of Mussolini's first year and a half of power showed that murder and intimidation were central to the regime's exercise of social and political control. Indeed, along with administering dozens of beatings with clubs, fascist thugs were responsible for twenty-three murders in November and December 1922 alone, the first two months after Mussolini seized power, and a further fifty-four in the following ten months. Moreover, Matteotti missed some murders (and many acts of intimidation) when he drew up his inventory of fascist violence against opponents, and he knew this. His first item in January 1923 records how the dissolution of the royal guard had led to many dead and wounded in Turin, Naples and elsewhere, but police chiefs in those places forbade publication of the news. Among the six murders that Matteotti noted in August 1923 was that of Don Giovanni Minzoni, a priest clubbed to death in Argenta, a small town in the province of Ferrara.

Some of the victims that fascists left seriously injured almost certainly died later from the gunshot and knife wounds or beatings they had received. Piero Gobetti, a writer and radical campaigner who thought Matteotti's noble mind distinguished him from the "notoriety of other socialist leaders", died in exile in Paris in February 1926, a heart condition having been caused or aggravated by several beatings in Italy. Gobetti was not yet 25 years old. (His wife Ada would write *Partisan Diary* about her experiences while fighting fascism with the Italian resistance in Piedmont.) Giovanni Amendola, a journalist and liberal politician, would die in Cannes after suffering at the hands of fascists in Tuscany. Carlo Rosselli, a university teacher, anti-fascist writer and politician, escaped from confinement on the island of Lipari and was able to reach Paris. Carlo and his brother Nello were murdered in June 1937 at Bagnoles-de-l'Orne in Normandy by French rightwing extremists, a crime probably commissioned by Mussolini's secret services in Rome.

Claudio Treves and Filippo Turati, fellow social democrats with Matteotti in establishing the Unitary Socialist Party, both died in exile in Paris, Turati in March 1932 and Treves in June the following year. The laws against Jews that the regime introduced in 1938 forced Treves's two sons into exile in London, where they spent the war years working for Radio London. Don Luigi Sturzo, a Roman Catholic priest and social activist who founded the Italian People's Party in 1919, a party launched in a call to "all free and strong men", went into exile in 1924, first in London and then in Paris and New York. Antonio Gramsci, one of the founders of the Italian Communist Party and its secretary from 1924 to 1927, did not die in exile but under arrest in a Roman clinic in April 1937. He had been arrested in November 1926, and a combination of prison conditions, a weak constitution and deteriorating health brought his death at the age of 46. His ashes were interred in the non-Catholic cemetery behind a section of the Aurelian Walls in Rome, at the far end of the cemetery from the tomb of John Keats, the English poet.

Abduction and murder

Matteotti's wife watched him as he left their apartment block at around half past four in the afternoon and crossed Via Pisanelli to walk up a short stretch of Via P.S. Mancini to the boulevard that runs beside the Tiber, in that section called Lungotevere Arnaldo da Brescia. Matteotti was alone. The state provided bodyguards not only for fascist politicians but also for some opposition figures. Yet Matteotti's only protection was a solitary policeman stationed permanently outside the apartment block. Matteotti intended to walk to Piazza del Popolo, about ten minutes away at a brisk pace, and then catch a tram for the longer part of his journey to Montecitorio. As he usually did, under an arm he carried a document case bearing the words Camera dei Deputati. A mystery surrounds what happened to the document case and the documents it contained, which were thought to be concerned with the Sinclair Oil scandal. Matteotti planned to work in the library of the budget commission in preparation for the following day's parliamentary session.

A group of boys was relaxing in the sun on steps by the river that afternoon in early summer as Matteotti turned the corner from Via P.S. Mancini, and two girls playing there saw Matteotti, whom they recognised, as he often passed. On this occasion they witnessed a frightening, unforgettable scene, an event that would be among the bleakest in the bleak period of modern Italian history when fascism took hold and Mussolini seized the opportunity for imposing a dictatorship. Walking quickly along the pavement beside Lungotevere Arnaldo da Brescia, Matteotti found his path blocked by two men who grabbed him and pulled him towards the road, where a Lancia Kappa saloon car was waiting. He fought back and was able to knock an assailant to the ground and free himself. But it was just a moment of freedom, as a third and heavily built attacker leaped forward and struck the politician hard in the face, causing him to fall. Although Matteotti continued struggling to break away and to shout for help, the three fascist thugs succeeded in bundling him into the car, punching him as they did so.

Zigzagging, the Lancia set off, with one of the gang still on a running board and Matteotti shouting and fighting his attackers. The strength he found in desperation was such that his kicking shattered a glass partition separating the driver from passengers in the rear. Perhaps to leave a trail, he threw his railway season ticket from the car and it was picked up by two agricultural workers on a passing cart. Trying to drown out Matteotti's cries for help and to warn other road users, the driver kept his hand on the horn as the car sped towards the Ponte Milvio. The bridge, restricted to pedestrian use half a century later, was barely wide enough for one vehicle, and a fortified gate on the northern side further narrowed the carriageway. Piazzale Ponte Milvio beyond the gate is the meeting point of two consular roads. The beginning of the Via Cassia lies ahead at the far side of the piazza, but the gang turned off to the right, to head northeast from Rome along the Via Flaminia, the ancient road to Rimini on the Adriatic coast. Other than a few houses, this was open land.

Narrow and winding, one hundred years later the Via Flaminia Vecchia would be flanked with shops, businesses and apartment buildings, mostly four- and five-storey blocks built in the late 1950s and the 1960s. How different the road would be in the 2020s to what it was in the mid 1920s, when land on either side was cultivated and provided food for Rome's growing population. Busy roads and heavy traffic were several decades ahead. And while few people were around, those few were too many for the gang to kill Matteotti and bury his body there, about five kilometres from Piazza del Popolo. So near the city, the place was risky. Murder and grave-digging needed quieter, less exposed surroundings. The gang had planned to take Matteotti far into the countryside before killing him. However, he wasn't going quietly and the kidnappers decided to murder him in the car. A dagger stab to Matteotti's chest pierced a lung and brought blood up through his throat and out of his mouth. He died a slow and painful death. As investigators would later find, the large amount of blood that Matteotti lost while dying stained his clothes and the seats and carpets of the car.

With Matteotti's body in the car, the killers drove around the countryside until dusk, looking for a burial place according to some accounts, although according to others they had already decided and knew the site. The shallow grave would be discovered on 16 August in a clearing of scrub between the Via Flaminia and the beginning of a dip where the land falls away into a valley. A wall of a brick-red road-keeper's house nearby carries a sign saying that the distance from Rome is 24 kilometres. Part of the village of Riano, the locality was then known as the Macchia della Quartarella. The four members of the gang and the car's driver were soon identified. The police quickly established that Matteotti had been abducted. Witnesses had seen the kidnapping. Investigations led to two concierges of an apartment building on Via P.S. Mancini who had noticed the killers' Lancia, which passed frequently on the day of the kidnapping. Suspecting that those in the car planned a robbery, the concierges noted its number.

The case of Giacomo Matteotti's abduction was near to being solved. The car had been hired by Filippo Filippelli, and his driver, who had not been involved in Matteotti's kidnapping, told the police where it was garaged. He also gave them the name of the gang's leader, Amerigo Dumini, who was a veteran of the Italian army's Arditi shock troops who served in the Great War. The gang's other members had been comrades. Many Arditi veterans had been drawn to fascism and the man who led it. All Dumini's gang had had tangles with the law and had gladly done dirty work for the Duce in the past. According to Borgognone, "All were well known to Mussolini and were tied to him in dealings that went back to 1918 when he was seeking friends and accomplices in Milan." Dumini had recruited them and covered the expenses incurred in the operation with funds received from Mussolini's chief press officer. Later in the evening of the murder, one of the killers met Mussolini's private secretary and told him how the killing had gone. According to another account, the gang went to the private secretary's home to wash and to deliver the documents they had taken from Matteotti. The Fascist Party's head of finance, a close colleague of Mussolini from the early days of fascism in Milan, had been responsible for recruiting the member of the gang who tailed Matteotti in preparation for the abduction.

Despite efforts to obstruct investigations, the five members of the gang were brought to trial, which the regime rigged through job changes for prosecutors and judges—being compliant helped careers—and the court sat in the town of Chieti, off the beaten track in the Abruzzo region. Dumini and two of his gang were found guilty of manslaughter. Defending lawyers claimed the killers had not intended to kill Matteotti but only to abduct him. Accepting this defence, the judges sentenced the three who had committed the murder to five years, eleven months and twenty days in jail and banned them for life from public office. The other two defendants were found not guilty. The sentences were reviewed after the second world war, but the killers had benefited meanwhile from the regime's largesse. Thanks to an amnesty introduced by a government decree, Matteotti's murderers served only two months in jail after sentencing. Dumini was rewarded financially on leaving prison, a large lump sum being part of his pay-off. After further blackmail, he squeezed a salary equal to that of a supreme court judge from the regime. Another killer became wealthy from state transport contracts in Abyssinia.

Colleagues of the Unitary Socialist Party were among the first to arrive after the burial site was found. Filippo Turati and Claudio Treves, who had helped establish the Italian Socialist

Party in 1895, identified Matteotti from what was discovered in the grave. Parts of the body were missing, and what flesh remained was in an advanced state of putrefaction, leading Turati to write to Anna Kuliscioff that he would spare her the details. Just as the killers' trial would be held far from the spotlight, so the government and civil authorities arranged that Matteotti's funeral should take place quietly to keep the number of mourners down and to minimise the opportunities for demonstrations against the regime. A company of Carabinieri military police guarded the cemetery at Riano, where the body was taken, and visitors were not allowed.

The funeral took place at Fratta Polesine, Matteotti's birthplace. The coffin holding his body did not go to Rome but was carried by train at night from the village of Monterotondo, whose railway station was on the line from Rome to Florence and the north. The authorities organised an overnight journey to limit public attention and in Bologna and Ferrara, where the train passed early in the morning, took special measures to keep people away from railway stations. However, several thousand mourners travelled to Fratta Polesine and non-fascist newspapers covered the funeral fully. Despite the regime's efforts to play down Matteotti's murder, there were murmurings of public unrest when the body of the Unitary Socialist leader was found and at the time of the funeral.

Mussolini tightens his grip

Mussolini and those around him knew that public reaction to the murder was a threat to the regime. Support weakened following Matteotti's kidnapping. Many Italians, particularly trade unionists and middle-level white-collar workers who had backed fascism, perhaps from sheer opportunism, turned away, Donations of money to the party fell sharply. To minimise scrutiny, parliament was rarely summoned in summer and autumn 1924. Mussolini relied heavily on government by decree and issued 247 decree-laws between 25 June and 25 November. In a preface to *Il fascismo tra demagogia e consenso* (Fascism between demagoguery and consensus), a collection published in 2020 of Matteotti's writings between 1922 and his death, Alberto Aghemo, chairman of the Fondazione Matteotti, reflects on what he describes as the decisive and tragic summer of 1924, "when everything could still happen and then nothing happened ... while Mussolini trembled and denied, seemed to wobble, but already had the measure of the weakness of his opponents, deprived of the charismatic and intransigent leadership of the Partito Socialista Unitario's secretary".

In his biography of the fascist leader, Richard Bosworth notes, "Mussolini rose to the occasion and, from the edge of disaster, steered a course which led to his re-affirmation as national leader." During the autumn and early winter of 1924 Mussolini was able to thwart, pacify, dodge or otherwise deal with the three constituencies that posed most threat: the old elites, centre-left opponents, and hard-line followers in fascist strongholds. (With the signing in February 1929 of the Lateran Pacts, which dealt with claims of the Holy See arising from the reunification of Italy, the fascist leader would mollify critics in the Roman Catholic Church and head off opposition from it.)

Mussolini began a speech in parliament on 3 January 1925 by saying that he would not be subject to a vote. He had had his fill of parliamentary votes, said Mussolini, challenging the chamber of deputies to file charges against him and his ministers with the supreme court, as they were allowed to do under the constitution. He and he alone took the political, moral and historical responsibility for everything that had happened. The centre-left politicians "on the Aventine", boycotting parliament in protest against Matteotti's murder, were subversive, anti-constitutional and seditious, and republicanism was a factor in their action, said Mussolini, with a nod towards Italy's royal family. He was making a great effort to return Italy to normality and was determined to repress illegality. Where there are two opposing groups, he said, referring to the Aventine politicians, force is the only solution. History had shown there was no alternative. "Fascism, the government and the party are at full efficiency," he threatened.

Mussolini and those around him had been working towards a dictatorship and, with his speech, they had almost arrived. Nine days later the king approved a major reshuffle of the cabinet and the non-fascists who survived that cull would be ousted in the following months. Mussolini had outflanked the liberals and conservatives who, since the parliamentary elections of 1921, had assisted and accompanied his rise. There would be no going back. With the exception of the Partito Nazionale Fascista, political parties would be abolished in November 1926, but Mussolini's dictatorship was already firmly established.

Provincial roots and British interest

Paradoxically, Matteotti's background had fitted him to be one of those conservative and liberal politicians and a fellow traveller of fascism. His family was well-to-do. His grandfather had built a successful metals-trading business and his father had diversified into land-owning and assembled a substantial portfolio. Giacomo Matteotti was a bright and conscientious student in the law faculty of Bologna University and might have made a successful career in academic life or have developed a thriving legal practice. Instead, after encountering socialist movements in Bologna, he returned to Fratta Polesine on graduation in 1907, became a member of the village council and began a career in politics. Two years later he was elected councillor in the far larger neighbouring village of Lendinara and in 1910 he was elected to the council of Rovigo province.

Matteotti was driven by the injustice that kept many people in the Po Delta, illiterate agricultural labourers and their families, in poverty or surviving precariously on the edge of it and exploited by landowners. The young Socialist politician's experiences in Rovigo province convinced him of the need to make education and literacy a priority of policy. His efforts to improve the lives of workers, particularly the agricultural labourers of his constituency, found a national platform after his election to parliament in Rome in 1919. On 31 January 1921 he addressed the chamber of deputies on behalf of the Socialist Party about the increasing level of fascist violence against working people, listing several such incidents against agricultural labourers in his constituency and more widely in the Emilia-Romagna region. He told parliament how lorries carrying armed fascists had left Ferrara for the countryside the previous Sunday on a mission of intimidation that had led to the injury of four agricultural labourers, two of them seriously, and the arson of two buildings belonging to labourers' associations. Injuries and damage apart, the fascists' mission had led to the arrest of twenty socialists but no fascists. Recently a fascist in Rovigo had shot three socialists and seriously injured one of his own band accidentally. A large number of police and Carabinieri, including two lieutenant colonels, stood by while fascists set fire to the offices of the workers' association in Bologna. There had been arson against the offices of the workers' association in Modena, despite the fact that the prefect of Modena had been warned about what was to happen.

The bourgeoisie possess numerous weapons, said Matteotti, including laws, Carabinieri, prisons, and handcuffs, and they use them. The violence and illegality of armed bands of fascists coincided with what the capitalist class considered to be its interests. "The landowners' associations organise the violence, provoke the violence, the most brazen violence, because those associations' members are the most backward section of their class, which to protect its wallets would even be happy to allow the state to perish, because nothing is more important to it than profit and immediate gain," Matteotti told parliament.

Yet he was not a revolutionary socialist. He didn't believe in overthrowing the system, as many of his party colleagues did and, in doing so, caused splits in the Italian left that would benefit Mussolini when, a decade after declaring himself a socialist revolutionary, he won power as a fascist by marching on Rome in October 1922. Earlier that month, Matteotti had joined Filippo Turati and Claudio Treves in leaving the Socialist Party to establish the Unitary Socialist Party (a moderate and reformist party, and forerunner of Italy's Social Democratic Party) and become its first secretary. While Mussolini joined the bosses, Matteotti continued his political struggle for working people. Indeed, opposition to fascism was, for Matteotti, in large part a struggle on behalf of the working class against powerful elites.

Provocation of social instability served fascism during the years immediately after the first world war. Mussolini claimed that only he and his followers could and would bring order to Italy, and landowners, businessmen, and the wealthy and privileged were mostly fascism's accomplices. (With plots and bombings to create instability, Italy's neo-fascists would play a similar card from the 1960s to the 1980s.)

Matteotti quickly became an international figure. In February 1924 he had published, semi-clandestinely, an account of Mussolini's first year of government. *Un anno di dominazione fascista* (A year of fascist domination) recorded incidents of fascist aggression and many misdeeds, lies, and acts of corruption and incompetence. A French translation was published in Brussels that same year and a German translation in Berlin in 1925. (Despite severe penalties against people who distributed or possessed it, more than 20,000 copies of Matteotti's book had been sold in Italy in the month after his abduction and murder.)

His standing was particularly high in left-leaning and reformist circles in Britain, where Italian radicals had long been welcome. Giuseppe Mazzini, a revolutionary republican, had spells of exile in London between the late 1830s and the 1850s, and Giuseppe Garibaldi, hero of the victory over the autocratic and decadent Bourbon monarchy in southern Italy and an architect of Italian reunification, was greeted warmly when he visited in April 1864.

The Independent Labour Party published an English translation of Matteotti's book the year it appeared in Italy. The publication of *The Fascist Exposed: A Year of Fascist Domination* had been one of the issues on Matteotti's agenda when he was in London in April 1924. He met leaders of the Labour Party, including Ramsay MacDonald, who was prime minister at the time, and the Trades Union Congress (TUC), and he addressed the party's executive committee and the trade unions' general council on what was happening in Italy. The news of Matteotti's abduction caused the committee and the council to send notes expressing serious concern to the Italian Socialist Party. They would write to Mussolini after Matteotti's body was found to say that, whoever had carried out the crime, Britain's labour movement considered the fascist leaders to be morally responsible.

At that time, not only before internet but also before television and radio, media interest in Matteotti's abduction and then his murder was solely a matter for print journalists and their newspapers and magazines. And the *Daily Herald*, a newspaper owned by the TUC and the Labour Party, which during the 1930s would have record daily sales of two million copies, paid close attention to the case of the Italian politician. Among its numerous articles related to Matteotti was one published after the discovery of Matteotti's body, in which the newspaper tied the killing to the fascists and their need to silence the politician before he published evidence of ministerial corruption in the Sinclair Oil affair.

THE KILLING OF GIACOMO MATTEOTTI

Remembering Matteotti

Giacomo Matteotti was in the spotlight of public attention for only a short period, but he was not forgotten in Britain. Founded on 1 May 1930, the Women's International Matteotti Committee was the result of the work of Silvio Corio, an anarchist who moved to London in 1901 and died there at the age of 80 in 1954, and Sylvia Pankhurst, a campaigner for women's suffrage and a prominent socialist. The story of their work—partners in the promotion of an anti-fascist movement in Britain, as well as sentimentally—is the subject of a book by Anna Rita Gabellone, a historian. *Giacomo Matteotti in Gran Bretagna, 1924–1939* was published in 2022 with the support of funds from the Italian government under legislation passed in 2017 promoting initiatives to preserve the memory of Giacomo Matteotti. A lengthy appendix contains nearly 150 previously unpublished letters, part of the correspondence between Corio and Pankhurst and leading socialists and anti-fascists, mainly Italians, among them Pietro Nenni, Carlo Rosselli, Francesco Fausto Nitti, Emilio Lussu, Gaetano Salvemini and Don Luigi Sturzo. To read them is to be carried back to that bitter period and to share the anxieties and idealism of their writers.

Giacomo Matteotti served for four and a half years in the national parliament, arguing vigorously and unceasingly for social democracy, and for three years he faced his principal opponent in the chamber as well as in the piazzas of Italian villages, towns and cities and in the countryside between them. When fascists murdered him, fascism was little more than five years old, and it had less than twenty-one years to run before Mussolini's corpse was strung head down by the side of a petrol station on Piazzale Loreto in central Milan. Neither would be forgotten, albeit Matteotti would be remembered less and less.

We can still be reminded, outside the pages of history books and guidebooks, and beyond television documentaries and cinema screens, of those tragic years and the people involved. In 2024, one hundred years after Dumini and his gang abducted Matteotti on a boulevard running beside the Tiber, and killed him as he struggled in the back of their Lancia Kappa car, Roman streets offer numerous mementoes of the fascist period. A small stone tablet fixed to the wall at the front of the four-storey apartment block where he lived, near the door through which he passed on his way to Lungotevere Arnaldo da Brescia, tells passers-by: "Here lived Giacomo Matteotti who, leaving home on 10.6.1924, went to meet death". The bridge over the Tiber, close to the spot where the killers seized him, now bears Matteotti's name and a tall, bronze spike-like sculpture stands nearby, at the top of stairs and a ramp leading down to the Tiber. This is the spot where the abduction happened, and there are several plaques at the sculpture's base, placed by social democrats on anniversaries of the murder.

Each year on 10 June, people gather by the sculptural spike to remember Giacomo Matteotti's killing. It's a sad small space, and not simply for the event that happened there and for how that event scotched hopes that in the aftermath of the first world war Italians would follow a harmonious path of economic recovery and social and democratic growth to national well-being. The location of the memorial, squeezed tightly onto the pavement at a junction by traffic lights on a busy stretch of road and close to the exit of an even busier underpass, brings distractions of noise and movement when attention might be better focused on remembering the man, his work, and his untimely and terrible end. And it's a sad space because little was done to maintain it in the decades after the spike was erected to mark the fiftieth anniversary of Matteotti's murder. In 2022 when I visited, it was a disorderly, scruffy place with the plaques set scrappily in the ground. Trees with cascading branches unpollarded for years, and a jungle of shrubs, weeds and bushes growing raggedly unchecked, obscured the memorial.

THE KILLING OF GIACOMO MATTEOTTI

The sky was overcast, patches of black cloud threatening a heavy downpour, occasional raindrops making blotches on pavements along Lungotevere Arnaldo da Brescia, when I returned to the memorial on 10 June 2024. As I arrived, two tall Carabinieri of Italy's presidential guard wearing black trousers with broad red stripes along their seams, white jackets and golden helmets with long black plumes streaming behind were placing a giant wreath at the memorial. Sergio Mattarella, Italy's head of state, was there to pay his respects to the murdered politician. Carabinieri and police were out in force by the memorial and on nearby streets. Around twenty photographers and journalists stood across the road from the memorial, about the same number as minor civilian officials and representatives of political parties who stood chatting near it. However, members of Rome's general public had not turned out to mark the centenary of Giacomo Matteotti's murder. There were perhaps a dozen, mainly casual passers-by. The city authorities had cleared the undergrowth, removed the ground cover and sawed off branches, but that small space of uneven beaten earth near stairs down to the Tiber was still far from dignifying the memory of the man whose assassination by thugs had marked the beginning of Mussolini's dictatorship and the fascist *ventennio*.

In contrast, a far grander sight comes into view when crossing the Tiber by the ceremonial Duca d'Aosta bridge, inaugurated in March 1939 to mark the twentieth anniversary of the Fasci Italiani di Combattimento. A tall, pristine white obelisk of Carrara marble stands outside the Foro Italico sports complex, the site of the Stadio Olimpico football stadium, the national swimming centre, the tennis courts of the Rome tournament and much else. The letters on the obelisk's front face spell the words MUSSOLINI DUX. On one side at the base are the words "Opera Balilla Anno X". The Opera Balilla was a fascist children's and youth indoctrination organisation that encouraged physical education, and put young Italians into uniform and drilled them at weekend parades. Anno X was 1932, the tenth year of the fascist era. Work began on quarrying the stone for the obelisk in July 1928 and Mussolini inaugurated the 300-tonne work on 4 November 1932. Building was then underway on the Foro Mussolini sports facilities for the planned but never-held Olympic Games of 1940. As pedestrians and motorists turn onto the bridge to cross to the Prati side of the Tiber, Mussolini's obelisk stands out smartly in its setting of well-kept buildings and stadiums.

The use of the word *dux* and a Roman numeral on the obelisk, and the Foro Italico's sixty large marble statues of athletes of different sports in various poses, are examples of the claims to an ancient Roman heritage that the fascists began laying in 1921, when Mussolini decided that the birth of Rome should be celebrated on 21 April each year. Fascism promised a rebirth of ancient Rome and a return to its military successes and the epic glories of its emperors and empire. Mussolini's daily newspaper *Popolo d'Italia* reported the Duce in April 1922 as saying that fascism revived the immortal spirit of Rome. Rome was fascism's reference point and symbol, he said. Not by chance the youngest children enrolled in the Balilla, those from six to eight, were called *figlie e figli della lupa*, daughters and sons of the wolf. And the straight right-arm salute was a Roman salute.

Anti-militarist and a believer in Italian neutrality, Giacomo Matteotti had opposed Italy's entry into the first world war. He would have opposed the Balilla and its militarisation of young people, and would certainly have stood firmly against Mussolini's adventures in Abyssinia and Spain and Italy's entry into the second world war. Matteotti's fight was for the freedom of working people in Italy, freedom from economic oppression and freedom of expression, not for foreign possessions. That fight ended during a car journey from Rome to Riano, where his murderers buried him in a shallow grave. A plain memorial to Matteotti now stands by the road near where the killers scraped his grave. Backed by a line of locust trees, with their delicate, pale green leaves and pendulous chains of small white flowers, like the bronze-spike sculpture in Rome, it's nevertheless a poor memorial to the man.

After it was found on the morning of 16 August 1924, Matteotti's body was taken to a cemetery a kilometre from the old village of Riano, a journey of about three kilometres, first north on the Via Flaminia and then east along the Via Rianese. One hundred years later, the untouched countryside that Filippo Turati and Claudio Treves saw when they travelled out of Rome to identify the body had been transformed. Houses and businesses stand on the Macchia della Quartarella near the Via Flaminia. A veterinary surgery and a car parts distributor are neighbours at the beginning of Via Quartarella, and only a few paces separate the memorial to Matteotti from Il Casaletto, a trattoria offering barbecued meat as its speciality. The steep valleys that characterise the landscape are heavily built up with villas and apartment blocks. There are shops of many types, cafés, pizzerias, beauty salons, branches of a rural and craftsmen's savings bank, established during Italy's economic miracle years after the second world war, and countless cars and vans.

The cemetery where Matteotti's body was taken is about two kilometres from Via Flaminia, through the narrow main street of La Rosta, a hamlet and part of Riano, then with a scattering of poor dwellings for poor labourers. Enlarged several times, with few of its many tombs holding the remains of people who were alive when Matteotti was murdered, Riano's cemetery reflects changes brought by time. Riano has grown considerably and much of the growth is recent. It is no longer a village. The population had increased from less than 4,000 in 1971 to over 10,000 in 2020. Perhaps some know the story of the Unitary Socialist politician who, after being brutally murdered, was buried in a shallow grave in the countryside nearby, but none are alive who can remember the four days when the cemetery was kept closed and guarded by a company of armed Carabinieri.

On the afternoon of 20 August 1924, a small convoy left Riano and headed towards the river Tiber. Then, like most roads outside cities and towns, the one from Riano was unmetalled. As well as leaving broken glass inside, the killers left their car plastered on the outside with dust when they returned it to the garage in Rome late on 10 June. Even in Rome itself some major roads were still unmetalled in the 1920s. In his novel *Quer pasticciaccio brutto de via Merulana* (translated in an English edition as *That Awful Mess on the Via Merulana*), set in Rome in early 1926, Carlo Emilio Gadda wrote of a funeral procession along Viale Regina Margherita between the capital's main hospital and the Verano cemetery "stirring up a bit of dust as the street there hadn't yet been asphalted". The asphalting of rural roads would arrive much later, well after the second world war.

Raising a cloud of dust in its wake, the convoy carrying Matteotti's body proceeded downhill along the unsurfaced road. Soon after passing the hamlet of Monte Perazzo the road reached a series of sharp bends surrounded by woodland. The broad valley where the Tiber snakes its way through fields, made hazy by the heat of high summer, lay spread out below. The village of Monterotondo and its railway station were on the other side of the river, about eight kilometres away. There a group of mourning agricultural labourers, railway workers and journalists knelt when the coffin passed, paying homage to a man who was murdered because he defended the weak against the strong, sought peace and fought for social justice. Giacomo Matteotti had briefly shone a beacon of decency and democracy. Twenty years of fascist domination and political darkness lay ahead.

II

CAPITAL CITY FOR A MODERN EMPIRE

Move the stones of Rome to rise

William Shakespeare, *Julius Caesar*

Benito Mussolini knew what he did not want in Rome. He did not want a large population of industrial workers threatening agitation and conflict in the capital. Mussolini had gained first-hand experience of class violence during his years in Milan. Indeed, he had fuelled it with his speeches and writings, and put his words into action through gangs of armed fascist thugs. He had been a leading figure in creating the turbulence and the social and political unrest that had scarred northern Italy particularly in the years immediately following the first world war, a war that had cost the country proportionately more than Britain. In "The Economics of World War I: A Comparative Quantitative Analysis", a paper published in 2005, Stephen Broadberry and Mark Harrison of the University of Warwick calculated that human capital destruction, measured in war deaths as a percentage of the pre-war male population aged 15 to 49 years, was 3.8 per cent in Italy against 3.6 per cent in Britain. Yet, even as veterans and bereaved families lived among them during the decades that followed the second world war, Italians would forget their country's losses of young and middle-aged men in the Great War.

There would be no regiments of potentially rebellious blue-collar proletariat in the capital. One of the first acts of economic policy of Mussolini's newly formed government at the end of October 1922 was a decree-law that dissolved Rome's industrial development board. Officially established in 1920, the board had been short-lived. Yet Mussolini had simply delivered the final blow once he put his hands on the levers of power. The ground for his decision had been prepared. Roman landowners had refused to contribute to costs and, fearing competition, business-men in northern Italy had lobbied against Rome's industrialisation. Moreover, Giovanni Giolitti, prime minister for nine years during the first two decades of the twentieth century, considered an inland industrial port "neither useful nor appropriate", and he preferred the capital to be without it. (Giolitti's tolerance, some critics say encouragement, of fascist violence and his slate of National Bloc candidates encompassing his Liberal Party, the Italian Nationalist Association and the Italian Fighting Fascists in elections of 1921 would open parliament's door to Mussolini.)

Industrial ambitions

For decades, Paolo Orlando, an engineer from Genoa, had dreamed of a modern industrial Rome, served like Manchester by a large inland port and connected by a navigable canal to the sea. A major seaport would be built for modern Rome, just as ancient Rome had had a port at what centuries later would be called Ostia Antica. And the capital would also be linked on land to Ostia by a railway line. Orlando drew up his first scheme in 1887, but this lay dormant and prospects for it only brightened seventeen years later with the creation in 1904 of a pressure group to push for construction of the canal and port. Such projects made slow progress in the Eternal City, however, and the uncertainty caused by the Great War didn't help. Orlando had to wait until 1917 before the public works authority approved the establishment of an autonomous board for Rome's maritime and industrial development. The decree-law that followed in 1919 must have seemed like success in overcoming the final administrative and legislative hurdles, and hopes and expectations were such that in June 1920 King Victor Emmanuel III, with a spade and great ceremony, initiated building works on dunes where the port was to be built. There were to be three wharves, and a depth of 10 metres of water would allow the port to handle deep-draught vessels. Mussolini's decree dashed the hopes and expectations of Orlando and the group of businessmen and politicians who backed him.

Even so, heavy industry did arrive near the coast at the end of the 1920s, in Ostia's northeastern outskirts, near the road that leads to Ostia Antica. But the Società Trattori Italiani e Macchine Agricole, which as its name suggests produced tractors and agricultural machinery, remained an isolated factory. Even before Italy entered the second world war, by focusing on its capacity as a steel foundry its ploughshares had been converted into output more suitable for swords. German soldiers failed in their attempt at demolition with explosive charges and the factory would limp on, eventually becoming part of a notoriously loss-making state holding corporation.

Yet just four years before Paolo Orlando first put forward his revolutionary scheme to take industry to Rome and the Roman coast, and to end the city's focus on the Roman Catholic Church and government administration, the authorities published a plan that laid out where and how factories should be stitched into the urban fabric. They decided that Testaccio, close to the Aurelian Walls at Porta San Paolo, should be an industrial area. Better known in the twenty-first century as a late-night haunt for young people, Testaccio would become thick with bars, clubs, discos and trattorias strung around the base of the large man-made hill of shards that ancient Romans created when they smashed amphoras used to import grain, oil and other foodstuffs. The Testaccio slaughterhouse between the hill and the Tiber, built between 1888 and 1891, would close in 1975 and be transformed in the early years of the twenty-first century into a centre for contemporary art and a campus for the architecture faculty of Roma Tre, the third state university in the capital. The city's 1883 plan was followed by another in 1909 that extended the industrial area outside the walls and into the Ostiense district beyond the pyramid at Porta San Paolo, and along Via Ostiense to where the river Tiber passes near the basilica of San Paolo fuori le Mura.

However, little of that old industry would remain in the area other than as sites of modern archaeology. A power station inaugurated in 1912 and then enlarged, the final addition being a 20 megawatt steam turbine in 1942, would be declared obsolete and decommissioned in 1963. The buildings would be brought back to life in 1997 as the Centrale Montemartini, becoming the city authorities' second archaeological museum with ancient artefacts placed alongside pieces of electricity-generating machinery. Opened in 1912, the wholesale market for fish, fruit, vegetables and other foodstuffs across Via Ostiense from the Centrale Montemartini would close in 2004 and, despite plans for its regeneration, would lie abandoned twenty years later. Natural gas would begin reaching Roman households in the early 1980s, making redundant a gasometer, a landmark in the Ostiense district, which had been erected in 1936. With coal brought up the Tiber in barges or by rail from the port at Civitavecchia, the gasworks by the river had begun producing town gas in 1910.

Despite the closure of the autonomous board for maritime and industrial development, the fascist *ventennio* did, however, take a small number of industrial ventures to the district that the city authorities had chosen for this purpose. A factory of Ottico Meccanica Italiana (OMI), a maker of cryptography machines and precision instruments for aerial photography and surveys, and for aircraft navigation, was built during the 1930s downstream from the gasworks, across the Tiber from the San Paolo basilica. And not far away, also in the 1930s, Alfa Romeo set up a maintenance centre for military vehicles and specialist workshop for building racing cars on Via Ostiense. Like the wing of the Testaccio slaughterhouse, both factories would find new roles as parts of Roma Tre University, and a similar end would arrive for a glassworks on Via Ostiense.

Although nothing would remain of the industrial ambitions that some politicians and businessmen had nurtured around the beginning of the twentieth century for Ostia and the area of Rome between Testaccio and the San Paolo basilica, the period left two important legacies as well as the industrial-archaeological sites. One of those legacies is the railway to Ostia with its Rome terminus at Porta San Paolo, across Via Ostiense from the pyramid. Romans had to wait for more than half a century after the first project for the railway was approved by the papal authorities in 1868, two years before Rome was taken by Italian soldiers. Probably glad to get away from the question of Giacomo Matteotti's murder in June 1924, Benito Mussolini inaugurated the line in August that year. The second legacy is the Ponte dell'Industria girder bridge across the Tiber near the gasometer. Built as a railway bridge in the early 1860s, it became a road bridge after the construction of a new station in Trastevere and a new bridge over the Tiber to allow rail traffic between this and the station at Ostiense.

Garbatella and other fascist housing

Yet Paolo Orlando did leave his mark on the city. He deserves much of the credit for the Garbatella project of social housing of good standard on a hill to the east of Via Ostiense, to provide homes for workers in the food market, the electricity power station, the glassworks, gasworks and other businesses that had already sprung up near the small river port by the gasworks. "Homes for Heroes" perhaps, the district was a small step towards placating progressive spirits and satisfying post-war hopes and expectations, and it is possible to see an element of idealism behind the creation of Garbatella and the decision to call it Concordia garden suburb. However, Concordia would be quickly forgotten and the district would always be known as Garbatella.

The site chosen for the Garbatella social housing estate was a fine one. Aerial photographs taken in the 1920s and early 1930s show the area as a township on a hill mostly surrounded by countryside. Speaking at the laying of the foundation stone by King Victor Emmanuel III in February 1920, the chairman of Rome's social housing authority, which worked in tandem on the scheme with the industrial development board until this was closed, described the location as charming. For Orlando, Concordia's small and cheerful houses on the top of a hill dominated "a vast and marvellous panorama over the lower valley of the Tiber and Rome itself". However, well before the arrival of the twenty-first century the view had been blocked by construction on the open land. Densely packed six-, seven- and eight-storey apartment blocks would be built in the decades following the second world war, both from the bottom of the hill towards the centre of the city and for several kilometres on countryside in the other direction.

There would be 7,400 homes in Concordia, said the social housing authority's chairman, some of them two-storey villas with attached gardens or allotments of between 100 and 200 square metres, others low-rise apartment buildings. The model used in Rome came from the English garden city movement of the late nineteenth century and places such as Bournville near

Birmingham, Letchworth, Welwyn and Hampstead Garden Suburb. However, the housing authority's initial plans were soon upset. The first houses were completed quickly and in January 1921 their occupants moved in. Yet within four years, in response to a housing crisis in Rome, the social housing authority had transformed what had been intended as a garden city, with each home having a small plot of land, into a district where villas were few and apartment blocks with modest communal courtyard gardens predominated. And a further, even bigger shift occurred at the end of the 1920s with the construction of four large buildings that were called suburban hotels. Completed too late for pilgrims who had travelled to Rome for 1925's Holy Year, their one thousand rooms found immediate use in housing people displaced by clearances in Rome's historic centre such as that around the Teatro di Marcello, and people living in shanty settlements like one near the Ponte Milvio.

Life for the residents of Garbatella's hotels, all situated in the lower part of the district, was different from that of those living in the well-aired villas at the top of the hill, many of which were occupied by managers of the industrial development board on whose behalf Orlando had obtained pre-emption rights. Where they housed wage-earners, the families crammed into single rooms or small apartments in the hotels mostly depended on the meagre and uncertain pay packets of men in casual work as porters at the food market or as general labourers. These families were vulnerable to the waves of hard economic times that fascist autarky couldn't hold back. They lived precariously and with few comforts. Communal kitchens and shared bathrooms served all the rooms on each floor. Custodians ensured both social and political control and, as the need arose, the hotels provided suitably restricted accommodation for the fascist regime's opponents.

Most homes in Garbatella lacked what would in the second half of the twentieth century, and decades earlier in northern

Europe, be considered the minimum of basic sanitary facilities. Overcrowding was frequent and large families, comprising numerous children together with grandparents and aunts and uncles, were served by small bathrooms measuring just one metre by one metre, barely space for a WC and a small handbasin. Had the fascist regime not actively sought to encourage personal hygiene in working-class districts, bath-time would have amounted to filling a tub with water heated on gas stoves for all the family rather than just elderly folk and children. Instead, among Garbatella's centralised social amenities were public baths where men would gather once a week for a proper bath. Many would use the occasion to meet friends and catch up with their news. The weekly trip to the public baths also offered an excuse to young people of both genders to get together. There was a cinema and theatre across the piazza from the baths. Both buildings date from 1929–30.

A few buildings would be demolished in the early 1950s, but the villas and apartment blocks would be much the same externally in the 2020s as they had been at the start of the 1930s when the final pieces of Garbatella, its schools and churches, were completed. Yet the district's warren of narrow streets, with steep uphill gradients and descents, and occasional sets of stairs between groups of buildings, would be far from a utopian Roman copy of the low-density English garden cities with abundant greenery that Orlando, the industrial development board and the social housing institute had imagined and hoped for. But, within the social, political and economic constraints of the 1920s, their efforts and those of the architects, planners and builders they employed gave Rome a new community with innovative housing in an integrated townscape. Like architects who worked on Hampstead Garden Suburb in London at the start of the twentieth century, those working on Garbatella were attracted by the Arts and Crafts movement and added picturesque decorative details in a style called *barocchetto romano* that gave buildings uniqueness. Turrets, classical columns on balconies, arches, porches, cast iron gates and quirky figures such as a lioness drinking from a downpipe, a devil's head, a putto supporting a drainpipe and a Tuscan lily would be part of the attraction for architectural tourists a century later.

Census figures underlined why Rome needed to build more homes. The city's resident population was 492,000 in 1911. Ten years later, the year before Mussolini's March on Rome, it stood at 611,000, and the 20 per cent increase over the following ten years would take the number of Romans to 735,000 in 1931. The million mark was soon passed, an increase of 41 per cent over five years, pushing the capital's population to 1,039,000 in 1936.

Under the fascist administration dense building continued in the Prati district, which neighboured the Vatican to the north and until the 1880s had offered a rural landscape of allotments, fields for pasture and swamp dotted by an occasional farmhouse near surrounding higher land. The district was and would continue to be convenient, within walking distance of Rome's historic centre and government offices located there. The supreme court, other courts and several large military barracks were located in Prati, and apartment blocks were built there with senior civil servants in mind. Similar reasoning lay behind the construction of an imposing condominium that was built in the 1920s at Piazza dell'Emporio, by the Tiber and at the foot of the Aventine Hill and neighbouring Testaccio. However, while residential blocks near the slaughterhouse were for working-class residents, the apartments in the building on Piazza dell'Emporio were for officials of the Fascist Party. In less than half an hour, those living in the inner wing of the block could close the doors of their spacious, comfortable, solidly built and solidly bourgeois apartments, take the rattling dark-wood lift with its manually operated doors to the ground floor, cross two inner courtyards, exit the block through a doorway onto the piazza outside, and walk to the Palazzo di Venezia where the Duce had his offices.

Yet whatever the size of the Fascist Party's organisation in the capital and the extent of government bureaucracy, clearly the principal demand for housing came from the working class rather than the middle and executive classes. Garbatella was one district that helped satisfy this demand. Another was Quadraro, an outlying district to the east of Rome beyond Porta San Giovanni, about five kilometres along Via Tuscolana. Not far from Garbatella and close to the San Domitilla catacombs, the fascist social housing institute built Tor Marancia, a district for housing displaced people in the early 1930s. The Donna Olimpia district near the Villa Pamphili park dates from the same period, while Primavalle on the northern outskirts was constructed in the second half of the decade.

Across the city, the group of massive seven-storey blocks on Via di Valle Melaina, their 530 apartments accessed by fourteen staircases, was even further from the centre and isolated from it. Like Quadraro, it also enjoyed a name for harbouring people whom the regime would have preferred locked in Regina Coeli prison or confined to distant and inaccessible islands or regions. Also known as Stalingrad, this working-class housing project was built at the beginning of the 1930s. On 23 April 1954, a tablet would be set in a wall to honour four men who lived there and who had been "barbarously murdered by nazi-fascists" when German soldiers occupied Rome in September 1943. The people of Val Melaina placed the tablet to remember the sacrifice of those who fought and gave their lives for Italy's freedom and independence and for peace. The city had been liberated a little less than a decade earlier, and memories were still fresh and raw for many Romans.

Garbatella, Prati, Quadraro, Piazza dell'Emporio, Tor Marancia, Donna Olimpia, Primavalle and Via di Valle Melaina are just eight of numerous places where construction under the fascist regime aimed to satisfy the demand for housing of a rapidly growing capital city. In the twenty-first century, observant visitors to almost any part of central or semi-central Rome can notice apartment blocks from the 1920s and 1930s: on and around Via Nomentana beyond Porta Pia; on streets just beyond the Aurelian Walls near the San Giovanni in Laterano basilica; in the Parioli district; on the Piccolo Aventino, where construction began in the late 1920s, not far from the Baths of Caracalla and only a few hundred metres from the Circus Maximus; and around Piazza Bologna. Inaugurated in 1935, the large post office that stands on one segment of the piazza was one of four approved in 1932. Another stands near Porta San Paolo and the Pyramid of Cestius, at the other end of Via Marmorata from Piazza dell'Emporio.

In Rome and around the capital, the fascist *ventennio* wrought change to the urban fabric that would last. Indeed, despite the closure of the autonomous board for Rome's maritime and industrial development, the 1920s and 1930s continued to add significantly to the huge changes that had transformed Ostia in the closing decades of the nineteenth century and the opening years of the twentieth.

Birth of a seaside resort

Nearest to the capital, its beach partitioned into numerous bathing establishments with rows of changing cabins, and with sunbeds, deckchairs and colourful umbrellas set out neatly in ranks almost to the water's edge in summer, Ostia Lido in the second half of the twentieth century would be one of many resorts along Rome's lengthy seaside playground of kilometre after kilometre of broad sandy beaches that runs from the Tuscan promontory of the Argentario in the north to Sperlonga in the south, more than halfway along the coastal road to Naples. However, with its tight grid of streets flanked by a dense mass of apartment blocks and countless cars parked bumper to bumper at kerbsides, the Ostia Lido municipality of modern Rome, a short distance inland from the beach, offers a picture far from seaside charm.

How different it had been in the 1870s when Ostia was untamed marshland almost without human presence. The engineering corps of the Austro-Hungarian army estimated that only fifty-three people lived in Ostia in 1843 and little changed in the following forty years. According to some sceptical commentators on Mussolini's regime, making trains run on time and draining swamps were the main, perhaps only positive achievements of his twenty-year dictatorship. Whether or not Italy's trains ran on time, land was certainly brought into agricultural use by the draining of the Pontine Marshes about 80 kilometres south of Rome, the principal example of fascist land reclamation. Goethe travelled across them in February 1787 when they were papal lands and found they did not look "as dreary as people in Rome usually describe them". Drainage operations had begun, and Goethe thought they were going to be successful. They were not. Effective reclamation of the marshes had to wait for implementation of the 1928 Mussolini Law, work beginning in 1930 with the clearance of scrub and the construction of drainage canals and pumping stations. The project was completed just before the beginning of the second world war.

Yet similar land between Rome and Ostia had already been cleared of typical Mediterranean marsh vegetation, drained and reclaimed well before the arrival of Mussolini. The first tentative steps had been taken by the Vatican when much of the wetlands around the Tiber between the city and the sea was owned by aristocratic Roman families, among them the Rospigliosi, the Torlonia and the Chigi, and the salt pans in Ostia were directly controlled by the Reverenda Camera Apostolica. This limb of papal financial administration, controlled by the Curia, would be abolished by Pope Francis in 2022, but in 1858 it established the Società Pio-Ostiense charged with bringing Ostia's saltworks into full production (and using the salt for producing other chemicals), draining the area's ponds in order to make land available for farming, and creating a modern commercially focused business. The Curia's scheme didn't get far before Italian unification caused upheaval in and around Rome and halted the project.

However, just fourteen years after the storming of the Aurelian Walls near Porta Pia by Bersaglieri soldiers and the seizure of Rome in September 1870, work began that would make Ostia habitable and the wetlands agriculturally productive. Indeed, in November 1870 a commission was established and tasked with proposing a plan for reclaiming the marshes close to Rome. Work on the land behind Ostia was contracted to a farm labourers' association that had been set up in 1883 in Ravenna in the Po Delta. Like many agricultural workers in that part of Italy, those around Ravenna had experience of dealing with land reclamation and protection, and management of the river Lamone, which enters the Adriatic a few kilometres north of the city, had been ongoing since a major flood in 1839.

An advance party of forty workers left Ravenna for Ostia in November 1884 and more than four hundred soon followed. It fell to them to grub up the tamarisks, alders, willows and holm oaks, and to clear the rushes and ground vegetation before beginning to level the dunes, dig drainage canals and build pumping plants. Accounts of that period tell of an inhospitable land offering harsh conditions, and of gruelling labour, disease and death. A virulent form of malaria was endemic, tetanus infections were frequent, lung problems common and viper bites far from rare. More than one hundred workers died during the reclamation of the swamps between Rome and the sea. Even so, once work was completed in May 1891 some of those who had taken part in the project preferred to stay and establish an agricultural colony there rather than return to the farmland around Ravenna.

The farm labourers' association in Ravenna entrusted the colony's establishment to thirty families. Piazza dei Ravennati would be the name of the square in the centre of the seafront where Via Ostiense ends and the resort's pier begins. Those first workers and their families initially lodged in Ostia Antica, the old village of Ostia whose medieval Rocca, the massive castle of Julius II, stands across the road from the entrance to the archaeological site. As at Ostia Lido, those people from Ravenna in the region of Emilia-Romagna would also be remembered at Ostia Antica. The main road around the Rocca would be called Viale dei Romagnoli and a tablet set in a wall by a small square would remember their work, the difficulties they faced and those who died. Unveiled in 1904, the tablet records: "Men, women and young maidens arrived from Romagna's pleasant fields, a peaceful army seeking bread and work through whose efforts cultivation, sanitation and civilisation were restored to an area abandoned for centuries through the indifference of princes and priests, and culpable governmental inertia." The tablet calls on Romans and foreigners who pass to lift their eyes from the ancient ruins, look up, and salute and honour the trailblazers of the new civilisation.

Yet what those men, women and young maidens found would be almost impossible to imagine in the twenty-first century. A page in an academic study of the draining of the land behind the coastal dunes at Ostia, published a century after the work was undertaken, contains a blurred photograph of a squalid straw shack that served as a home, and on another page a photograph shows a patch of watery marshland where cattle grazed. A few photographs of women in a field receiving quinine tablets to combat malaria, of women reaping, of a watermelon harvest, of the first workers of the agricultural colony outside its building, and of the first grain harvest after threshing in 1893 illustrate the years that followed soon after land reclamation was completed, when men and women were planting the reclaimed land and harvesting the results. However, the study offers nothing to illustrate the early years when the men were clearing trees and vegetation and digging drainage canals, and its oral history is mostly second-hand, the words of children and grandchildren remembering what parents and grandparents had told them.

About thirty years passed before Ostia began to take the shape it would have in the twenty-first century. Some workers from Ravenna and their children discovered the benefits of living near the sea, but Ostia would only become a seaside resort in the mid 1920s. Less than thirty buildings are visible in an aerial photograph taken in 1922 from above the centre of what would be the seafront promenade. However, mostly a large expanse of empty ground lay inland from those few seafront buildings, albeit the railway station stood out in the background. The arrival of trains from Rome was crucial to development, and construction boomed after Mussolini inaugurated the line. Taken in the winter of 1923/4, a photograph showing many more buildings suggests that some Romans guessed what would happen once trains were running, and invested early in prime sites of seaside real estate. Construction of the extravagant and exclusive "Roma" beach establishment, with a long pier and a huge pier-head palace, was well advanced by September 1924. Soon after it was completed the following year, its impact was seen in significant erosion of the beach immediately to the south. Man's meddling with nature coupled to coastal currents in the vicinity of the mouth of the Tiber would be a constant problem at Ostia. Far worse would happen in the future.

By the beginning of the 1930s, large expanses of Mediterranean maquis covering the dunes had been grubbed up in what would be the Lido's heart, the dunes themselves levelled, and numerous bathing establishments had taken over the central part of the beach. Construction had covered plots for around two kilometres along the coast and for about 300 metres inland from it. And building continued during the decade leading to the second world war, taking the built-up area inland to where the main post office stands. With a design marrying rationalist to futurist styles, the post office, inaugurated in 1934, features sharp horizontals and verticals, with a deep canopy supported by reinforced concrete columns faced with red brick around an open courtyard with a fountain in the centre. Ninety years later the building still looked strikingly fresh.

Much of what would be architecturally interesting or meritorious in Ostia, of which the post office is an example, was built in the 1920s and 1930s. Unsurprisingly and certainly not to everyone's taste, *barocchetto romano* with its cocktail of renaissance, baroque and art nouveau, widely employed in Rome during the 1920s and most notably in Garbatella, also found favour with architects designing buildings for the centre of Ostia during that decade. Typical are the municipal authority's Palazzo del Governatorato, which was built in the mid to late 1920s; the offices of the Istituto Case Popolari (Social Housing Institute); and some villas along the central part of the promenade and on a few streets behind it. In matters of architectural style, Ostia had moved on little when the huge Colonia Vittorio Emanuele III, for children for whom the sea air was thought advisable for health reasons, opened in 1932. Used for social and religious purposes, but seemingly empty at the time of writing, it continued to dominate a long section of the northwestern part of the promenade.

All that was erected in Ostia from 1922 until the war can be described as having been built with the architecture of the fascist regime, and by the early 1930s, when work began on the Casa del Balilla, a centre for the indoctrination of children and youth, approved style had progressed from *barocchetto romano*. The simple clean lines and elegant curves of a building that stands on Corso Duca di Genova seem to be owed equally to art deco and Italian rationalist style. However, the Casa del Balilla was neglected and abandoned before the arrival of the twenty-first century. By the start of the 2020s, there were rough-edged holes in scruffy and fading brick-red walls where once there had been window frames fitted with glass. External plaster was missing, the forecourt was covered with litter, weeds were flourishing and, at risk of collapse, the canopy over the spacious entrance portico was propped up by several scaffolding poles. And just as the salt in the seaside air had rusted the exposed steel rods in the columns of reinforced concrete supporting the canopy, corrosion had affected the columns and the beams they supported which marked the Casa del Balilla's grounds.

How different the building had been on a sunny Wednesday at the beginning of September 1935, when Benito Mussolini, wearing an immaculate white suit over a black shirt, white shoes, a black hat with tassel and soft black leather gloves, stepped out of a black Lancia limousine and strode quickly up a few stairs towards the entrance of the new building. Cameras of the Istituto Luce (Institute of Light) state propaganda body, there for the Duce's visit, recorded pristine walls in a white to match his uniform. And the interior—sparkling washbasins in a bathroom, rows of neatly made beds in a dormitory, the tables in a dining room laid in an orderly fashion—matched what was outside.

While Mussolini inspected them, the young apprentices of fascism stood smartly on parade, boys dressed in dark blue sailors' suits, skinny bare-chested youngsters of eight or nine or perhaps a little more in black shorts, and girls in short black skirts and white blouses, all lined up in ranks with excitement and enthusiasm lighting up their faces. Those young Romans had no notion of what the future would bring them as that summer of 1935 was drawing to an end. Yet, with the Great War almost two decades in the past and memories of it fading, they had every reason to hope, indeed expect, that their future would be as bright as the surroundings where they were passing those days, the beach and the Tyrrhenian Sea visible beyond the vacant plot of land across the road. Instead, the future soon darkened for them, for Italy's European neighbours and for much of the rest of the world. Less than a month after visiting the Casa del Balilla in Ostia, Mussolini launched 200,000 Italian soldiers into an invasion of Abyssinia. Meanwhile, in Germany on 15 September, Adolf Hitler had promulgated the notorious Nuremberg Laws against Jews. The road to the second world war had been signposted.

In March 1936, Hitler gave the order for German troops to march into the Rhineland in a breach of what the Treaty of Versailles had decided should be a demilitarised zone. Hitler and Mussolini would help reactionary Spanish generals after they began the Spanish Civil War by moving against a democratically elected republican government in July that year. A few months later, in October 1936, the Rome–Berlin axis came into being with the formalisation of a coalition between fascist Italy and nazi Germany. Those children and adolescents who were staying in Ostia's Casa del Balilla at the time of Mussolini's visit would find their lives touched by war, with most of the Roman boys who had been wearing sailors' suits soon in adult military uniforms. Wounding and death probably arrived for some of them.

At Ostia as much as on the Piazza Venezia and the Foro Italico, and in Garbatella, Rome's fascist past would live on and be clearly visible, particularly to people of a certain age and from certain backgrounds. I would wonder, as I looked and photographed from across the street, if the couple, probably in their early seventies, waiting at the bus stop near Ostia's market had noticed the date, eroded and fading in plasterwork on stairs leading to a small villa slotted tightly between two apartment blocks. There, one above the other were the years: 1929—Anno VII. Mussolini had seized power seven years before the villa was built. Yet, in the mid 2020s, did that couple know and, if they did know, were they interested in or did they care about what the fascist *ventennio* had brought Italians?

Certainly the lido's development was part of fascist notions of rebirth of ancient Roman power. On a personal level, in March 1926, the Duce himself had been given membership of the agricultural cooperative of Ravenna residents in Ostia. According to Edda Mambelli, who was born in 1930, he often visited the farmhouse of her grandparents who came from Predappio, Mussolini's birthplace, about 45 kilometres southwest of Ravenna. And, in promoting the Borghetto dei Pescatori (Fishermen's Village), built towards the end of the 1920s at the side of a major drainage canal into the sea at the southeastern end of the lido, the Duce had a tie to the sea as well as to the land. He kept boats there for his seaside jaunts. And a trip to Ostia brought a significant change in his private life. On a windy Sunday towards the end of April 1932, Mussolini had found his car being followed closely by another as he drove to Ostia along Via del Mare, the road that begins in Rome and ends in Ostia as Via Ostiense. On stopping at the seafront he discovered an enthusiastic young woman supporter among its passengers. The woman was Clara Petacci, about whom he recorded in his diary, "Sublime and marvellous moment, my unforgettable pearl. A sunny smile in an impetuous gust." (Petacci would be at Mussolini's side when partisans shot him on 28 April 1945 near Dongo, a village on the northwestern shore of Lake Como, and her body would be hung head-down beside his on Piazzale Loreto in central Milan.)

Photographs of Ostia in the decade before the storm of war broke over Italy in June 1940 show people enjoying the sun while sitting or lying on the beach or strolling along the promenade. For a select minority, however, Ostia meant the seaside glamour of "Roma", the elegant bathing establishment which offered everything that the aristocracy, the wealthy, high-level diplomats and top-ranking members of the regime enjoyed in the city and might wish for when they travelled out to the seaside near the capital. The establishment's promoters expected that the sophistication offered by "Roma" would rival whatever could be found on the French Riviera in Nice, Cannes and Monte Carlo. In fact, bathing and the beach were only part of the business at "Roma". Standing at the end of a pier and topped by a large copper dome, the ornate building reminded one critic of the Hagia Sophia in Constantinople. With orchestras playing and elegantly dressed guests served by regiments of formally dressed waiters at parties, receptions, balls and gala dinners, this secular cathedral was dedicated to high living. War brought that to an end and, after German soldiers set off demolition charges on the night of 12 December 1943, "Roma" would host no more events like those that found space on the society pages of Italy's newspapers and magazines in the late 1920s and 1930s. Other bathing establishments ended similarly, destroyed in order to prepare defences and ensure clear lines of fire for defenders. And German troops, now occupation forces, transformed sandy beaches into minefields.

EUR—a world fair district

While a few parts of Ostia and many places in central and semi-central Rome are dotted with unobtrusive but clearly identifiable items in the architectural legacy of the fascist *ventennio*, two districts in the city stand above all for the architecture of the period. One is the Foro Italico sports complex between the Prati district and Ponte Milvio, where the marble obelisk with the inscription "Mussolini Dux", mentioned earlier, is a notorious item in the legacy. The 1940 Olympic Games for which the sports complex was built were not held, and war forced suspension of work on the second district noted for its fascist architecture. Designed to be the Esposizione Universale di Roma—EUR, an acronym that would stick—it was meant to host a World Fair in 1942 to celebrate fascism's first twenty years.

* * *

Late one evening early in April 1972 I had stepped off an Egypt Air flight from London into a wall of heat at Fiumicino airport. I wondered if summer had arrived early in Rome that year, or if the beginning of April in the Eternal City always seemed like high summer. The journey from the airport in a taxi, a small, shaky and rattling Fiat, provided another of those unforgettable experiences: no street lamps then to illuminate night's darkness on the autostrada, windows down, a hot gale blasting through the car, a carefree Roman driver, cigarette in one hand, the other often off the wheel, one or the other often on the horn, the car steering itself at 90 miles an hour. After about twenty death-defying minutes, I was left outside the Residence Garden, a block of late-1950s serviced apartments on Viale dell'Arte in EUR.

I awoke the following morning to a blue sky and bright sunshine. On my right when I left the Residence Garden was Viale della Musica, an avenue of low-rise, stylish, upmarket apartment blocks set well back from the road, whose pavements were flanked by oleander bushes thick with buds of what would soon be flowers, white with pink flush, pink and deep red. Dodging traffic, I crossed Viale dell'Arte and on the other side was faced with the rear of the Palazzo dei Congressi, a conference hall that was planned as one of EUR's principal buildings, and whose construction began in 1938 but was only completed fifteen years later. I was heading to a long-fronted four-storey building about 200 metres further on, across the square from the Palazzo dei

Congressi's imposing facade. Over the next five years I would get to know the building well. It was the main offices of the Cassa per il Mezzogiorno, the development fund for the south of Italy. Simply standing in its airy and luminous courtyard of marble flanked by thirty-six columns of rose-coloured granite from Baveno on the western side of Lake Maggiore in Piedmont provided an exotic introduction to Roman working life. There was a constant to-and-fro of people at the main entrance, and a buzz of staff chatting busily as they made their way to and from the fund's café off the portico surrounding the courtyard. Dressed smartly but casually in light-coloured clothes, many men wore sports jackets and were tieless. This was very different from offices in London where men then wore dark suits with white shirts and ties tightly knotted at their collars.

The rear of the Cassa's building overlooked Via Cristoforo Colombo, a ten-lane highway lined with dark green umbrella pines from the Aurelian Walls to EUR, three central lanes in each direction plus parallel carriageways of two lanes both ways. It was originally known as Via dell'Impero (Road of the Empire). As planners had decided in the late 1930s, the offices for the Istituto Nazionale Previdenza Sociale (INPS, the state pension scheme)—the letters INPS engraved on the ends of the building's two arms—were across the road from those occupied by the Cassa. Mirroring the INPS building, the letters INA were engraved on the end walls of what were the offices of the Cassa, although the Istituto Nazionale delle Assicurazioni (INA, a large state-owned insurer) never occupied the building that had been designed and built for it.

The INA and INPS buildings are among around twenty that appear prominently on open land across which the principal road axes of the district are clearly visible in an aerial photograph taken immediately after the war. According to Vieri Quilici, an architectural historian, the two buildings were among the most significant relics of fascism's project, which was halted, touched by the passage of war, suspended and then abandoned. With Rome's widest road between them, the INA and INPS buildings form a piazza in a striking entrance to what would have been the World Fair. The principal architect, Giovanni Muzio, a proponent of restrained classicism, was assisted by two younger architects, Giulio Pediconi and Mario Paniconi, who leaned towards modernism. The result was a felicitous marriage of the two styles. The curved porticoes of the two buildings, surmounted by a double order of columns, make four arms in a way that "embraces visitors arriving from Rome". Fountains placed between the curves of the porticoes occasionally play. Set above the letters INA and INPS, square high relief sculptures in Roman travertine decorate the ends of the arms, *The Conquest of the Seas* and *The Fascist Empire* on the INA building and *The Marine Republics* and *Rome against Carthage* on the INPS building.

* * *

In late spring 1935, leaders of the fascist regime had begun discussing the idea of celebrating their twenty years in power with a World Fair in Rome, and in June the following year, despite the Italian invasion of Abyssinia in October 1935 and consequent but futile and ineffective international sanctions, the Bureau International des Expositions in Paris approved Italy's application. Rome's World Fair was a litmus test for the regime. It needed to show that it was efficient and capable of building and organising the fair. The regime wanted to use the fair to express fascism's ideas of modernity. The fair offered an opportunity to demonstrate the best of Italian culture and business, and the regime allocated the resources needed to do so. Those who oversaw the project were people of proven managerial ability and energy, while the architects responsible for the master plan and for designing the buildings were leading figures in their profession. Although they presented Mussolini with a list of the most prominent Italian architects, the three-man managing director-ate probably nudged him towards the team of five architects whose names appeared on the master plan that was subsequently developed. Marcello Piacentini, well established and the oldest, leaned strongly towards monumentalism, but the others were modernists, among them Giuseppe Pagano, a leading proponent of rationalist style. (Pagano turned against fascism in December 1942 and died, not yet 50 years old, at Mauthausen in Austria, thirteen days before the concentration camp was liberated.)

The choice of site fell on an area of undulating open country-side about five kilometres from the Porta Ardeatina in the Aurelian Walls. Mussolini envisaged Rome as an outward-look-ing city, and the site, close to the Tiber and in the direction of Ostia on the coast, fitted his vision. The zones mapped out in the original plan prepared in April 1937 and the definitive plan of the following year show a shape that would be recognisably EUR more than eighty years later, with Via Cristoforo Colombo bisecting the site, its carriageways separating to cross an artificial lake and joining again after about 800 metres. Most of the build-ing undertaken before war brought a halt was close to the first decumanus (an east–west axis) beside the INA and INPS build-ings, which runs from the Palazzo dei Congressi to the Palazzo della Civiltà del Lavoro, which is also known as the Palazzo della Civiltà Italiana. English guidebooks would often call it the Cheese Grater or Square Colosseum (from the Italian "Colosseo Quadrato"). The post-war aerial photograph mentioned earlier shows nothing lying between the two extremes of the second decumanus, the church of Santi Pietro e Paolo at the western end and what was intended to be the Piazza delle Forze Armate (Armed Forces Piazza, now Piazzale degli Archivi) and the build-ings that enclose the eastern end of it.

As visitors in the twenty-first century would see, Piacentini's monumentalism won the battle for the architectural style that would characterise E42 (Esposizione 42), and the younger, more numerous group of modernists with their rationalist projects were the losers. Few of the monumentalist buildings represent the style's dull weightiness better than a group of museums, including the museum of popular arts and traditions, the prehistoric ethnographic museum and the museum of Oriental art, and the triumphal arch that stand on the eastern side of what was called Piazza Imperiale. This piazza was planned as the central nucleus of E42, and the museums on the eastern side are mirrored by equally massive buildings on the western side. An obelisk standing at its centre, it was renamed Piazza Marconi after the war. More monumentalism marks the buildings around the piazza which ends the broad avenue that goes eastwards from the arch by Piazza Marconi. A similarly monumental arch, with Museo della Civiltà Romana (Museum of Roman Civilisation) engraved on it, closes that piazza.

Fortunately, the future was bequeathed an iconic, imaginative and unforgettably quirky monument by E42's monumentalist obsession: the Square Colosseum. Perhaps even those who dislike EUR's monumentalism cannot help being won over by it. The reinforced concrete structure clad in white travertine, which positively glows in the sunshine, beat fifty-two competitors for what would be E42's emblem. Sixty metres high on a base 53 metres by 53 metres, it is big and it dominates its surroundings. It's an unmissable landmark, visible when seen from the final kilometres of the highway from Fiumicino airport as this rises above other roads before crossing the Tiber. Each of the building's four equal faces is pierced by fifty-four arches, six vertically and nine horizontally. It's certainly monumental, yet it's also rationalist with none of the bombast that goes with EUR's monumentalist buildings. Despite its size it has elegance. That's not surprising as Ernesto La Padula, who headed the team of three architects responsible for the design, was a founding member in 1928 of the

Movimento Italiano per l'Architettura Razionale that gave birth to Italian rationalist architecture. It was in La Padula's offices on Piazza del Popolo that the movement held its first meetings. La Padula grew up in a socialist family, and the fascist regime didn't change his ideas or the circle of people in which he moved. Perhaps there is a trace of tongue in cheek in the words engraved in three lines above the top nine arches, a tribute to Italians: "a people of poets, of artists, of heroes, of saints, of thinkers, of scientists, of navigators, of migrants".

There's elegance also in two buildings close to the Palazzo della Civiltà del Lavoro. E42's planners intended that a two-storey building by its base should be a public restaurant and café, albeit with private facilities for staff of the body administering E42. It was designed by Ettore Rossi, one of the young rationalist-style architects who worked with Piacentini on the master plan. There's airiness and luminosity to the building, which has porticoes on three sides, the porticoes' slender travertine columns extending the building's full height. The Caffè Palombini began occupying one side of the ground floor in 1963, so part of the planners' intentions has been met. The smart café claims to be a meeting place for all generations, an essential reference point for those seeking the best in coffee, aperitifs and pastries, to be enjoyed on an open terrace, where soaring masses of purple-flowered bougainvillea plants climb the walls, in its conservatory or sitting at one of the tables in its large and comfortable lounge.

I occasionally drank cappuccinos at Palombini when I came to know the building in the middle years of the 1970s. Housing the department of the Cassa per il Mezzogiorno that designed aqueducts and water supply and drainage systems for the south of Italy, the building had probably been offices for more than a decade. It would have been during that early period—I imagine immediately before the development fund's staff moved in—that significant architectural vandalism was done to what Rossi intended and to what was there in 1953, when photographs still showed the porticoes created by the travertine columns. Possibly to squeeze more working space from the structure, windows had been reinstalled further out.

The other notably elegant building, the offices of the EUR administrative authority, the only building completed before war interrupted work, stands across the road from the bougainvillea-clad wall of Palombini's terrace. It comprises two elements: one a square, plain three-storey office block built around an internal courtyard, the other a rectangular building containing a reception hall that overlooks a piazza in which fountains play in fine arcs above shallow pools neighbouring pavement mosaics reminiscent of those at Ostia Antica. The style of the facade, with its adornment of slender rectangular columns in travertine, has been described as restrained monumentalist, which might easily be translated as rationalist. Engraved above the sixteen columns are the words "La terza Roma si dilaterà sopra altri colli lungo le rive del fiume sacro sino alle spiagge del Tirreno" (The third Rome will spread across other hills along the banks of the sacred river to the beaches of the Tyrrhenian Sea). Such were the dreams of some of those who conceived E42. Propaganda was a central instrument of the fascist regime, in architecture and in words.

Although Mussolini planted an umbrella pine in EUR in April 1937 to symbolise the beginning of work on the World Fair, architects and designers were still busy tackling the challenges of fascism's grand celebratory project. Since July 1936, Spain had been in the grip of a civil war between democratic republicans on one side and rightwing nationalists and monarchists on the other, and a far wider war threatened the whole of Europe. The detailed plan for EUR would be completed in 1938, the very year that the gulf separating European democracies on one side from the continent's extreme-right dictatorships on the other was made glaringly and undeniably clear by the programme of a state visit to Rome.

SCENES FROM A ROMAN CENTURY

Hitler visits Rome

Tuesday, 3 May 1938, ended like any other working day for officers and men of Italy's Regia Marina serving in warships anchored or berthed at Naples while the fleet was preparing for manoeuvres. They had recited the sailors' evening prayer, asking the Lord to "bless us who keep armed watch on the sea". Those on upper decks had turned aft to face towards their ships' sterns where ensigns flew. They had come to attention and removed headgear while ensigns were slowly hauled down as the sun slipped below the horizon. Liberty men were already ashore and the duty watch on board had carried out daily fire drill. The sunset ceremony had brought the day to a close. Almost an hour and a half later, a train carrying Adolf Hitler pulled alongside platform number one at Rome's Ostiense railway station. He had been met that morning by Filiberto of Savoy (Duke of Pistoia and cousin of the king), a guard of honour, Italian flags, banners carrying swastikas, and cheering crowds when his train stopped at Brenner, near the mountain pass of that name on the Italian–Austrian border. Then spring weather and organised crowds on station platforms and in towns and the countryside beside the tracks had accompanied his journey south. But night had fallen and darkness had arrived when, to the sound of a saluting gun being fired, Hitler's train drew to a halt in Rome.

As the door to his carriage was opened, a party led by King Victor Emmanuel III stepped forward to welcome him, the scene filmed by the Istituto Luce. The commentary of the propaganda newsreel of Hitler's arrival and stay in Rome described the greeting offered by the king and Mussolini as the "solemn moment of meeting between the Führer of the new Germany, the king-emperor and the Duce, founder of the empire". Background shadows and camera flashes were caught in the filming of handshakes, bows, military salutes, straight-armed Roman salutes by fascist hosts, and nazi salutes by German guests, accompanied by a clicking of jackboot heels. The German party of several hundred included most of the nazi top brass, notably Joseph Goebbels (minister for propaganda), Rudolf Hess (deputy Führer), Heinrich Himmler (head of the SS) and Joachim von Ribbentrop (foreign minister). As at Brenner, all on the platform were in uniform, and all were men. Mussolini wanted uniforms and military matters to be the focus of Hitler's visit. He wanted to show that, like the ancient Roman empire, fascist Italy was based on martial power.

The lighting effects the regime had prepared for the German dictator were striking. Flickering theatrically in the breeze, hundreds of blazing oil flares, perhaps thousands of them, provided atmospheric illumination along the roads that the horse-drawn carriage carrying Hitler and the king travelled to the royal residence at the Quirinal Palace. The Istituto Luce described the spectacular show as being designed to match the grandeur of the occasion. When editing, propagandists may have added the soundtrack of roaring crowds and an occasional burst of loud parade-ground music to accompany the commentary, but the large number of Italians, filmed as the king's carriage passed, was indubitably there and waving flags. Escorted by columns of mounted Carabinieri, the cavalcade followed the newly renamed Viale Adolf Hitler to the Porta San Paolo Roman gate, and then down Viale Aventino to the Circus Maximus. Along Via dei Trionfi, the Palatine on the left, the Arch of Constantine and the Colosseum ahead, this tour of Rome by night aimed to impress. It passed beside the Roman Forum, the heart of ancient Roman power, along Via dell'Impero that had until recently been a district of medieval buildings. The area's clearance on Mussolini's orders opened a broad avenue for military parades between the Colosseum and Piazza Venezia, where the Duce gave speeches from his balcony. Hitler was being shown "the road that joins Old Rome to the forum of the most solemn ceremonies of fascist Italy".

A meeting with Mussolini at the Quirinal Palace began the nazi leader's first full day in the Eternal City. For the Istituto Luce, this was a meeting of two *condottieri*. Tourism gave Hitler visits to the Pantheon, one of Rome's best known attractions with its vast cupola and imposing entrance portico, and to the Vittoriano monument on Piazza Venezia, where he laid a wreath on the altar of the *patria*, the tomb of Italy's unknown soldier of the Great War. During the days that followed, Hitler was shown the museum of Roman civilisation, the Ara Pacis of Caesar Augustus, the Villa Borghese museum and the Palatine as well as being treated to a display of folk dancing at the Piazza di Siena in the Borghese gardens. But the regime's emphasis was squarely on military matters. It laid on manoeuvres at Centocelle airport, an air base in Rome's southeastern outskirts about ten kilometres from the centre, more manoeuvres the following day at Furbara, a grass strip aerodrome about fifty kilometres north of the city where, according to the Istituto Luce, the air force demonstrated its readiness for war, and a day on board a battleship in the Bay of Naples watching the Regia Marina show off its ships and fire-power. And on the day before he left Rome, Hitler's Italian hosts organised a huge military parade that passed a saluting base on Via dei Trionfi and brought tens of thousands of soldiers to march, ride or drive from the Circus Maximus to the Colosseum and beyond.

The summit between the two dictators in May 1938 was their third meeting. They had met in Venice in June 1934 and in Berlin in September 1937, but Hitler had introduced a new factor into their relationship since Mussolini's journey to the German capital. In March, nazi forces had invaded Austria and Germany annexed its neighbour, thereby moving its own frontier up to the border with Italy. And Hitler had given Mussolini no warning of his plans. Many Italians viewed the German annexation of Austria with concern. Others were angry at what seemed an affront and disappointed by Mussolini's meek acceptance. However, Hitler offered conciliatory words when he appeared one evening with Mussolini on the Duce's balcony. The Alpine frontier was untouchable, he assured his host. As for Mussolini, Hitler's visit to Rome had consecrated the Rome–Berlin axis and cooperation between fascist Italy and nazi Germany.

The first of those Roman days, just fifteen months before the second world war engulfed Europe, would be remembered nearly forty years later by the film director Ettore Scola. *Una giornata particolare* (A special day) gave cinema-goers outstanding performances from Sophia Loren and Marcello Mastroianni, both winning 1978's Globo d'Oro awards, while Mastroianni was nominated for best actor in 1978, both for an Oscar and a Golden Globe. The film won Scola a Golden Globe for best foreign film. A social, political and sentimental drama, the film's action takes place over just a few hours of Hitler's first full day in Rome. Apart from footage from Istituto Luce's coverage of Hitler's arrival, the location for external and some internal shooting was the Palazzo Federici, an enormous residential complex in Rome's Nomentana–Bologna district that was completed in 1937. There's no mistaking the building's style: Italian rationalist architecture on a vast scale. Had he seen it, perhaps the Palazzo Federici would have appealed to Hitler, who considered himself an expert on urban planning and architectural matters.

What impressions did Hitler take away? Reports from German diplomats and military officers in Italy had already advised him that Italy's military strength was mostly illusory and was mainly bluff. And the parades, military manoeuvres and air force exercises highlighted the obsolescence of the equipment in service with the Italian army and air force. The German army and air force could call on hardware that was more modern and more effective. There was illusion also at the Ostiense railway station, and Hitler had probably been told about this. Although his attention may have been taken mainly by the crowds, the movement and noise and the illuminations beyond the station's entrance, perhaps he glanced at the station's new walls and columns, and saw them for what they were. Hitler's arrival in Rome was staged, with the station, erected in just forty-five days, little more than a theatrical set. What at first sight seemed travertine stone was a plaster surface applied to wood chipboard panels that had been fixed to steel scaffolding tubes.

Time had been insufficient to build what Mussolini considered a suitably impressive station for Hitler's arrival in Rome. The invitation was only decided after Mussolini's visit to Berlin, when the grandeur of the German capital had left a deep impression on him. The railway station where Hitler would be welcomed to the Eternal City had to leave a similarly strong impression on the German leader. It had to be monumental as well as close to important archaeological sites in order to give Hitler an unforgettable arrival in the city. Stazione Termini, Rome's main station, whose building took place between 1868 and 1874, was unsuitable. It wasn't near major archaeological sites and, above all, it was typical of many railway termini in major European cities, a relic of the second half of the nineteenth century. Not far from the Porta San Paolo terminus of the railway line from Ostia, the new Ostiense station replaced a modest building on the Rome to Pisa coastal line, alongside the Scalo San Paolo marshalling yards and about seven kilometres down the track from Stazione Termini.

Whatever the materials used to build the station where Hitler arrived in Rome, the work of the architect Roberto Narducci was well received, and his design would be retained for the permanent building that replaced 1938's temporary station. The 110-metre facade, with its central portico of twelve slender columns, is entirely clad with travertine, and its unadorned verticals and horizontals provide a fine example of Italian rationalist style. A bas relief sculpture of Pegasus and Bellerophon enhances a wall to the right of the portico, and the floor within the portico is decorated with a series of black-and-white mosaics that tell part of the story of Rome. The station, a luminous, spacious and agreeable building that was inaugurated in 1940, still welcomes travellers in the 2020s, as well as people wanting to use the passageway beneath the fifteen tracks to cross from one side to the other. After being renamed Via A. Hitler in honour of the Führer at the time of his visit, the road joining the piazza outside the station to the Porta San Paolo would have another name change at the end of the second world war, to Viale delle Cave Ardeatine. This was the quarry where German SS soldiers murdered 335 Italians in a reprisal for an operation by partisans. And, losing the name of the nazi leader, the piazza outside the station would commemorate the partisans themselves by becoming Piazzale dei Partigiani.

Public buildings and fascist symbols

When Hitler travelled to Naples to watch the Italian navy's manoeuvres, he used the Stazione Termini. And he used it again four days later when leaving for a day of sightseeing in Florence with Mussolini before beginning his return to Germany. With only six tracks, and with Rome as Italy's capital and its population growing rapidly, the city's original main station had soon proved too small, and work began on expansion shortly after its inauguration. However, even after enlargement, the station was insufficient for Rome's needs, and this was recognised in the 1930s. The decision was taken that a new terminus should be built, and the project for this was approved in 1939.

Favoured by many fascist decision-makers, monumentalism was the essence of the design. A massive portico-facade was to stand in front of a vast atrium of 12,000 square metres, which is about half as big again as the football pitch at Wembley stadium, one of England's biggest. The architects and engineers, and the fascist politicians who encouraged them, were aiming for effect rather than functionality. Efficiency was secondary to their thinking. Because the station was planned as a showcase for the nation, top-quality Italian marble was to be used for wall facings and floors. Work began with demolition of the old building and the siting of a new building about 200 metres down the tracks, thereby giving space for a large piazza in front of the terminus. Construction of parts of the wings was completed before a worsening war situation caused the government to suspend work in 1943. Suspension would offer an opportunity to post-war decision-makers to reconsider the project, and their rethinking would be radical. The heart of the new Termini station, still in use in the 2020s, would bear no resemblance to the dreams of Mussolini's architects.

Understandably, two or three generations in the future, most of Rome's residential buildings from the *ventennio* would go unnoticed. Equally unnoticed would be buildings in the centre of Rome that had housed fascist ministries and state organisations, the economic development (at one time, industry) ministry on Via Veneto, built between 1928 and 1932, and the national institute of insurance on Via Bissolati, built between 1936 and 1944, being typical examples. Just outside the centre, at the southeastern end of the Circus Maximus, the building that would become the headquarters of the United Nations Food and Agriculture Organization (FAO) had been destined for the ministry of Italian Africa. Construction began in 1938 but was only completed in 1952, nine years after the Italian empire in Africa ended. The Axum obelisk that Italy looted from Abyssinia in 1937 would stand in the central reservation of the road outside the FAO building until being dismantled for return to Ethiopia in 2003.

Those curious about the organisations that decided and controlled how Romans lived during Mussolini's dictatorship may sometimes wonder where those decisions were made and controls exercised. Where, for example, were offices of the Opera Nazionale Maternità e Infanzia and the Unione Fascista Famiglie Numerose, bodies concerned with maternity, childhood and large families? Where was the special inspectorate, usually referred to as OVRA, established by the Arturo Bocchini, the police chief, to uncover and stamp out anti-fascism, or the ministry of popular culture, the infamous but risible Ministero della Cultura Popolare (MinCulPop) which, through propaganda and censorship, had the responsibility for totalitarian control over news, speech, writing and thought? And where were the central and district offices of the Balilla, Avanguardisti and Giovani Fascisti organisations for children and young people, and the Gioventù Italiana del Littorio, their umbrella successor from 1937?

With the parents whose children who took part, many of them reluctantly, in the Saturday *sabato fascista* gatherings of those organisations with their creed "*credere, obbedire, combattere*" (believe, obey, fight), and most of the children too, having passed to *miglior vita* (better life), the organisations themselves had by the 2020s simply become paragraphs or a few lines in history books. And while buildings may pass unrecognised as reminders of the *ventennio*, symbols that the regime drew from ancient Rome still survive in the marks that fascism left on the Italian capital.

From December 1926, castings or stone sculptures of a *fascio littorio* (a bundle of wooden staves strapped together by leather strips with an axe at the side) were added to walls of government buildings, and the following year the *fascio littorio* became the badge of the Italian state. The Italian term comes from the Latin *fasces lictoriae*, the arm carried by lictors and a symbol of state power. For the *Shorter Oxford Dictionary*, a lictor is "an officer whose functions were to attend upon a magistrate, bearing the fasces before him, and to execute sentence of judgement upon offenders". Above the first-floor windows of number 323 Via del Corso are the much-faded words Libreria del Littorio, a relic of the years when Mussolini was in power. At some point the book-shop became the Hotel Regno (Kingdom Hotel), though this was shuttered in the wake of the Covid-19 pandemic.

The symbol would survive on the sides of decorative vases in stone gate-pillars to the Monte Esquilino park behind the Colosseum. It would, however, be chipped away from the sides of drinking fountains inside the park, although their outlines would continue to be visible. The *fasci littori* would also be removed from what remained of a fountain set into a wall of the Antiquarium Comunale on Via di San Gregorio, opposite the entrance to the Palatine. In 1926, a column was placed at the centre of each quadrant of the pond that stands at the centre of Piazza Mazzini in Rome's Prati district. The columns were capped with imperial eagles and three *fasci littori* decorate their sides, between them the words "Honor, Virtus, Imperium", Latin that can be translated as "honour, courage, authority". The *fasci littori* would be defaced by the obliteration of the axe heads. A brick wall providing support to the Teatro di Marcello and visible from Via del Teatro di Marcello would continue to carry a stone inset of three *fasci littori*, the letters A, VII, E and F beside and between them to say that the wall was built in 1929, the seventh year of the fascist era. Nearby, on a wall of Rome's central registry office, another stone, topped by the Roman wolf suckling Romulus and Remus, and the letters SPQR below the wolf, was placed to commemorate Benito Mussolini Duce and Petrus Columna Præf Urb. Those names would remain visible, but the name of Victor Eman III Rege Imp (Victor Emmanuel III king-emperor) would be barely visible after obvious attempts to remove it.

The imperial eagle was another fascist symbol. The badge on officers' caps, like that worn by Mussolini, was an imperial eagle clutching a *fascio littorio* in its talons. A carving of an imperial eagle would decorate the facade of the Nuovo Sacher cinema in Trastevere, alongside the words "Dopolavoro dei Monopoli di Stato". Built between 1936 and 1938, the theatre had been part of a recreation centre for workers employed by state monopolies that had offices and factories nearby. The *fascio littorio* would be removed from the eagle's talons. However, eagles would be present together with *fasci littori* at the base of tall grey flagpoles near Piazza della Repubblica. Five large maps in stone showing how the Roman empire grew were set into the wall of the Basilica di Massenzio at the side of Via dei Fori Imperiali, then Via del Impero, and inaugurated by Mussolini in 1934. Only four would remain after the fifth, which showed how Italy developed its empire in the first four decades of the twentieth century, was removed from public view following the second world war.

A reminder of other territory lost because of Mussolini's adventures is visible on a terrace of the Victor Emmanuel monument that overlooks Piazza Venezia. Alongside an inscription of the victory bulletin issued on 4 November 1918 by Armando Diaz, the commander of the Italian army, are the names of six provinces that were taken by Italy from Austria-Hungary in the post-war settlement. Zara, Pola and Fiume, the three Istrian provinces, would pass to Yugoslavia after the second world war. Who can imagine what Italy's capital city would have become and how it would have appeared had Mussolini, like Francisco Franco in Spain, opted for neutrality after Germany forced a war on its European neighbours and the world in 1939? Instead ...

III

WAR IN ROME

You'll see your Rome embrac'd with fire

William Shakespeare, *Coriolanus*

From the terrace of the Vittoriano, the monument to King Victor Emmanuel II that looms above Piazza Venezia, a camera panned left across crowds below, thousands of waving banners adding movement to a mass of black, white and greys, Via del Corso ahead solid with people. It settled briefly on the fifteenth-century Palazzo di Venezia. Another view was captured by a camera placed opposite the Vittoriano and filming people packed on the monument's stairs and along Via dell'Impero towards the Colosseum. The newsreel service of the Istituto Luce, the fascist regime's cinematographic propaganda arm, was busy that day, 10 June 1940, preparing for and filming an announcement by the Duce. More cameras recorded the scene. One was focused on a small second-floor balcony above the door in the centre of the Palazzo di Venezia's plain facade. A figure dressed in a black uniform appeared in the room behind the balcony, and the cheering increased as he came out, raising his arm in a Roman salute.

With one step Benito Mussolini was leaning forward to place his hands on the balcony's ledge. A camera positioned in the room framed him for an over-the-shoulder shot, a bulky figure, lifting his right arm again in a Roman salute. "Saluti al Duce!" (Salute the leader), ordered a beige-uniformed man on the balcony, turning towards Mussolini with his right arm raised. Thumbs stuck in belt, lantern jaw thrust out, the Duce began: "Combattenti di terra, di mare e dell'aria! Camicie nere della rivoluzione e delle legioni! Uomini e donne dell'Italia, dell'Impero e del regno dell'Albania! Ascoltate!" (Fighters on land, at sea and in the air! Blackshirts of the revolution and the legions! Men and women of Italy, of the Empire and of the Kingdom of Albania! Listen!)

A moment of destiny had crossed Italian skies, Mussolini told the crowd. This was the moment of irrevocable decisions. "The declaration of war has already been delivered to the ambassadors of Great Britain and France," he announced. The nation was entering the fight against the West's plutocratic and reactionary democracies that had always stood in Italy's way and often threatened its existence. For Mussolini, Italy's conscience was absolutely clear. The country had done everything possible to avoid a war that would devastate Europe, but in vain. Honour, interests and the future itself imposed the decision to accept risks and sacrifices. The struggle was between the young and fertile and the barren and declining, between two centuries and two ideas. "The dice have been rolled," said Mussolini. Yet, arguably, the ending for the regime began that day when, believing that the victory of Hitler's armies in northern Europe had cleared the way for Italy to have its place in the sun among the world's great powers and for him to participate in sharing the conqueror's spoils, Mussolini announced Italy's declaration of war on France and Great Britain. Even so, as the historian Richard Bosworth notes in his biography of the Duce, this was not a decision of one man alone, and circumstances were such that "Mussolini had made a 'decision' from which few demurred". For the superstitious, however, 10 June 1940, the sixteenth anniversary of the murder of Giacomo Matteotti, was an inauspicious day to roll the dice of war.

For the next eighteen months, thanks to European allies in exile and the forces of the Commonwealth and empire, and with lend-lease support from America, Britain held out and, despite setbacks, the Allies managed to cling on in the Mediterranean and North Africa. Then, standing on his balcony above Piazza Venezia on 11 December 1941, Mussolini told the crowds below that Italy had widened its war, and that its new enemy was America. Within a year Allied forces had landed in Morocco and Algeria, and the British Eighth Army had defeated Axis armies at El Alamein in Egypt. In July 1943 the Allies landed in Sicily. They crossed to the mainland on 3 September, the day that Italy signed an armistice. This became public five days later. Italy's war had lasted just over three years. However, the war in Italy would bring nearly twenty more months of bloodshed, and Rome, where a committee for national liberation was immediately established, was the first major city to suffer in a phase of the war that set Italians against Germans, and Italians against Italians.

The defence of Rome

The Allied landings in Sicily had brought the end for Mussolini, who was overthrown on 25 July 1943 and followed as prime minister by Pietro Badoglio, the army chief of staff between 1925 and 1940. And the announcement of the armistice brought the end of government in Rome. The king and his entourage, and senior military and political figures, including Badoglio, fled the city early on 9 September, leaving behind confusion, uncertainty and a leaderless army. Germany's army suffered no such handicaps, and their paratroops were soon in action. About 14,000 were stationed at the military airfield of Pratica di Mare near the coast, about 30 kilometres south of the capital, and within an hour of the announcement of the armistice they had seized valuable stocks of fuel and taken key positions close to the Alban Hills.

German forces quickly pushed strongly towards Rome, moving inland close to the bank of the Tiber and through the district where construction was well advanced on what would be two key buildings on high points of the site of the World Fair planned for 1942. Germans occupied the Palazzo della Civiltà Italiana, and were engaged in fierce fighting around the church of Santi Pietro e Paolo. The church occupied a position of tactical value, as visitors can imagine many years after war briefly touched that part of Rome. Long flights of broad ceremonial stairs lead from significantly lower ground to the front of the church, an imposing building with a large dome, the city's third highest after Saint Peter's basilica and Sant'Andrea della Valle. Two further flights of stairs follow to a raised platform on which the church stands, with wide passageways at each side that lead around the building to the rear. From there, despite the umbrella pines growing on a slope that drops away steeply towards the river, the position dominates the Tiber upstream and down, as well as providing lines of sight to hills behind the Tiber's northern side.

However, on the morning of 10 September German soldiers passed beyond EUR, both along Via Ostiense, which follows the river towards the city centre, and across open land around Via Imperiale, which passed through EUR and joined Rome to the sea at Ostia, the post-war Via Cristoforo Colombo. A five-kilometre march along Via Ostiense took the Germans past the San Paolo basilica and the city's wholesale food market. Close by, about 500 metres beyond the Rome-to-Pisa railway line, was the section of the Aurelian Walls that runs from the Porta San Paolo, and the neighbouring Pyramid of Cestius, to the Baths of

Caracalla. There, at the Roman walls and the pyramid the Germans faced a hastily organised defence. And there, helped by civilian volunteers, Italian soldiers, among them troops of the Sardinian grenadiers, the Montebello lancers from Piedmont, and Carabinieri of the Rome legion offered the fiercest resistance to the German advance. It was a valiant but vain and short-lived effort and, given how the armistice was announced and the behaviour of the Italian leaders, it could not have been otherwise.

Close to the pyramid, commemorative tablets fixed to the wall of the non-Catholic cemetery tell part of the story of desperate fighting against battle-hardened German forces on 10 September 1943. About one-third of almost 600 defenders killed by the Germans in the Battle of Porta San Paolo were civilians. Just four years later, memories still fresh of what happened, partisans of the Lazio region placed a tablet to recall how for seventeen centuries the walls had been a defence against Barbarians and how, guided by faith, soldiers from many regiments and civilians from all walks of life showed Italians the path to honour and freedom by opposing the German invaders. Unveiled on 9 September 1990, a nearby tablet acknowledges the role that women played in defending their city against the German onslaught: "To the women of Rome who, fighting alongside soldiers and citizens through days of extreme danger and with fearless resistance, defended the city and the patria, helped the wounded, comforted the dying, each one of the women facing death, many of them dying, the City of Rome and the National Association of Italian Partisans place this stone in everlasting memory and honour of their courage, compassion and commitment to freedom and peace."

Maria Teresa Regard was 19 years old when she joined the ranks of women trying to hold back the German forces at Porta San Paolo. She had been a member of a Trotskyist group while at school and joined the outlawed and underground Italian

Communist Party in 1941. Her role in September 1943 was that of dispatch runner and supply orderly. After the German army took control of Rome, Regard continued her fight as a partisan. Remembering that blood-soaked day at Porta San Paolo, she later noted that because the thrust of German forces was along the southern bank of the Tiber, "this first mass participation in resistance to nazi-fascism involved working-class Roman women from San Paolo, Garbatella, Testaccio and districts between the Roman Walls and EUR such as Montagnola and Magliana". How many women took part? There are no contemporaneous rolls or official records, but perhaps several thousand women participated in the attempt to defend Rome. Fifty-five of them were victims of the German attack. On 8 September 2010, the city's cultural heritage department planted fifty-five roses "to keep alive the memory of the sacrifice of 55 mothers, wives, sweethearts, students, workers and pensioners".

A section of road separating the pyramid from the Porta San Paolo, just a few tens of metres beside which no buildings stand, would be named Via Raffaele Persichetti in memory of a young officer who died on 10 September 1943 near that spot. Persichetti had been discharged as a war invalid but went there on being told that defensive action was underway and, arming himself with a pistol, took command of a leaderless group of soldiers. Fighting alongside him was a medical student, Adriano Ossicini, a practising Catholic who frequented a neo-Marxist group, had co-founded a clandestine newspaper (*Pugno Chiuso*—Closed Fist) and would help establish the Catholic Communist Movement immediately after Rome fell to the Germans. On the evening of 8 September, with Luigi Longo, who had fought with the Garibaldi Brigade in the Spanish Civil War and would later become secretary of the Italian Communist Party, Ossicini had collected a small quantity of arms from various barracks. These were distributed the following day.

At around three o'clock in the afternoon of 10 September, Ossicini accompanied Persichetti, whose jacket was covered with blood from the battle, and led him towards Viale Giotto, a broad avenue inside the walls that runs uphill towards the area above the Baths of Caracalla. And it was there, on that lower section of Viale Giotto near Porta San Paolo, that Persichetti was seen to fall and die. About three hours later, as German soldiers won control, Ossicini guided a group of fighters to safety through the non-Catholic cemetery. Like many involved in the attempt to defend Rome, he went into hiding and helped organise resistance, always on the move and usually staying in religious institutions. He was caught in a check on Via del Corso in February 1944 but, thanks to being the last among those arrested, he managed to slip away and escape. The citation for the silver military medal for gallantry notes that Ossicini organised a strong and courageous partisan group that committed numerous acts of sabotage and guerrilla actions. Ossicini was a "fine example of brave fighter and capable organiser". The street sign fixed to the wall by the Pyramid of Cestius, placed in honour of Raffaele Persichetti, simply says that he fell in the defence of Rome in September 1943 and was awarded the gold medal for gallantry.

The German high command had wasted no time in dispatching its paratroopers from Pratica di Mare to Rome. And the SS and Gestapo wasted little time before rounding up Rome's Jews. On 10 September, with the noise of gunfire echoing in the streets near the Porta San Paolo, the Porta San Giovanni and around the Piazza dei Cinquecento in the heart of Rome, Herbert Kappler, a lieutenant colonel in the SS and the Gestapo's chief in Rome, received a message from Heinrich Himmler. Writing from Berlin, the principal architect of the elimination of Jews told Kappler that developments of the war in Italy required "an immediate solution to the Jewish problem" in territory recently occupied by German armies. Two weeks later Himmler wrote again to Kappler to say that all Jews "irrespective of age, nationality, gender or condition" should be transferred to Germany for liquidation. Himmler said that surprise action was needed to ensure a successful round-up.

Villa Wolkonsky

On 26 September, Kappler summoned leaders of the Jewish community to his office at the German embassy in the Villa Wolkonsky, close to the San Giovanni in Laterano basilica. Unless they delivered 50 kilos of gold within thirty-six hours, he told them, he would immediately order the deportation of two hundred Jews to Germany, and the rest of the Jewish community would follow. In exchange for the gold, the Jewish community would be safe, Kappler promised. At six o'clock in the afternoon of 28 September, a slippage of four hours to which Kappler had agreed, Jewish leaders took the gold to Villa Wolkonsky and then, with an escort, carried it about 400 metres to a plain, flat-fronted, four-storey 1930s building on Via Tasso. Leaving the villa down a steep slope and passing through the main gates, the party turned right onto Via Ludovico di Savoia. After about 100 metres they reached Viale Emanuele Filiberto. Across the street, Via Domenico Fontana led uphill to a turning onto Via Tasso, opposite the rear of the Scala Santa and a small section of the Neronian aqueduct, a branch of the Claudian aqueduct built to supply Nero's Domus Aurea residence on the Oppian Hill.

Number 145 Via Tasso would carry a grim significance. It had been leased by the German embassy in 1941, and Kappler took over the whole block for Gestapo and SS units in September 1943. The part at number 155 held nazi offices and accommodation, while that behind the entrance at number 145 was a prison, and the two parts were linked by corridors. Conditions were unspeakable. Torture and brutality were normal. In the 2020s, a long vertical banner hanging beside the door at number 145 says that the building is the Liberation Historical Museum. A commemorative tablet had been fixed to the wall on 5 June 1945 by the National Association of Italian Partisans in eternal memory of all fighters for freedom, the inscription noting that it "consecrates for all time the place where nazi ferocity raged strongest and the heroism of martyrs shone brightest". Neighboured by two large church schools, the Istituto Santa Maria and the Istituto Suore Carmelitane, the block on Via Tasso where Kappler was in command is close to the San Giovanni in Laterano basilica and within easy walking distance of the Santa Maria Maggiore basilica and other churches and convents. The Gestapo and the SS were based in a district thick with religious institutions.

Other than the museum, in 2022 the mustard-coloured block which would always be associated with the barbarities committed within its walls held the offices of the Sindacato dei Lavoratori d'Europa, the union of European workers. Above the list of occupants and their bell-pushes at number 155 was a metal plate to say that the Relais 155 guest house was on the first floor. How many of those who stayed there knew the building's gruesome history, and were those who did able to sleep easily when they turned out the lights? And perhaps those who lived in the Villa Wolkonsky, once the centre of nazi power in Rome, also wondered about what Germans did there when the building housed officers like Herbert Kappler.

Set in four and a half hectares of gardens, the villa is a grand building that owes its name to Zenaïde Wolkonsky, a Russian princess. She oversaw the transformation of agricultural land into a large romantic garden and the construction of a small house within arches of a long section of the Neronian aqueduct that passed across the land. During the 1830s and 1840s, the Villa Wolkonsky became a place of parties and salons frequented by leading literary and musical figures, including Sir Walter Scott and Gaetano Donizetti. It is said that Nikolai Gogol wrote much of *Dead Souls* while staying at Villa Wolkonsky. Following Wolkonsky's death in 1862, the property passed first to her son and then to one of his adopted children, Nadia Campanari, who sold a substantial part of the land before ministerial intervention blocked further sales.

The palatial building that twentieth-century visitors would know as the Villa Wolkonsky grew from a project of the Campanari family who, towards the end of the nineteenth century, built a new villa in the southern part of the gardens. They sold the property to the German government in 1922 after diplomatic relations were resumed following the end of the first world war, and it became the German ambassador's residence. Wings and another floor were added during the next decade, and this was where the SS lieutenant colonel Herbert Kappler worked before moving to Via Tasso. Despite the presence of the Gestapo, Eugen Dollmann, a colonel in the Waffen SS and a senior liaison officer on the German military staff in Rome, described the Villa Wolkonsky as a kind of paradise, "an oasis of peacocks, roses and chirping crickets". The non-diplomatic use of the Villa Wolkonsky and German occupation of Italy after September 1943 allowed the Italian government to seize it after Rome was liberated in 1944, and the building served the Swiss legation for a short period and subsequently as quarters for the Italian Red Cross. It was then leased to the British government for use as a temporary embassy and ambassadorial residence after Irgun terrorists blew up the villa housing the chancery and ambassador's residence at Porta Pia in October 1946. The government in London purchased the Villa Wolkonsky five years later.

Sir Ivor Roberts, then ambassador in Rome, hosted a luncheon party for a small group of journalists in the summer of 2006, shortly before he retired to take up the presidency of

Trinity College Oxford. He seemed more interested in making the occasion a social one than for gathering information to feed back to London, and the journalists were similarly inclined during a long and agreeable meal washed down with liberal quantities of wine. At about three in the afternoon, as coffee was being drunk, one of the group suggested that Sir Ivor might like to show them around the cellars where small, dim spaces were said to have been used as cells for prisoners the Gestapo tortured in the villa's outbuildings, and so he did, in a disquieting tour of a place whose atmosphere was in marked contrast to the beauty and serenity of the gardens above. Making their way out of the villa, down the southern ramp from the building's imposing entrance and onto the drive leading to the gate, a steep slope with two sharp hairpin bends, perhaps some of those journalists wondered how many nazi jackboots had trodden that same path and how many nazi victims had been guests in the villa, their lives later to be snuffed out by their hosts. This was the path along which, on 28 September 1943, the party of Roman Jews had carried their tribute of 50 kilos of gold that the SS lieutenant colonel Herbert Kappler had extorted behind the false promise that they, their families and their community would not be harmed.

The round-up of Jews

Instead, less than three weeks later, early on Saturday 16 October, a Jewish day of rest, about 400 nazis began their barbarous work of rounding up members of Rome's Jewish community, concentrating on Via del Portico di Ottavia and the narrow streets nearby, an area behind the Great Synagogue known then, and as always would be known, as the ghetto. This was a task in which they were helped by the census that Italy's fascist regime had undertaken shortly before the war. The regime had cast a wide net in its four criteria to define who was a Jew, but the census found that the Jewish community in Italy numbered only 47,000, about a tenth of one per cent of the population. Even so, this was enough for the Germans who had occupied Rome and central and northern Italy to put into motion the machinery to arrest and murder them after transportation to Germany.

Jews had lived in Rome since the second century before Christ. However, in 1555 Pope Paul IV ordered that they should be confined from dusk to dawn in the area between the Tiber and the Portico di Ottavia. The ghetto was enlarged in 1825, during the papacy of Leo XII, and this was followed by complete liberalisation in 1848, when Pius IX abolished limitations on where Jews could live, albeit the ghetto and surrounding area continued to have mainly Jewish residents. Access roads were sealed on that terrible black Sabbath in 1943 and, block by block, the Gestapo ordered people, the old, the young, women with babies, children, invalids and the sick, from their homes. At half past five in the morning many had been in bed. They offered no resistance.

Reporting the outcome of the operation, Kappler said that the passive resistance of Romans often became active assistance to their Jewish neighbours and that in one case nazis found a black-shirted fascist with an official document in a building where Jews were listed as living. Twin sisters who lived there were saved. Another fascist allowed sixteen families to escape the nazi cordon by entering his house through a service door and exiting through the main door into a street beyond the German net. The January–June 2004 issue of *Rivista di Storia della Chiesa in Italia* (Journal of the history of the Church in Italy), published by the Catholic University, provided some figures. Grazia Loparco, a lecturer in church history at the Pontifical Faculty of Pedagogy, wrote that 3,500 Jews found safety for many months in religious institutions while Rome was under German occupation, and that others were kept by parishes in the city. In September 2023, the

Vatican's press office reported on newly discovered documents examined by researchers from institutions which included the Gregorian University, the Yad Vashem holocaust research institute and the department of culture of Rome's Jewish community. The researchers had been able to identify with certainty by name 3,200 Jews among more than 4,300 who were given refuge.

Kappler complained about the complete unreliability of the Italian police. Police chiefs had advised Mussolini of public discontent at the racial laws enacted in 1938, and they had tried to prevent the police from becoming simply a tool or offshoot of the Fascist Party. Richard Bosworth describes Arturo Bocchini, the chief of police from 1926, as a fascist non-believer. The evening that he died, at the age of 60 in 1940, Bocchini had eaten a substantial dinner and was enjoying the company of his 25-year-old mistress. Nevertheless, working on their own, the nazis rounded up 1,259 people of whom, after the release of mixed-race individuals, 1,021 were loaded into railway livestock wagons and transported to Germany. Only 16 returned.

The last survivor died on 26 October 2018, seventy-five years after the train carrying the first group of Jews from Rome arrived at Auschwitz. A total of 2,091 Jews, of whom 743 were women and 281 children, were taken by the Germans in Rome between October 1943 and June 1944 and deported. Only 73 returned, none of them children. Fixed to a wall of the Jewish school, just around the corner from Via del Portico di Ottavia in the heart of the ghetto, a commemorative marble tablet is inscribed with the words (in Hebrew and Italian):

Hear, I pray you, all people, and behold my sorrow:
my virgins and young men are gone into captivity.
(Lamentations 1:18)

In everlasting memory of the 112 pupils of this school
who were slaughtered in nazi murder camps.

The armistice that Italy and the Allies had signed, and so precipitously announced, consigned all central and northern Italy to German occupation and the horrors that this brought. Allied armies were still deep in the south of Calabria, the toe of the Italian boot, and not only facing determined German defenders but also having to contend with difficult terrain. The "tyranny of distance", which the French historian Fernand Braudel ascribed to the geography of eighteenth-century France, applied to southern Italy until well after the second world war. The infrastructure that Allied soldiers found was that of a backward, agricultural society. Narrow and unmetalled roads clung to mountainsides and descended into and climbed out of deep, steep-sided valleys. And German demolition squads had been busy making Allied progress even harder. After putting up fierce resistance German defenders were eventually overcome at Salerno, where landings took place on 9 September to bypass central and northern Calabria. By the second week of September 1943, Allied aircraft had made three major bombing raids on Rome, the first of these on 19 July when more than 500 aircraft targeted the San Lorenzo railway marshalling yards and killed around 1,500 civilians, a raid repeated a month later that also caused many civilian deaths. Yet, although British forces entered Naples on 1 October, the German high command had by then established a strong defensive line, the Gustav Line, which passed through Monte Cassino.

Bombs on Rome

Among the bombers' targets in the autumn–winter campaign of 1943/4 was the town of Palestrina, the birthplace of the High Renaissance composer Giovanni Pierluigi da Palestrina, about 30 kilometres southeast of Rome. The civic authorities would fix a stone tablet to an ancient wall, part of a huge sanctuary built between the middle decades of the second century BCE and the beginning of the first century BCE and dedicated to the goddess of fortune. The tablet remembers ninety-one townspeople who were killed in an Allied bombing raid on 22 January 1944, the day that waves of landing craft ran up to the sandy beaches on the Tyrrhenian coast at Anzio, about 50 kilometres southwest of Palestrina. As well as killing local people, the Allied bombs caused considerable damage, including the destruction of the house where the writer Thomas Mann spent two summers and where he began *Buddenbrooks* and set part of *Doctor Faustus*.

One fine early-May morning I stood above the sanctuary's ruins and understood the significance of the Valmontone Gap in the military strategy behind the Allied landings at Anzio. The view is extraordinary. A magnificent panorama lay spread out below and in front of me. Rome's urban mass was visible on the plain away to my right. A huge shark's fin of a costly, unfinished and abandoned sports centre, designed by the Spanish architect Santiago Calatrava, was rather closer. Sited beside the section of autostrada that joins the capital's GRA ring road to the Roma Sud toll station for the Autostrada del Sole highway to Naples, it stuck up like a sharp white peak. Yet the four features that truly mark the view from where I stood, almost 500 metres above sea level, are natural and not man-made: the Alban Hills in the middle distance to the right; a broad, unobstructed, gradually descending slope towards Rome between the Alban Hills and Palestrina; the Lepini Mountains in the middle distance to the left; and a wide, seemingly flat valley between the Alban Hills and the Lepini Mountains that affords a glimpse of the far-off Tyrrhenian Sea.

The landings were the beginning of a bitter struggle lasting more than three months. The Commonwealth War Graves Commission's Anzio War Cemetery overlooking the sea holds the remains of almost 1,100 British and Commonwealth servicemen, and there are more than 2,000 graves at the commission's

Beach Head War Cemetery nearby. America lost a similar number of dead during the landings and in the battles of the weeks that followed to secure the beachhead and to break out from it. Most of them are buried in an American war cemetery in Anzio's neighbouring town of Nettuno. In its account of that part of the war, in 1990 the United States Army Center of Military History published *Anzio Beachhead: 22 January–25 May 1944*. This noted that American units lost "at least 2,400 killed" and that the losses of Germany's Fourteenth Army in defending its possession of that small patch of Italy included "at least 5,500 killed". Germans and the Allies each suffered wounded and missing of over 30,000.

Perhaps those losses were unavoidable once a stalemate had been reached in the foul weather that set in following the establishment of the beachhead. That winter was among the coldest in Italian memory, which added to the problems of soldiers bivouacked in trenches and foxholes, clinging on to the beachhead gained when landing. But some military strategists believe that if Mark Clark, the American general commanding the forces at Anzio, had obeyed the instructions he had been given by Sir Harold Alexander, the British commander-in-chief of Allied armies in Italy, then the war against Axis forces in that theatre would have been shortened and many lives would have subsequently been saved.

Alexander had given instructions that, after breaking out from Anzio, Clark's forces should drive northeastward to take the town of Valmontone, which sits astride the Via Casilina, a strategic ancient road from Rome to Capua, on the plain not far north of Naples. As I saw from Palestrina, Valmontone lies at the confluence of two valleys. The first lies southwest to northeast between the coast and Palestrina. The second lies from southeast to northwest along the Via Casilina, to Rome from Valmontone and the south, between Palestrina and the Monti Prenestini mountains behind it, on one side, and the Monti Lepini and the Alban Hills across the valley, on the other.

Plugging the Valmontone Gap, where German forces were weak, would have cut their communications to and from the south and blocked the retreat of those holding the Gustav Line at Cassino. Instead, eager for the news-making prestige of liberating Rome, Clark swung northwestward to the seaward side of the Alban Hills, where he was slowed by strong German defences. In so doing he prevented the Allies from springing the trap that Alexander envisaged for German forces, which had obstructed Allied progress throughout the winter. For one war correspondent, Clark's decision was "as militarily stupid as it was insubordinate ... the worst vainglorious blunder of the war".

Air raids by Allied bombers intensified in attempts to disrupt rail transport of supplies and reinforcements to German forces south of Rome. But the city's hopes of early liberation were dashed when progress stalled at Anzio. Allied air superiority following the landings was not enough. In March 1944, as Allied armies tried to break through the Gustav Line at Cassino and break out from the Anzio beachhead, bombers again attacked railway marshalling yards in Rome. The Scalo Ferroviario San Paolo yard in the Ostiense district, which also served the wholesale food market, was one of them. After decades of inactivity, these marshalling yards would close in 1980 and be cleared, and apartment blocks would be erected on the site. In the twenty-first century, the goods and passenger trains that pass on their way from or to the coastal line to Genoa and the north are reminders of why the tracks were once targets for American bombers and why bombs landed in that part of Rome.

The first of two raids on the Ostiense district was on 3 March 1944, and was carried out by two of the US Army Air Force Bombardment Groups that formed the 42nd Bomb Wing and flew Martin B-26 Marauder twin-engined medium bombers. With the

Ostiense yards as their target, twenty-eight aircraft belonging to the three squadrons in the 320th Bombardment Group took off from the Decimomannu base near Cagliari in Sardinia between four minutes and fifteen minutes past nine o'clock. They overflew Capo Carbonara, Sardinia's southeastern point, and followed aircraft of the 319th Bombardment Group to rendezvous with Spitfire fighter cover above the island of Montecristo in the Tuscan archipelago. After altering course to 106 degrees, the bombers made landfall on the coast about 30 kilometres west of Rome. This was the initial point for the bomb run. Continuing the account of the raid in his mission report, James Wagar, a second lieutenant bombardier in the lead aircraft, wrote that they were flying mild evasive action from the coast in.

> At first it was impossible to pick up the city of Rome due to cloud cover but as we drew nearer the Tiber river was easily picked up and the general location of our target was determined from the curves in the river. About a minute from the target we could distinguish it fairly well though a cloud was over the first part and billows of black smoke covered the rest due to the bombs dropped by the 319th Group. Our target was long and narrow and due to our axis of attack, it was necessary to have our drift completely killed ... As the bombs dropped we broke sharply to the left around and over the city to avoid the flak which the 319th Group was getting because they didn't break fast enough. Our flight's bombs dropped a little short but other flights did an excellent job.

Wagar had begun his report by noting that the raid on the marshalling yards had been preceded by "a very complete briefing because of the danger of damaging world famous religious buildings that were near the target area". Indeed, the 319th Bombardment Group received a Distinguished Unit Citation for carefully avoiding religious and cultural monuments that day. As for the results that the 320th Bombardment Group achieved, its intelligence officer reported that its aircraft had dropped one hundred and thirty-one 500-pound demolition bombs from an altitude of 11,100 feet as they flew southeast above the centre of the marshalling yards. The report said that the aircraft destroyed the railway track, the Ostiense station and at least 75 of the 180 railroad cars in the area. Several fires, including one from an oil tank, were observed. All the B-26 aircraft returned safely and undamaged. All except one, which landed in Corsica to refuel, were back at Decimomannu by a quarter past one. The return flight, on a constant bearing from the mainland to Sardinia, was about 260 statute miles, against 380 statute miles flown on the outward run.

The 42nd Bomb Wing mustered a total of eighty-four B-26 Marauders for the raid on 3 March, and as well as inflicting damage on their target, the aircraft caused considerable damage and loss of life in the area near the tracks and around the station. According to Rome's police headquarters, bombs caused 140 deaths and injuries to a further 157. Four days after the raid, an Italian newspaper reported that the death toll amounted to more than 400. A food warehouse had received a direct hit, said the police report, and two buildings in the Garbatella district were destroyed. The 42nd Bomb Wing would cause large loss of life in the Garbatella district on 7 March, the Albergo Bianco—a social housing block that included a nursery and a maternity centre—being among the buildings hit by stray bombs. In his report on the raid, the group intelligence officer of the 320th Bombardment Group wrote that some bombs landed south of the target and parallel to it. The housing block lay about 400 metres south of the marshalling yards.

The report Wagar wrote on his return to Decimomannu seems to solve a minor mystery of who caused a significant alteration to traffic management at the Porta San Paolo. A poorly aimed bomb that morning hit the short stretch of the Aurelian Walls that joined the Porta San Paolo to the pyramid, and badly damaged the oldest section of the non-Catholic cemetery where John

Keats was buried. The small patch of ground between the pyramid and the Porta San Paolo, which was opened by the bomb and strewn with the wall's rubble, was cleared and levelled, asphalted and made into a road to allow the passage of traffic from Via Marmorata onto Piazzale Ostiense by dog-legging around the Roman gate. Wagar wrote that bombs from "A" flight, in which he flew and which led the raid, had dropped a little short, which, given the bomb run's approach from 16 degrees north of west, would have placed the bombs around the pyramid. Perhaps the flak that the 319th Bombardment Group received and that Wagar reported was a reason why the bombs were released early.

Joseph Heller, an American writer, flew sixty missions over Italy as a bombardier in B-25 Mitchell twin-engined medium bombers and drew on his experiences in writing *Catch-22*, in which Yossarian, the principal character, is a bombardier: "There was no established procedure for evasive action. All you needed was fear, and Yossarian had plenty of that, more fear than Orr or Hungry Joe, more fear than Dunbar, who had resigned himself submissively to the idea that he must die someday. Yossarian had not resigned himself to that idea and he bolted for his life wildly on each mission the instant his bombs were away, hollering, '*Hard, hard, hard, hard, you bastard, hard!*'"

Partisan resistance

Romans mostly coexisted with the nazi occupiers as they waited for the Allies, but a small number of partisans engaged the Germans as best they could, their actions a way to help restore Italian pride in the nation and themselves after the tragic folly of the preceding twenty years. The Gruppi di Azione Patriottica (GAP, Patriotic Action Groups) were the partisans most active in the city. Their targets included sentry posts that guarded barracks and restaurants used by Germans, and they bombed the Barberini cinema at the bottom of Via Veneto in central Rome and the Hotel Flora at the top of the boulevard, which nazis used for a court. However, the Gapists' shootings and bombings were simply irritants for the Germans and Italian fascist soldiers of the Repubblica Sociale Italiana (RSI, Italian Social Republic), the regime's rump and German puppet that Mussolini led from the town of Salò on the western shore of Lake Garda. They weren't going to change the course of the war or bring the liberation of Rome closer.

Yet to read of the Italians who opposed fascism and the nazi German occupiers is to be reminded of their courage and moral strength. Piero Calamandrei, a Florentine lawyer who had opposed the war, joined the Giustizia e Libertà (Justice and Freedom) movement in 1941 and was a founder of the Partito d'Azione (Action Party) the following year. Soon after the outbreak of the war, he complained about how "Italy's tragedy is this general moral putrefaction, this indifference, this singular systematic cowardice". Even so, Calamandrei himself wrote of a Tuscan judge who continued to serve justice as best he could during Mussolini's dictatorship, "Someone, in the early days of fascism, called him the red judge. Really, he was neither red nor grey. He just had a clear, proud conscience, and was unwilling to deny justice in order to satisfy the fascist thugs who invaded the courtrooms. He was simply a just judge. For this he was called red because, among the many sufferings that await a just judge, there is always that of being accused, when unwilling to serve one faction, of being at the service of the opposing faction."

Typical of many anonymous, dim and narrow backstreets in central Rome, a road of *sampietrini* cobblestones running between tall buildings that seem old but are of indeterminate age, there's nothing special about Via Rasella. It leads off Via delle Quattro Fontane, opposite the entrance to the Palazzo Barberini, and falls away, steeply at the beginning, to end near the entrance to the tunnel under the Quirinal Hill. By the mid 2020s, it had become a street with a handful of trattorias serving inexpensive food and numerous short-let, bed-and-breakfast businesses with names like Domus Rasella Suites and Night and Day. A stone arch at number 155, with a passageway wide enough for a car to pass into a small courtyard beyond, stands out from other doors and entrances. The Palazzo Tittoni was built at the end of the six-teenth century on a cardinal's vineyards. It was enlarged towards the end of the seventeenth century and again at the start of the twentieth century. Like rooms in those other, far more modest, nearby buildings, it too is for hire, its ballroom, music room, library and winter garden available for weddings, dinners, recep-tions and concerts, and as film sets.

Palazzo Tittoni is about a third of the way down a street that won notoriety towards the end of the German occupation of Rome. It stands opposite number 156 Via Rasella, a building that early in 1944 was semi-abandoned. It was outside this that a com-mando of GAP partisans planted a bomb on 23 March 1944 that was triggered when a company of about 150 military policemen of the Bozen regiment was passing early in the afternoon. The partisans chose that place because the height of buildings and narrowness of the street would amplify the effect of the explosion. Franco Calamandrei, the son of Piero Calamandrei, was the head of one of the GAP networks and leader of the action on Via Rasella. (He would be a journalist after the war and serve in four legislatures as a Communist senator, while his father would be a member of the post-war constituent assembly that wrote the con-stitution of the newly founded Italian republic.)

Altogether, the GAP partisans in Rome numbered just over thirty, about the size of an infantry platoon in the British army, and they were split into two networks with two groups in each. Seventeen of them, including two women, were involved in preparing and carrying out the ambush on Via Rasella. They had not reckoned with the arrival of a gaggle of children who had decided to play at soldiers by marching behind the military policemen, but the partisans were able to draw them away from the column and to safety. Calamandrei had already given the signal and a fifty-second fuse to set off the bomb had been lit. The explosion was amplified not only by the location on Via Rasella but also by the triggering of grenades carried by soldiers in the column. Twenty-six soldiers died immediately, a further six had died of wounds by the next morning, and another died soon after. Eight bystanders were also killed. The German reaction was immediate and bestial, a reprisal in which they murdered 335 people on 24 March, the day after the attack.

Barbarity at the Fosse Ardeatine

The mass killing took place at a pozzolana quarry on Via Ardeatina, close to the Santa Domitilla and San Callisto catacombs, a slaughter that began around two o'clock in the afternoon and continued until about eight o'clock in the evening. Both Kappler and a close aide, Captain Erich Priebke, participated in the murders, which they tried to hide by having engineers dynamite the two entrances that led to the gallery where the victims were killed and their bodies piled. However, the explosions were heard by members of the Salesian religious order who had noticed an unusual movement of German vehicles and investigated during the night. Rome's city authorities decided immediately after the war that the quarry should be transformed into a memorial for those who died, and this was inaugurated on 24 March 1949.

As befits the event that happened there, the memorial to the victims of the Fosse Ardeatine is a sombre, saddening, thought-provoking place. Two openings in the rock face, which visitors see immediately when entering the large courtyard that lies behind heavy steel gates in a high wall running beside Via Ardeatina, lead to the gallery where the atrocity was committed. The tombs of those who died are set in ranks in a dim concrete vault at the side of the yard. Narrow horizontal slits beneath a thick concrete roof allow slender rectangular beams of light to enter. Most of the tombs carry the names of those whose remains they hold, their ages and occupations. Early in 2022, just seven carried the word *ignoto*—unknown. Some came from towns and cities in northern Italy, from Venice, Parma, Modena and Milan, others from the south, from Naples, Palermo and Foggia, and some were born abroad, in Berlin, Odesa, Paris and Lviv. But mostly they were Romans: shopkeepers, students, bricklayers, painters, carpenters, clerks, lawyers, doctors and professors. Some were soldiers, including generals, who had joined the clandestine opposition to German occupation. Some of them had been active with the partisans. And many belonged to the Communist or Socialist parties and were anti-fascists. Seventy-five were murdered because they were Jews.

The German barbarity of that day in March 1944 has not been forgotten. The murders are remembered on some Roman streets with memorial tablets. There's a wreath on the wall at number 104 Via Merulana, the block of apartments where Carlo Foschi lived, beneath a stone tablet that tells passers-by that he was a member of the Communist Party and that he was butchered in the Fosse Ardeatine because of his part in the struggle against fascism. And on the wall of an apartment block on Via Giambattista Vico, about 100 metres from the building where Giacomo Matteotti lived, a tablet carries a dedication to Colonel Giuseppe Cordero Lanza di Montezemolo of His Majesty's Engineers who lived there from 1940 to 1943. Awarded the Medaglia d'Oro, Montezemolo was head of underground military resistance in Rome, and the tablet records that "believing in God, he suffered with heroic resolve the tortures of the prison on Via Tasso and the barbarous mass murder of the Fosse Ardeatine". Commemorations are found in unexpected places. Fixed to a wall of the Teatro dell'Opera along Via Torino, a tablet recalls how the singer Nicola Ugo Stame, who had refused to join the Fascist Party, was arrested for anti-fascist activities in 1939 while rehearsing the role of Prince Calaf, the leading tenor role in Puccini's opera *Turandot*. Imprisonment and special surveillance followed. Stame joined Rome's partisans following the armistice in September 1943, was captured in January 1944, tortured by the Gestapo in the block on Via Tasso, imprisoned again, and murdered at the Fosse Ardeatine.

The crime at the Fosse Ardeatine is remembered each year when Italy's head of state pays homage to the victims at the place where they died. Schools hang banners outside that carry words like "335 thorns in the heart". The youngest of those murdered was a 15-year-old boy. The three Germans held most directly responsible, Field Marshal Albert Kesselring, head of the German forces in Italy, and the SS officers Kappler and Priebke were put on trial. Kesselring was sentenced to death in 1947 but reprieved and released from jail in 1952. Free and widely esteemed, he died in Germany in 1960. Kappler was sentenced to life imprisonment in 1948, escaped from a military hospital in Rome in 1977 and died at home in Germany. Priebke spent fifty years living in Argentina but was eventually caught, extradited and, after mistrials, was sentenced to life imprisonment. He served his sentence in the comfort of an apartment in Rome until his death in 2013. All three died in old age, Priebke at 100.

Despite the German reaction, and after heated arguments about the merit of continuing their actions in Rome, GAP partisans carried out several attacks in April 1944. But liberation was close. On 25 May Allied units from the south, which had broken through the Gustav Line, met those which had broken out from the Anzio beachhead, and Allied soldiers entered Rome on 4 June. There was some shooting as Germans retreated. The American general Mark Clark got what he wanted by heading a victorious entry into the Eternal City, albeit a small party of British officers was also there, causing Italians to spread the word that the English were in the Grand Hotel. Across the Tiber at Saint Peter's the pope gave thanks. For Romans, the peace was beginning. For Italians north of the mountains between Florence and Bologna, the war had almost eleven months to run.

PART TWO

POST-FASCISM'S *CHIAROSCURO* DECADES

1945–2024

IV

HOLLYWOOD ON THE TIBER

Was't not a happy star led us to Rome?

William Shakespeare, *Titus Andronicus*

There's a small baroque church about a kilometre along the Via Appia Antica, the consular road to Brindisi, the Adriatic port from where ships sailed to Rome's ancient empire in the east. The church's facade is plain and its interior modest, with neither fine marble sculptures nor great works of art. The pews in its compact nave seat forty-eight. Santa Maria in Palmis is not a place of pilgrimage, yet it's special for some Christians. The doors are open throughout the day, and the church is a stopping point and curiosity for tourists exploring the Appia Antica. A few votive candles usually flicker on stands near the stoup of holy water by the entrance and at the altar rail.

Protected by an iron grille, a stone dented with foot-like impressions is set in the floor inside the doors. According to some readings of early Christian writing, the church stands where Peter the Apostle, fleeing Rome and Nero's persecution of Christians, encountered Jesus Christ. A marble tablet fixed to a wall near the stone tells how, surprised by Christ who was walk-ing towards Rome, Peter asked, "Domine, quo vadis?" (Lord, where are you going?) and Christ replied, "Venio Romam iterum crucifigi" (I come to Rome to be crucified again). His spirits boosted by the meeting, Peter turned and began his way back to the city, to his own crucifixion, and as he turned Christ van-ished, leaving footprints in the stone where he had stood.

Wall paintings at the middle of the nave show the two figures, Jesus Christ arriving from the countryside on the right, Peter the Apostle leaving Rome on the left, with the words they are said to have spoken beneath the figures. Paintings of their crucifix-ions decorate side walls near the altar: Christ upright, arms out-stretched, hands nailed, with feet crossed and nailed, and Peter, who believed himself unworthy of being similarly crucified, nailed to the cross with his head down and feet above.

Neither the Circus Maximus, where many Christians died because of their beliefs, nor Saint Peter's basilica or the basilicas of Santa Maria Maggiore and San Giovanni in Laterano have direct associations with Jesus Christ. One can imagine the roots of Western Christianity as having been planted at the spot where Peter the Apostle is said to have met Christ and to have turned back to his own crucifixion on what would be called the Vatican Hill. (Some say the site of crucifixion was on the Janiculum Hill.) As much as any part of the city, the start of the Appia Antica provides evidence of the beginnings of Christianity in ancient Rome. Stretches of well-preserved, red-brick Aurelian Walls soar on both sides of the Porta San Sebastiano gate, a fine sight, particularly to the right towards the Porta Ardeatina, while the first few metres of the Appia Antica lie ahead, narrow, hemmed in by high walls and dropping away downhill towards a bend. An entrance to the San Callisto catacombs where sixteen early popes were interred is close to Santa Maria in Palmis. The San Sebastiano catacombs and basilica, which keeps the original of the stone set in the floor of Santa Maria in Palmis, are two kilometres further on.

Alas, politicians, planners and Romans themselves treated the city badly in the second half of the twentieth century. The road's history and its archaeological riches counted for little, as several kilometres of the Appia Antica, despite a long section of bone-shaking surface of *sampietrini* cobblestones and a tight fit for vehicles, became the end of an important commuter route from and to the south, with cars forming peak-hour queues at the Porta San Sebastiano. A brick railway bridge was built over the road not far from the gate in the early 1900s, and a concrete viaduct carrying a four-lane highway was added nearby towards the end of the twentieth century.

How different the Appia Antica and its surroundings appeared when unspoiled countryside lay beyond the gate, as it did until the 1950s when developers began packing tall apartment blocks close together along kilometre after kilometre of open land flanking major roads to the south from Rome. A black-and-white newsreel that Castle Films, a part of Universal Pictures, made in 1950 to tell Americans about the *Jubilaeum Maximum* Holy Year included a clip of a party of young priests. Wearing black cassocks and broad-brimmed *cappelli romani*, they were walking on ancient flagstones against an unmistakable backdrop of umbrella pines and Roman ruins. According to the soundtrack, the group of priests was aware that countless millions had passed that way before them, "martyrs and infidels, the humble and the great. Yes, even Saint Peter himself."

With the camera focused on the church's facade, the narrator described Santa Maria in Palmis as the tiny chapel of Quo Vadis, standing on the spot "where Christ appeared to Saint Peter to give him renewed faith and courage to continue his divine mission and brave the threat of a martyr's death", the voice-over synchronised to images of a horse and cart passing in front of the church. The clatter of hooves and the crunching and scraping of iron wheels on stone were familiar noises along the Appia Antica during that Holy Year, like church bells that started the day, marked midday and began the evening, and the occasional, insistent tolling of a funeral bell. Many of the sounds were those that had broken the quiet of the Roman countryside for centuries: the crack of hammers on stone or thud of mallets on stakes, cockerels crowing, birds singing, the creaking leather harnesses of horses pulling carts and wagons, dogs barking, sheep bleating, the braying of mules and the shouts of people calling across fields. The rumble of motor traffic didn't disturb the silence. The total number of registered cars in Italy was then less than half a million, and those mostly in the northern towns and cities of Lombardy, Piedmont and Liguria, industrial regions still recovering from the devastation of a world war that had ended just five years before.

This was the Appia Antica in 1950, and traces of the atmosphere of timelessness, of the different and distant world shown in that newsreel film, still lingered when I arrived in Rome early in April 1972 to find colourful, bustling street markets enlivened by singing stall-holders, as well as roads enlivened by the anarchy of Romans behind the steering wheels of cars, but pedestrians unhurried and taking life easily. A substantial part of the city's southern outskirts inside the ring road was still farmland, and sheep grazed suburban patches of open ground. Traffic-free Sundays in the twenty-first century could do little to recapture the Appia Antica of the early 1970s and would be far from what must have been an Arcadian tranquillity in 1950 when not only were Castle Films at work in Rome but so also were Metro-Goldwyn-Mayer, with the director Mervyn LeRoy shooting the studio's version of *Quo Vadis*. Work on the film led *Time* magazine, in an article headlined "Hollywood on the Tiber" in June 1950, to link Rome and Los Angeles. This was the beginning of more than a decade during which producers, directors, screen-writers, designers, film stars and supporting casts arrived from California to work in the Eternal City, bringing with them customs and trappings of the American movie industry.

Quo Vadis

The film was mainly shot at Rome's Cinecittà studios, but numerous Italian locations were also used, the Appia Antica among them. It's easy to imagine that actors visited the small church that gave its name to the film they were making. A bust of Henryk Sienkiewicz, the Polish author of the book on which the film was based, would be placed there in 1977. And although his book *Quo Vadis* helped Sienkiewicz to win the Nobel Prize in Literature in 1905, nine years after its publication, I wonder how many of the actors, before or after reading their lines, hacked their way through a wordy undergrowth of over 500 pages of historical fiction and its long list of characters. With a silent movie of the same subject from 1924 to help, writing the film's treatment probably didn't stretch Hollywood's literary talent. As for the writers who wrote the screenplay for the three-hour epic, the cinema critic of the *New York Times* would complain of the film's banality, pretentiousness and verbal boredom. Yet it was a major commercial success.

Perhaps some among the production crews, writers, designers and partly British cast of *Quo Vadis*, which included Peter Ustinov, Leo Genn, Felix Aylmer and Rosalie Crutchley, who went to Rome had been there before. But perhaps the film gave its stars, the 38-year-old American actor Robert Taylor and the 28-year-old British actress Deborah Kerr, who had moved to California in 1947, their first experience of the city. International tension, heightened by the Italian invasion of Abyssinia in 1935, Benito Mussolini's pact with Adolf Hitler and their military support for rightwing Falangist rebels in the Spanish Civil War, and the approach of the second world war had been disincentives to travel in the second half of the 1930s. Then came the world war and its aftermath of austerity, reconstruction and recovery. Holy Years notwithstanding, European tourism was not a priority.

As well as horses and carts on the Appia Antica, in sharp contrast to limousines on Sunset Boulevard, those involved in shooting *Quo Vadis* found in Cinecittà, a studio complex that owed itself to Italy's fascist regime, a cinematic world remote from Hollywood. By the spring of 1944, the chaos and upheaval of a war of movement along the Italian peninsula had taken the number of refugees in Rome to around half a million and, although most would return to their homes when peace arrived, many remained. Cinecittà had hosted around 6,000 of them and several thousand were still living there in 1950. Many were recruited, put into Roman costumes to form the crowds for *Quo Vadis* and, according to one account, paid with a daily basket of food.

The availability of inexpensive extras was one advantage that American film-makers enjoyed when they worked in Rome. Another was a pool of low-cost but skilled craftsmen: carpenters, upholsterers, plasterers, cutters, tailors, seamstresses and metalsmiths, many of whom had been displaced to the southeastern part of Rome by the regime's clearances of the old centre, during which their homes and workshops were demolished to make way for grandiose roads like those running from the Tiber to Saint Peter's and from the Colosseum to Piazza Venezia. Large numbers of those craftsmen (and women) were kept busy. Thousands of costumes and accessories were needed, outdoor sets had to be constructed, sound stages built and decorated, chariots and other props made, and much else. While the production's low-technology, high-craft requirements were met in Rome, local shortages meant that MGM had to bring equipment from California.

Quo Vadis was shot in 1950 and released in November the following year, in time to be eligible for Academy Awards in 1952. It was nominated for eight, including best motion picture and two nominations for best supporting actor, the British actors Leo Genn, who played Petronius, and Peter Ustinov in the role of Emperor Nero. The film was up against stiff competition in Elia Kazan's *A Streetcar Named Desire*, which won four awards, including three acting awards, and John Huston's *The African Queen*, for which Humphrey Bogart won best actor award. *Quo Vadis* won none, but MGM had the satisfaction of winning the Oscar for best film with another of its productions, Vincente Minnelli's *An American in Paris*. Moreover, with box office earnings of three times its production cost, *Quo Vadis* amply recompensed the studio with its commercial success.

And perhaps the film's economic results softened the blow of the ferocious review that Bosley Crowther wrote for the *New York Times*, which was published the day after the film's release. For Crowther, Charles Laughton, who played Nero in *The Sign of the Cross*, the Cecil B. DeMille film of 1932 based on the Quo Vadis story, had been a master of restraint compared with Ustinov whose mouthing and screaming might have been endurable had it been halved. The *Times*'s critic found the presentation of Christianity trite and believed the tableaux of scenes from Christ's life would cause sensitive members of audiences to cringe. Crowther thought, however, that the film had not been made for the overly sensitive or discriminating, but for those who like "grandeur and noise—and no punctuation". Yet the fact that it was filmed in Italy enabled *Quo Vadis* to offer brilliance, colour, excitement and geographical authenticity. "The opening shot of Roman legions pounding along the dusty Appian Way in a beautiful Technicolor haze sets the tone and, indeed, the massive tempo for the motif of power that gives this film its one claim to artistic stature. And this merits thanks to Italy."

Crowther described the film's scenes of Roman gatherings in honour of the empire's heroes or at circuses where lions clawed Christians to death as "rendered intoxicating by the magnificence of the sets and the massing of thousands of extras, which shooting in Italy has allowed Metro to afford. On the strength of its crowds and architecture, this *Quo Vadis* would tip any scales."

However, the film's pre-eminence in terms of crowds and architecture would survive less than a decade. MGM would return to Hollywood on the Tiber to make another epic set in ancient Rome: *Ben Hur*, which was directed by William Wyler and which, unlike *Quo Vadis*, won wide approval from the Academy of Motion Picture Arts and Sciences. Against competition that included Billy Wilder's *Some Like It Hot* and Alfred Hitchcock's *North by Northwest*, of the twelve 1960 awards for which it was nominated, *Ben Hur* won a record eleven, among them those for best motion picture, best director, best actor in Charlton Heston, best supporting actor in Hugh Griffith, best music (composed by Miklós Rózsa, who had also composed the music for *Quo Vadis*), and best costume design.

Epics, swords and sandals, romantic comedies and dramas

Production of *Ben Hur* exceeded *Quo Vadis* in its search for the spectacular. It needed 300 sets, several being recycled from Mervyn LeRoy's film. Costumes were required for 10,000 extras. Making sets and costumes gave work to hundreds of skilled craftsmen and wardrobe staff. Chariots were built for a dramatic, action-filled race lasting almost ten minutes, the sequence for which the film is best remembered. Robert Surtees, who had been cinematographer for *Quo Vadis*, would win an Oscar for his work on *Ben Hur*, the filming of the chariot race being a factor. Two Roman galleys, a fleet of miniature ships and an artificial lake were built for a sea battle, and hundreds of animals—sheep, horses, donkeys and camels—were procured in efforts to provide the film with geographical, social, technological and temporal authenticity. In running just over three and a half hours *Ben Hur* comfortably beat *Quo Vadis*'s running time. The film was in many respects a blockbuster. Released in November 1959, it enjoyed great success at the box office.

Between the filming of *Quo Vadis* and *Ben Hur*, Cinecittà was production home to numerous sword-and-sandal films that had varying levels of American involvement. Shot in 1954, with Paramount Pictures partnering Lux Film, *Ulysses* had joint American–Italian production companies, for example. The film starred Kirk Douglas and Anthony Quinn, and Irwin Shaw contributed to its screenplay. However, direction and production were Italian and Italian actors predominated. As for *Hercules*, released in Italy in February 1958, this was, other than Steve Reeves, an all-Italian film. Reeves, an American bodybuilder from Montana, a former Mr America, Mr World and Mr Universe who turned Hollywood actor briefly in a small part in 1954, was lured to Italy three years later to star in the title role of *Hercules*. Reeves was kept busy at Cinecittà. Five sword-and-sandal films in which he starred were released in Italy in 1959 alone, the year that *Ben Hur* began to fill widescreens and draw to cinemas a public seeking "the entertainment experience of a lifetime".

Hollywood on the Tiber created two epics between *Quo Vadis* and *Ben Hur*. Robert Wise's *Helen of Troy* for Warner Bros was released early in 1956 and King Vidor's star-encrusted notions about Leo Tolstoy's novel *War and Peace* in August that year, albeit the Italian contribution to *War and Peace*, produced by Dino De Laurentiis, was substantial. According to *Treccani*, Italy's national encyclopedia, six truly colossal films came out of Hollywood on the Tiber. Strangely, the list omits (or forgets) *Quo Vadis* but includes Anthony Mann's *The Fall of the Roman Empire* (released in March 1964) for Paramount Pictures, which was mainly shot in Spain, and Carol Reed's *The Agony and the Ecstasy* for 20th Century Fox, which was released in October 1965 and whose plot hardly merits the description "epic".

Cleopatra brings *Treccani's* list of epics to six, and the film is widely seen as representing the end of the era in which Hollywood was also on the Tiber. Shooting this notoriously troubled production, starring Elizabeth Taylor in the title role, Richard Burton as Mark Antony and Rex Harrison as Julius Caesar, began in September 1960 at Pinewood Studios in England under director Rouben Mamoulian, but was soon suspended due to Taylor's ill health. Production was transferred to Cinecittà where filming, which had resumed in September 1961 under Joseph L. Mankiewicz, continued until July the following year. More filming was needed early in 1963 and *Cleopatra* was eventually released in June that year.

Although the encyclopedia claims that Hollywood on the Tiber extended for two decades until 1969, its beginning and end points are best taken as *Quo Vadis* in 1950, when filming took place and the *Time* article appeared, and *Cleopatra* in 1963, when filming wrapped. A total of about forty American films were shot at Cinecittà during the 1950s and 1960s and, while the public associated Hollywood on the Tiber with blockbusters, the films were mainly mid-budget affairs, romantic comedies and dramas in contemporary costume. And these have mostly slipped forgotten into cinema history. *Roman Holiday* is one that hasn't.

Directed by William Wyler, who also produced it, the film stars Gregory Peck and an almost unknown Audrey Hepburn, making her first performance in an American film. Cinema-goers were captivated by what they saw of Hepburn in a romantic comedy, released in August 1953 and the winner of three Academy awards, including one for her as best actress. *Roman Holiday* provided the production team with an opportunity for a cinematographic tour around the Eternal City's best-loved tourist sights and they seized it, exploiting the photogenic qualities of the Piazza di Spagna, the Trevi Fountain, the Colosseum, the Bocca della Verità (Mouth of Truth) in the portico of the Santa Maria in Cosmedin church and much else. Edith Head's costume designs won her an Oscar, and the story by Dalton Trumbo would eventually be recognised with an award. Imprisoned in 1950 for contempt of Congress, Trumbo had been placed on Hollywood's blacklist and studios did not employ him directly. With a belated Oscar for the story in 1993 and credit for his work on *Roman Holiday*'s screenplay in 2011, the Hollywood establishment tried to make amends for its acquiescence in the McCarthy anti-communist witch hunt. Trumbo had died in 1976.

In its piazzas, palaces, pizzerias, bustling cobbled streets, archaeological sites, basilicas, churches and chapels, great works of art, fountains and fashionable shops, Rome offers film producers an abundance of colourful, historic and cultural locations. But northwards up the Italian boot in cities like Florence and Venice, on various rivieras and at top ski resorts, and south to Naples, Capri and the Amalfi Coast, Italy itself is well endowed with urban and rural scenery and atmosphere to make cinema-goers wish they were there. *Three Coins in a Fountain*, which was released in May 1954, less than a year after *Roman Holiday*, also made much of its Roman location. It tells the story of three American women hoping for and finding romance in the Italian capital, the city where they work. After various sentimental misadventures and adventures, including a trip to Venice, the film closes with the three women and their men-friends by the Trevi Fountain.

In contrast, a bleaker atmosphere pervades *The Barefoot Contessa*, released a few months after *Three Coins in a Fountain*. Ava Gardner played the title role, the barefoot countess being a dancer transformed into film star by a down-on-his-luck movie director, played by Humphrey Bogart, whose fortunes were then revived. She was murdered, and the film, directed by Joseph

L. Mankiewicz, is composed of flashbacks of her life remembered by mourners at her funeral. Filming of *The Barefoot Contessa* took place at Cinecittà and on location in Italy, at Portofino, an elegant resort on the Ligurian Riviera di Levante; at San Remo, a Ligurian coastal town with a casino close to the border with France; and in an olive grove at Tivoli, just to the east of Rome.

Light-heartedness is also in short supply in *Two Weeks in Another Town*, directed by Vincente Minnelli and produced by John Houseman, which was released in summer 1962 and which was one of the last productions from Hollywood on the Tiber. Despite starring Kirk Douglas, Edward G. Robinson, George Hamilton and Cyd Charisse, it was poorly received by the public, partly perhaps because of the critical savaging it received. Bosley Crowther of the *New York Times* led the attack, beginning his review, "It is well known that a class of trashy movies of a certain lush, synthetic sort is made in Rome—usually big, cheap costume pictures of tiny intelligence." Crowther complained about a screenplay "slapped together by Charles Schnee from the novel by Irwin Shaw ... as aimless and arbitrary in its development of a plot as the script for one of those crowded Cinecittà spear-and-sandals spectacles." He found the film "a lot of glib trade patter, ridiculous and unconvincing ... like something out of a Hollywood cartoon". Crowther wrote that Minnelli and Houseman had tried to simulate significance or substance by crowding the film with Rome's atmosphere. Shaw's book had been published in January 1959 to decent reviews, one describing it as "lusty, obsessive, bitter, driving ... vibrant with life".

Out of print in English, *Two Weeks in Another Town* appeared in an Italian translation in September 2021. In an introduction, Mario Fortunato, a literary critic and former head of the Italian Cultural Institute in London, describes Shaw as being widely considered an honest craftsman who knew how to produce novels that one reads with pleasure from the first line to the last. "Even so, in good craftsmanship, in the lack of presumption that char-acterises his work, it is sometimes touched by authentic great-ness." According to Fortunato, rather than simply being what academic criticism described as a popular American author, at times Shaw had a vision that was far more sophisticated, ambig-uous and definitely European than that of many of his fellow countrymen. That's not surprising given that, after blacklisting as Dalton Trumbo had been, Shaw moved to Europe in 1951 and spent much of the next three decades living there.

La dolce vita

However, the alcohol consumption and abuse described in *Two Weeks in Another Town* and central to its plot are not typical of Italian literature, and neither is heavy drinking a feature of Italian social or domestic life. The novel describes the making of a film in Rome and the difficulties caused by the leading male actor's boozing, albeit Minnelli's film assigns the drink problem differ-ently. Shaw provided a vivid scene early in his book in which a drunken American tourist (not the leading male actor) staggers from his hotel on Via Veneto and punches the book's central fig-ure on the nose. Yet in December 1960, beginning an account of bars and drinking on Via Veneto, the writer Ennio Flaiano noted that nobody in Rome drank alcohol other than with meals and that the Via Veneto's bars numbered few alcohol drinkers among their customers. Indeed, one was hard pressed to encounter a drunk on streets at night. According to Flaiano, that small group of alcohol drinkers who frequented the boulevard's bars became subjects of admiration, particularly by barmen, because their drinking was evidence of having travelled and acquired a cosmo-politan lifestyle. Others drank coffee, orangeade or even milk.

Although its consumption in bars on Via Veneto may have been unusual during the *dolce vita* years, alcohol coloured Shaw's writing in many places. His extensive output of short stories, mostly peopled by Americans, offers examples. The main character in "The Eighty-Yard Run" found solace in solitary drinking, going to the nearest bar and having five drinks by himself before his money ran out. The mental states of two characters in "I Stand by Dempsey" improved when they reached a bar and each drank two Old-Fashioneds. Another solitary drinker, in "Preach on the Dusty Roads", found pleasure in visiting an empty bar in the morning, hearing the sound of ice clinking in a mixer, smelling a faint aroma of gin, and finding that the drink dealt effectively and immediately with the sour taste in his mouth. Not unfairly, Salka Viertel, actress, screenwriter and active in Hollywood's central European intellectual émigré community in the 1930s and 1940s, took Shaw to task over alcohol's prominence in his writing and the apparent endorsement of heavy drinking. Why, Viertel wondered at a dinner party in 1970, did Shaw scatter bars, beers, whiskey, champagne, cocktails and drinkers around his work? Quite simply, in enjoying a close relationship with alcohol it provided a subject about which he knew a lot and could write with intimate knowledge. A biographical note by Brooklyn College, whose library would hold some of his papers, recorded that he was drinking heavily and his health was deteriorating by the middle of the 1970s. Peter Viertel, a writer like his mother Salka and a close friend of Shaw for four decades, would come to see a self-destructive strain in Shaw's character that helped bring his premature end.

Interviewed by the *New York Times* after Shaw's death in 1984, the American writer Gay Talese spoke about Shaw's generosity in Switzerland and in cafés along the Via Veneto in Rome. Shaw certainly enjoyed first-hand experience of the atmosphere of the *dolce vita*, which was partly framed and fostered by Italy's economic miracle that began in the early 1950s and extended into the 1960s. Hollywood on the Tiber and the *dolce vita* overlapped.

And given his place in American and European literary and movie circles, Shaw probably knew about Federico Fellini's preparations for his film *La dolce vita*. Crowther would think highly of Fellini's work, which was widely praised as a cinematographic masterpiece when it was released in February 1960, and mention it in his savage review of the film of *Two Weeks in Another Town*.

Shaw's book and the film that Minnelli made from it helped record and colour Rome's *dolce vita* years, but the true record and brightest colours, despite being shot in black and white, are in Fellini's work whose title, after all, would define the era. Other than Fellini himself and the writer Tullio Pinelli, no one was better placed to describe the genesis of *La dolce vita* than Ennio Flaiano, who wrote in June 1958 about how he, Fellini and Pinelli worked that month on an idea for a film about a young man from the provinces who arrives in Rome with hopes of becoming a journalist. Their idea was one they had considered in the past, and Fellini wanted to refresh it, to bring it up to date and draw a portrait of Rome's café society, a society alienated, bored and fooling around with eroticism and suddenly acquired wealth. A cocktail of the sacred and profane and the old and new, together with a flood of foreigners and the film industry, gave the city, which had grown larger, wealthier and more corrupt over the preceding years, an exotic and edgy character. Flaiano, Fellini and Pinelli did not write a line during that meeting but strolled around to sharpen their memories of places and note how they had changed. It seemed that hordes had taken over the streets, cinemas and trattorias. Piazzas whose architecture once enchanted had become open-air garages for the cars of the invading crowds. The three writers decided that Via Veneto, so different from the quiet boulevard Flaiano had known in 1950, had to be a location and settled on the film's title, *La dolce vita*.

Soon they had outlined the character of the journalist. He would be one who was well paid for writing sensational stories about scandals and the awful things that people did. He had abandoned earlier ideals and allowed himself to be seduced by the very part of society that he despised. Fellini had a clear idea of the photographer who would be the reporter's inseparable companion. A vulgar society that expressed its desire for living more by performance than by true enjoyment needed a photographer who was a persistent know-all like the photographers who were already busy along Via Veneto. As for his name, according to Flaiano, Fellini opened *By the Ionian Sea*, George Gissing's travel book from 1901, and chanced on that of a hotel-owner in Calabria. The photographer in Fellini's film would give the hotel-owner's name to his side of the photo-reporter's trade: Paparazzo.

Working at the seaside, the writers had finished their screenplay for *La dolce vita* within three months. Problems then arose in turning it into a film. Flaiano wrote in September 1958 that Dino De Laurentiis, the producer, had refused to go ahead with the project. He passed the screenplay to a small group of critics for their opinion. They said that what the screenwriters had given De Laurentiis was fragmented, chaotic, false, flip and pessimistic, whereas what the public wanted were a few rays of hope. Neither did De Laurentiis approve of Fellini's choice of Marcello Mastroianni in the role of the journalist. And two months later, in November, Flaiano was sure that the film would not be made, albeit Fellini was talking to actors and preparing for production, as well as getting better acquainted with the shady undergrowth on and around Via Veneto. Fellini wanted to film a surrealistic portrait of Rome, recreating everything or allowing reality only to the little that was already surreal in itself. And that is what he did. He found new producers and began shooting at Cinecittà in March 1959. Flaiano went there in June, noting that production finance had paid for a set to be built on a section of Via Veneto, not the part where poets and intellectuals met but the busy corner by the Café de Paris. Flaiano was shown some of the rushes

that Fellini had shot and was struck by the baroque sumptuous-
ness and colourful imagery that Fellini had drawn from the world
of Via Veneto.

Shooting finished in August 1959 and the film was released
six months later, the scenes of Mastroianni and Anita Ekberg in
the Trevi Fountain and of a stripper at work, and rumours that
the film would be seized by Italian prosecutors as obscene, helping it to an immediate and huge box office success in Italy.
Although critics at home would be divided, *La dolce vita* would
earn critical acclaim as well as commercial success abroad. The
jury at the film festival in Cannes awarded it the Palme d'Or in
1960, and early in April 1962 at the 34th Academy Awards ceremony, Piero Gherardi won an Oscar for his costume design. He
was also nominated for best black-and-white art director. Fellini
himself was nominated for best director. Flaiano would complain
about being the target of criticism for his part in showing Rome
as a sump of vice but, along with his fellow writers, he was nominated for the story and screenplay. That was only the beginning.
In the future, *La dolce vita* would appear in many lists of best
films and favourite films. About the time of the Oscars ceremony,
Flaiano was writing how Via Veneto was increasingly unrecognisable, submerged by its own notoriety and attracting only tourists, those seeking casual sexual encounters, and film-makers.
Jet-setters had begun arriving in autumn 1958 with the start of
transatlantic flights by commercial jet aircraft. The intellectuals
and writers who once met and passed their time in cafés along
the boulevard had moved away to join the artists in the cafés of
Piazza del Popolo.

Could Fellini have made his masterpiece had American actors,
directors, designers, screenwriters and cinematographic assistants
and hangers-on from California not added international glamour
and movie glitz to the ambience on and around Via Veneto by
staying for long periods in the area's luxury hotels and frequent-

125

ing its bars, restaurants and nightclubs during the decade before *La dolce vita* was made? Perhaps, but unlikely. In taking the lifestyle, the excesses and extravagances of the American original to Rome, and by fostering a Roman expression of this distant exoticism, Hollywood on the Tiber was essential to the creation of the very *dolce vita* that allowed Fellini to make his film. Italy's economic miracle alone was not enough.

Images of the dolce vita

While the films themselves provide the principal commemoration of the work of Hollywood on the Tiber, its main record of achievement, it is possible, without watching them or reading books about that period, to immerse oneself in nostalgia for it through the many photographs held in the archives of the Istituto Luce at Cinecittà. And there is no need to visit Rome and trek out to the studios as the archives' photographic collections are available online. Two collections in particular capture for ever people who made news in those years: the Fondo Vedo, whose 179,000 images were snapped between 1948 and 1965, and the Fondo Dial with 71,000 images dating from 1951 to 1967. These huge archives of black-and-white photographs bring back not only the film stars of the 1950s and 1960s, but fashion designers and their work in those distant times.

Stars of the cinema shine from among many dull politicians, statesmen and businessmen. In November 1952, Dial-Press photographed an elegantly dressed Errol Flynn, trilby hat on his head, smiling by the door of a Wagons-Lits sleeper carriage when he arrived at Termini railway station. He had travelled to Rome to star with Gina Lollobrigida in Milton Krims's swash-buckling *Crossed Swords*, an Italian–American joint production released in July 1954. A photographer for Vedo took a series of ten shots of Humphrey Bogart at Ciampino airport after his arrival on a Trans World Airlines (TWA) flight on 4 January 1954, one of the photographs showing him characteristically with cigarette in mouth. The same collection contains shots of Ava Gardner at Ciampino, leaving Rome at the end of March. She and Bogart had been in Rome to film *The Barefoot Contessa*. Charlton Heston and William Wyler, star and director of *Ben Hur*, were photographed arriving at Ciampino in 1959. Dial-Press had photographed Heston, on set and in costume at Cinecittà in September 1958, while he was running with an oval ball like those used in American football. The collection contains photographs taken four years earlier of Kirk Douglas and Silvana Mangano, the stars of *Ulysses* on the film's set.

With Hollywood on the Tiber in its second decade and moving towards its end, Dial-Press photographed the arrival in Rome of Cyd Charisse, one of the leading actresses of *Two Weeks in Another Town*. Film stars were no longer arriving at Ciampino. The aircraft that brought Charisse landed in September 1961 at Fiumicino airport. The new airport near the coast had opened in January that year and had welcomed a rather bigger star a few weeks before Charisse. Greeted by director Joseph L. Mankiewicz, Elizabeth Taylor had arrived for filming the much-delayed *Cleopatra*. She was accompanied by her husband Eddie Fisher. Unaware that the jinx that had affected the film would soon destroy his marriage, he was relaxed and smiling. On 14 December, the actor Richard Burton arrived on a TWA flight to play his part in shooting *Cleopatra*. Burton was accompanied by his wife Sybil Williams. Taylor and Burton were caught on film by a paparazzo while on a yacht in the Gulf of Naples in June 1962, but their marriages had effectively ended when the couple began filming in January. Dial-Press photographed Fisher trailing disconsolately after Taylor on the deck of a large motor yacht berthed at Civitavecchia, north of Rome. And Vedo photographed an unsmiling Williams at Fiumicino on 2 May 1962 when she was leaving for London with the Burtons' four-and-a-half-year-old daughter Kate, who clutched an *Almanacco Topolino* Mickey Mouse cartoon book.

Many years later, in November 2013, a luxury Roman jeweller held a press conference at a hotel in London that carried its name. Bulgari was sponsoring an exhibition, *The Glamour of Italian Fashion, 1945–2014*, at the Victoria and Albert Museum and was hosting the press conference to launch it. While Burton and Taylor were filming *Cleopatra*, Burton is reported to have said, "The only word Liz knows in Italian is Bulgari." According to the jewellery firm, both Burton and Fisher indulged her in "the most sought after, stylish and precious Bulgari jewels". A necklace of diamonds and emeralds set in platinum that was on display in the exhibition had been an engagement gift from Burton, and Taylor wore it on their wedding day.

Hollywood on the Tiber provided a transatlantic boost to the upper reaches of Italian style and Italian fashion. A maker of men's luxury clothing, Brioni opened its first shop on Via Barberini, a few hundred metres from Via Veneto, at the end of the second world war. It attracted numerous movie people as customers. Kirk Douglas and Henry Fonda were two of them. Clark Gable, who was in Rome in 1959 filming *It Started in Naples* with Sophia Loren, was another. Paulette Goddard was photographed shopping on Via Veneto in 1957, Kim Novak shopping with her mother the following year. Cyd Charisse was the subject of a long photographic session while trying on dresses in the atelier of a smart couturier.

The collections of photographs in the archives at the Istituto Luce hold many showing American film stars out and about in Rome. The Piazza di Spagna, close to Bulgari's shop on Via dei Condotti, and the stretch of Via Veneto outside the Hotel Excelsior and opposite the Café de Paris were favourite loitering areas for paparazzi. As for those locations that provided what was considered the full flavour of the *dolce vita*, nightclubs drew Judy Holliday, who was photographed dancing in July 1955, and Steve Reeves in 1958, while Robert Mitchum was caught sitting in a bar in 1954 and so, in 1959, was Henry Fonda. In Rome as producer and star of the 1954 film *L'amante di Paride* (Paris's lover), to whose screenplay Salka Viertel contributed, Hedy Lamarr was photographed at dinner with others involved in her film. Raoul Walsh, Joan Collins and Richard Egan were in Rome in summer 1960 to film *Esther and the King*, a co-production in which 20th Century Fox joined forces with the Italian Galatea, and among the restaurants they favoured was Da Meo Patacca, a tourist trap in Trastevere.

Wrap for the dolce vita

Its walls now covered with black-and-white photographs of film stars and celebrities at dinner, Alfredo alla Scrofa was much frequented by people who had crossed the Atlantic to film in Rome. Not far away, overlooking the Piazza Navona, the Tre Scalini was closely watched by paparazzi, and in spring 1962 one of them photographed Taylor and Burton as they left. Two decades after being in the vanguard of Hollywood on the Tiber, Deborah Kerr would remember Tre Scalini as a restaurant where she "put on many a pound eating pasta". Clark Gable was photographed at Cacciani, at Frascati in the Castelli Romani hills, its excellent Roman cooking served in unpretentious surroundings. Sixty years later the white linen was still crisp, the lighting stark and the wooden furniture plain and light-coloured. Little was changed from when Gable was there, eyes twinkling and a slight smile playing on the lips beneath a thin moustache, although, as one looked northwards from the restaurant's terrace, developers had plastered the Roman plain below with an enormous urban sprawl.

Shot in 1959, *It Started in Naples* was Gable's penultimate film. He would diet to shed the effects of too many plates of pasta and to get trim for his next film, which would be his last. *The Misfits*, in which he played an ageing cowboy and starred with Marilyn Monroe and Montgomery Clift, was released posthumously in 1961. It was also Monroe's last film. Hollywood's studio and star systems had ended, and the golden age of Hollywood was nearing its end. And so was the *dolce vita*.

The strange political stability-instability that brought frequent changes in Italian government, with ten different ones in the 1950s and a further ten in the 1960s, the conservative Christian Democracy always the dominant partner in coalitions, was joined in the 1960s by an increasing level of social and industrial unrest. Established by a referendum in June 1946 that decided the country's discredited monarchy should go, Italy's young republic was under stress. Students stood alongside strikers in 1968 in joint protests against economic and social injustice. Police shot and killed two strikers near Syracuse in Sicily in December 1968 and injured another five, including a child. At Battipaglia, about 70 kilometres southeast of Naples, police killed two people during a demonstration against the closure of a tobacco factory in April 1969.

Growth in Italy's gross domestic product had slowed from an annual average of 6 per cent in the 1950s to 3 per cent in the middle of the 1960s. The economic miracle was over. And a severe shock would arrive in October 1973 when, in response to the Yom Kippur War between Israel and Egypt and Syria, the Arab members of OPEC, the oil-producing countries' cartel, placed an embargo on sales which caused the price of crude oil to soar from $3/barrel to $12/barrel. Italy was dependent on roads for goods transportation, and heavy fuel oil was the main input for electricity production. Inflation surged. The economy stalled. Austerity returned. At the beginning of December 1973 the government decreed that bars, cafés and restaurants should close and television channels should shut down at eleven o'clock in the evening. The use of private cars was banned on Sundays, and the bicycles and horses seen on Roman streets brought back memories of the years immediately after the end of the second world war and the opening years of Hollywood on the Tiber. Bloody drama was added to austerity's restrictions on 17 December when a Palestinian terrorist gang, having shot and killed two people in a terminal building at Fiumicino, tossed grenades into a Pan American Boeing 707 aircraft that was preparing to depart for Beirut and Tehran. Thirty people died in the fire the grenades started. The terrorists killed two more when hijacking a Lufthansa Boeing 737 waiting to leave for Munich. Moreover, the Years of Lead of Italy's home-grown terrorism had begun and far worse was to come.

Sitting at pavement tables outside bars on the Via Veneto and sipping *aperitivi*, I lived a small postscript to the *dolce vita* era soon after arriving in Rome. The city's authorities would place a stone tablet above a street sign at the crossroads with Via Ludovisi to remember the film director Federico Fellini, who "made Via Veneto the theatre of the Dolce Vita". Yet by the mid-1990s, when the stone tablet was unveiled on the wall by the Café de Paris, decline was evident. The decline would continue. In July 2009, prosecutors seized and shuttered the heart of *dolce vita* nightlife, which had fallen into mafia hands. In their control of hotspots of that superficially untroubled and frivolous time, Calabria's mafiosi were making a statement about their power, and a headline in a newspaper thirteen years later said that they again controlled the Café de Paris. Other places closed, even before the Covid-19 pandemic created problems for many cafés, bars, restaurants and hotels. Broken slabs would make Via Veneto's pavements hazardous. Gun-bearing soldiers on guard, and concrete and steel barriers around the American embassy on a corner at Via Veneto's junction with Via Ludovisi, would tell of a harder, harsher world than that of the *dolce vita*.

V

INTO A NEW MILLENNIUM

A Roman now adopted happily

William Shakespeare, *Titus Andronicus*

By releasing the film *Quo Vadis* on Friday, 2 November 1951, the Hollywood studio Metro-Goldwyn-Mayer hoped to capitalise on American cinema attendance over the forthcoming weekend and to kick-start a box office success. Meanwhile, on the other side of the Atlantic Ocean, Italian households were preparing for an administrative ritual that had last been performed fifteen years earlier, before a world war had disrupted the lives of their members and those of many hundreds of millions of people in other countries. Sunday, 4 November, brought an appointment with Italy's census. Analysis of the count was published in nine volumes between 1954 and 1956 by the Istituto Nazionale di Statistica (ISTAT, National Statistics Institute), albeit the key figure was soon known. The census revealed that the country's population was 47.5 million. According to the census returns of April 1936, Italy had then been home to 42.4 million people. Despite the war, the population had grown by 12 per cent.

SCENES FROM A ROMAN CENTURY

A question of jobs

However, growth in the capital city was of a different order from that of the country as a whole. Rome's population boomed. Its population swelled from 1.1 million in 1936 to 1.7 million in 1951, an increase of 55 per cent. By 1961 it stood at 2.2 million, an advance of 30 per cent over the preceding ten years. Strong growth would characterise the subsequent decade. It was fertilised by the clientelism of politicians who secured jobs in Rome for supporters and constituents from around the capital and the provinces, most often in the south, boosting a central bureaucracy that ran ministries and state agencies like the railways, the Istituto Nazionale per l'Assicurazione contro gli Infortuni sul Lavoro (INAIL, the national insurance scheme against workplace injuries), the state-owned insurer (INA), the courts and prosecutors' offices, the postal service, the Istituto Nazionale per l'Assicurazione contro le Malattie (INAM, the national health insurance board), the national pension fund (INPS) and much else.

For about half a century after the second world war around two-thirds of Italy's banking system was in public hands, which meant that the government in Rome and politicians made the key decisions and decided who should manage the banks, and not only at board level. Political influence often contributed other names to banks' payrolls, even in the lower ranks. Finance was simply a part of Italy's economy in which politicians and political parties played a central role. The state and the country's politicians also dug their claws deep into, or wrapped their tentacles around, manufacturing and service industries.

Rome was home to the headquarters of three state holding corporations and their substantial and politicised bureaucracies. With significant stakes in defence manufacturing, food, glass and aluminium, the Ente Partecipazioni e Finanziamento Industrie Manifatturiere (EFIM, Board for Investment and Financing in Manufacturing Industry) was large and diversified but it was the smallest of the three. The Istituto per la Ricostruzione Industriale (IRI, Institute for Industrial Reconstruction) and Ente Nazionale Idrocarburi (ENI, National Hydrocarbons Board) were giants whose vast and varied interests included, in the case of IRI, the national airline Alitalia, the broadcasting corporation RAI, steelmaking, shipbuilding, toll highways, cement, civil engineering and construction, three big banks of national interest, food groups Motta and Alemagna, telecommunications and Alfa Romeo. In controlling Agip, Snam, Italgas, Snamprogetti, Saipem and Nuovo Pignone, ENI was essentially a diversified energy and engineering group. But it also owned a chemicals subsidiary, the ubiquitous Agip Motel hotel chain, the Lanerossi textiles and clothing group, and a small media empire.

Unsurprisingly, the state holding corporations were well practised in exercising their political connections and influence. Decision-makers at the Cassa per il Mezzogiorno, the development fund for the south of Italy, were on the receiving end of many efforts. The holding corporations and the companies they controlled were among the businesses, small and large, that treated the Cassa as a *vacca da mungere* (a cow to be milked). Sandro Petriccione, a professor at Naples University and one of the directors of the fund's small executive board from 1963 to 1976, would remember the intense lobbying by ENI, whose headquarters in EUR were a few hundred metres from his office at the fund. Petriccione recalled how the assistant to ENI's chairman was "mostly to be found loitering at the Cassa and pushing ENI's interests". Principally there for lobbying, representative offices abounded in Rome. The payrolls of the political parties swelled to provide the staff needed for ensuring that clients were satisfied, the parties' finances were healthy and wheels were kept greased. Strongly manned trade unions and the muscular employers' association were rarely absent from the smoke-filled corridors of power.

Drivers were needed for thousands of ministerial, institutional and company cars. This was one segment of Rome's labour market in which the burgeoning bureaucracy involved considerable amounts of low-skilled clerical work or unskilled jobs like office cleaning or portering. Porters were kept busy as the bureaucracy produced enormous quantities of documents and mountainous paper archives, but there was no shortage of people to do the work. The pool of low-skilled or unskilled labour on which the city could draw was deep, as people from towns and cities with high unemployment in the south joined others from rural areas who decided that agriculture, often precarious, always poorly rewarded, was not for them. Many expatriate Italians who returned to Italy from colonies in Africa when the war ended set up home in the capital. There were also refugees from Istria and Dalmatia who had lived in the post-1919 Italian provinces of Fiume, Pola and Zara. (These were provinces on the Adriatic's northeastern corner that would belong to Slovenia and Croatia when Yugoslavia broke up at the beginning of the 1990s.) About 2,000 Italian refugees from Istria and Dalmatia moved in 1955 to a southern suburb of Rome that neighboured EUR. What they would call the Quartiere Giuliano-Dalmata had been built as housing for workers on the site for the 1942 World Fair. A small advance party of refugees had arrived there in 1947.

Embassies in the Italian capital resumed normal business after the war, albeit with a Cold War setting in and a front line running through the centre of Europe. Italy's northeast frontier with communist Yugoslavia was perceived as fragile and a potential hotspot. Moreover, for some of Italy's Western allies, none more than the United States, the country's large and flourishing Partito Comunista Italiano (PCI, Italian Communist Party) made Italy especially vulnerable to internal upheaval. The sizeable diplomatic, military and intelligence mission at the US embassy on Via Veneto was fully occupied. A paper in the winter 1983 edition of *Diplomatic History* would describe how intensive covert and overt American activity on both sides of the Atlantic interfered in Italian parliamentary elections in April 1948 to ensure victory of the conservative and Vatican-influenced Democrazia Cristiana (DC, Christian Democracy) over the PCI. Alcide De Gasperi, the DC's leader and Italy's prime minister from 1945 to 1953, had close ties to the Vatican. Thanks to the Bishop of Trento, De Gasperi had obtained employment in the Vatican library after being arrested, accused of attempting to escape abroad, and imprisoned in 1927.

Expatriate staff of foreign corporations eager to exploit the Italian market set up offices in the capital and added to the Eternal City's throng of diplomats, spies and military people. Airlines from across the world opened offices on Via Bissolati, a street off Via Veneto, and the global oil majors kept close to the political and business action. Founded in Quebec City in Canada in 1945, the United Nations Food and Agriculture Organization (FAO) moved to Rome in 1951, taking with it international civil servants, economists, agronomists, engineers and experts in the sciences of farming and food. Their numbers would grow. Established in 1961, the World Food Programme, an international humanitarian organisation within the UN to provide food assistance, would also be based in Rome. In 1977, another UN food organisation would be established in Rome. The International Fund for Agricultural Development (IFAD) works in partnership with the Organization of the Petroleum Exporting Countries (OPEC) and the Organisation for Economic Co-operation and Development (OECD) in focusing on rural areas of developing countries and food security.

With adults came children and teachers from other countries. The Overseas School Rome, which would change its name to the American Overseas School, and the Marymount International School were established with help from the US embassy in the two years after the war. Owned by parents, St George's English School was set up in 1958 and six years later St Stephen's School opened on Via Aventina behind the FAO's offices. An American university opened in 1969 and a second followed three years later.

And with people, Italians and expatriates, came demand for goods, services and housing. More grocers, butchers, greengrocers, shoe shops, hardware shops and clothing shops were among the retail outlets that Rome needed to satisfy the demand generated by its growing population. The city also needed more barbers and hairdressers, cobblers, schoolteachers, lawyers, surgeons, doctors and nurses for hospitals, plumbers, electricians, cooks and waiters for trattorias, bakers, chambermaids, desk staff and cleaners for hotels, bus drivers and conductors, and waste collectors. An increase in the number of jobs in Rome's bureaucracies had a multiplier effect on the local economy. And the Italian capital needed homes: architects, engineers and quantity surveyors to design them; cement, steel, wooden fixtures, tiles, paint, wiring, electrical fittings, piping and bathroom fittings among the materials needed for them; workers with the skills to build the homes; and land to build them on.

Homes for new Romans

The results of Rome's post-war building boom can be easily picked out decades later in the densely packed six-, seven- and eight-storey gardenless apartment blocks whose entrances open directly onto the pavements of streets that fill much of what had been open ground outside the Aurelian Walls. The broad strip of land between Garbatella and the San Paolo marshalling yards and the railways lines passing through Ostiense station offers a typical example of residential building during the 1950s. Via Carlo Citerni in northern, post-war Garbatella is one such street in the district. The shop at number nine proudly notes that Marco

Donati ("Oro e non solo") has been there since 1960, although sixty years later the jewellery business is run by a future generation of the family. Further down the 150-metre-long street other businesses, such as Magrelli the butcher at number twenty-one and D'Alisera's car workshop, proclaim that they have been serving customers for more than fifty years.

Across Via Cristoforo Colombo, which provides an eastern border to that post-war strip in northern Garbatella, and on the other side of the Appia Antica park, are Via della Caffarelletta, Via Carlo De Bildt and Via Latina, and beyond them is a residential district of similar 1950s and 1960s apartment blocks. The same style of high-density habitation fills what had been pre-war open land on both sides of Via Cristoforo Colombo heading towards EUR and Ostia, behind Trastevere in Monteverde Nuovo and Colli Portuensi, around Viale Marconi, which runs from Trastevere railway station to EUR, in the Magliana district and in the Aurelio district northwest of the Vatican, as well as to the sides of other consular roads that lead from Rome. And significant residential development had spread legally beyond sections of the Grande Raccordo Anulare (GRA, ring road) by the end of the twentieth century.

However, much of what was built on a huge expanse of Roman countryside during the first three decades after the war was illegal, apartment blocks and houses constructed without planning permission and with little regard for building regulations. Reliable statistics are hard to find and uneven. One study estimated that about 10,000 hectares of Rome were subject to "territorial aggression" between 1949 and 1962. The City of London with its modest 290 hectares and the neighbouring boroughs of Camden with 2,179 hectares, Islington with 1,486 hectares, and Hackney with 1,905 hectares together cover less than 6,000 hectares. Territorial aggression in Camden alone would hit Bloomsbury, Fitzrovia, Primrose Hill, the eastern side of Regent's Park, Belsize Park, Hampstead and all its heath, and much else.

Rome's city authorities worked between 1976 and 1985 to regularise the situation. They estimated that about 15,000 hectares of floor area in Rome were outside the law, and that almost one million Romans, a third of the city's population, lived in housing that lacked legal permits. What was done in Rome would in London have been the illegal building of tightly packed seven-storey blocks of apartments, with shops, hairdressers, post offices, doctors' surgeries, driving schools, bank branches, workshops and more at street level, to cover every square metre of the 2,149 hectares of the City of Westminster: Westminster itself, Belgravia (including Buckingham Palace and its gardens), Mayfair, Soho, Paddington, Marylebone, St John's Wood, St James's Park, Green Park, Hyde Park, and most of Regent's Park, plus all the 107 hectares of Kensington Gardens and around a further 140 hectares of the Royal Borough where the gardens stand.

Open land further out was not spared the urbanisation that covered countryside near the city. Aerial photographs taken in the early 1950s showed that Ostia had grown little in the decade after August 1943, when British reconnaissance aircraft photographed Ostia Levante to the southeast of its centre and Ostia Ponente to the northwest. Both towards the southeast and northwest, large open areas lay inland and along the coast from the central section of the seafront. Rome's city authorities had approved a town plan for Ostia in 1926 and, although the concept of a "garden city" with low density of construction of high quality remained on paper, the effect of the plan, in keeping with the regime's aim of expanding Rome's boundaries towards the sea, was to boost speculation, increase building density and reduce quality. While the plan had not yielded significant results before war intervened, Greater Rome's seaside municipality of Ostia would participate fully in the city's steep post-war growth in population. Indeed its growth would be even more rapid.

INTO A NEW MILLENNIUM

Ostia finds new roles

Recovery from the war needed time. There were national institutions to be created following the defeat of fascism and a referendum that abolished the monarchy to establish a republic. There was an economy that needed to get back on its feet, infrastructure to build everywhere in Italy, and the capital itself absorbed significant resources. Even so, the 1950s, 1960s and 1970s were boom decades for the seaside municipality. A post-war plan, approved in 1962, brought far higher housing density and effectively shaped Ostia into its twenty-first-century form. Census figures show that Ostia's resident population increased from 14,000 in 1951 to 25,000 in 1961 and 60,000 in 1971. What had become an important dormitory for Rome was home to 87,000 people at the end of 2000, with 48,000 of them living in Lido di Ostia Ponente, the northwestern and always less desirable part of Ostia, and 38,000 in Lido di Ostia Levante. There were only 1,000 in Lido di Castel Fusano, further to the southeast and the third of Rome's seaside administrative districts that together make up Ostia.

Just as the arrival of trains boosted the arrival of day-trippers, so Ostia's link to the city encouraged commuting from the seaside, albeit much of the inland part of the town is short on charm and a fair distance from the beach. The bourgeois *barocchetto romano* and art deco of buildings along a few streets around the centre of the seafront are a small and fortunate part of Ostia. Mostly residents live several hundred metres from the shore, in densely packed medium-rise apartment blocks that line grids of dull streets where cars are parked bumper to bumper. So much for bracing sea air.

Twenty-five kilometres, eight stations and at least thirty minutes separate Lido Centro from Metromare Roma—Lido's city terminus at Piramide. Commuters face an alienating daily calvary of travelling by train on a line characterised by cancellations, delays and disservice. Many alight at EUR Magliana to travel on Rome's Metro B line to the centre, rather than continue to Piramide or the intermediate station at Basilica San Paolo where transfers to Metro B are also possible. For several years in the late 1980s and early 1990s, I often travelled in the latter part of morning peak, one stop from Tor di Valle to EUR Magliana, squeezing myself into a dense mass of strap-hangers. Even well before the peak, however, carriages fill with commuters, among them immigrants from Latin America and Asia, office cleaners, domestic helpers and baby-sitters, nurses and other hospital staff, all with early starts to their days. Some finish their work towards the end of the morning or in the early afternoon, others later in the day, some fall asleep if they are fortunate to find seats for their journey home. Many faces reveal the tiredness brought by the hard daily grind.

Yet they might be thankful that their after-work travel does not coincide with young people heading to the seaside in the morning when schools are closed for holidays. Only robust Romans, the less fortunate, tourists with a sense of adventure or the unknowing are willing to compete with the heaving crowds of noisy youngsters who surge into carriages from packed platforms at the Piramide terminus as soon as doors are opened.

At weekends, while trains departing for Ostia pulsate with their human cargoes, better-off youngsters riding motor scooters or motorbikes join endless streams of cars carrying families along the 25 kilometres of the Via Cristoforo Colombo highway that separate the Aurelian Walls from the sea and Ostia's 15 kilometres of sandy beach. Perhaps as they start their journeys back to Rome, the observant among them notice the stubby column of travertine at the beginning of the narrow strip of grass and umbrella pines that separates the two carriageways which lead to the city from Piazzale Cristoforo Colombo, a large piazza on the seaside promenade, with the beach just beyond. And perhaps some of them stop to read the two weather-worn words engraved in it: Via Imperiale (Empire Way). The capital of Mussolini's new Roman empire did reach the sea, to launch the transformation of land around the small agricultural settlement established in the final decade of the nineteenth century into a completely different future.

On the capital's doorstep, with safe swimming beaches where the water's cleanliness wins awards, Ostia is a major amenity that is enjoyed by many tens or hundreds of thousands of Romans who flock there from June to September. It's not smart. If Ostia ever had a fashionable name, that was in the 1920s and 1930s. The search for elegance and style has not since then been the reason Romans go there. Ostia offers no competition to Cannes or Saint-Tropez, but it is several cuts above Clacton and Skegness. From late autumn to early spring, with the sun lower in a blue sky, and the temperature hovering around twenty degrees, Ostia offers the slightly melancholic out-of-season charm of a seaside resort. And perhaps those quiet, cooler days are the best for visiting, to enjoy a lunchtime plate of spaghetti alle vongole on the uncrowded terrace of a beachside restaurant staffed by unhurried waiters, take a leisurely walk along the promenade or the beach, and return to the city in light traffic.

With such a location so close to the city, film producers and directors have often exploited Ostia. Almost one hundred filmmakers did during the half-century between *Domenica d'agosto* in 1949 and *Gallo cedrone* in 1998. Many were light fare, particularly in the early post-war years, offering stereotype characters with uncomplicated stereotype plots for unsophisticated cinemagoers who simply wanted amusement they could easily understand. However, other films have provided the cinema-going public with food for thought. Much of Federico Fellini's *Le notti di Cabiria*, a film about a prostitute, was shot at Acilia, about midway between Ostia and Rome. It won Fellini the Oscar in 1958 for best foreign film and gave a high-level start to Pier Paolo Pasolini, a leftwing creative polymath and intellectual (best known outside Italy for his work in film, mainly as a director), as co-writer with Ennio Flaiano and Tullio Pinelli. Pasolini would direct an episode of *Le streghe* in 1967, which was shot on location among the shanty dwellings along the road that follows the final stretch of the northern bank of the Tiber to its mouth. The area across the Tiber, on its southern bank, would provide a similarly suitable downbeat location for shooting *Ostia* in 1970, a film about two delinquent homosexual brothers which ends with one murdering the other. Pasolini co-wrote the screenplay with Sergio Citti, the director.

Indeed, it seems contradictory that hyper-luxury super-yachts for which high-net-worth individuals spend millions of dollars should be associated with that neck of Ostia. Yet the industrial complex that dominates the final kilometre on the southern bank of the Tiber belongs to Canados (Cantieri Navali di Ostia), which, soon after the second world war, took over what had been Rome's base for military and civilian flying boats during the 1930s and the war. Visits to the boatyard probably provide an out-of-the-ordinary experience for the customers who show up during the construction of their boats. There's an element of slumming when visiting that part of the seaside municipality. Potholes crater the road that follows the final kilometre of the Tiber as it makes its way to the sea. Untrimmed and littered verges, an expanse of sandy scrub, a boat storage, maintenance and repair centre, tall stands of rushes, and high walls hiding and protecting low-rise houses near the river's mouth, the result of unplanned building and some simply shacks, lend the district a distinctly gritty edginess.

In several areas of the seaside community, there's a sense of neglect that tends towards degradation, but the road where Canados has its yard is a particularly scruffy corner of Ostia. It's the kind of place where novelists might imagine that drug dealers meet, sex to satisfy all tastes is for sale, and murders are committed. Close to the Canados factory, on a corner of the road that takes buyers of luxury motor yachts back to Ostia's centre and fixed to gates in iron railings, a small metal sign informs the curious that this is the entrance to I Parchi Letterari—Pier Paolo Pasolini. It was there on scrub that Pasolini was murdered in the early hours of 2 November 1975.

Although mystery surrounded the murder, there was certainty about Pasolini's arrival around midnight in that squalid part of Ostia in his Alfa Romeo 2000 GT Veloce sports car, accompanied by a 17-year-old youth from a town just northeast of the capital. They had met at Rome's Termini railway station after Pasolini had eaten dinner, but the meeting was not a casual pick-up, as the 53-year-old and the youth, for whom he bought dinner before driving to Ostia, already knew each other. And the cause of death was also beyond doubt. Pasolini had been violently beaten and then run over with his own car. Police soon stopped the 17-year-old, who drove it away from the murder site. He was known to the authorities as a car thief and a *ragazzo di vita* (young male prostitute). There had been an argument about sexual services and this had become violent, the youth told the court at the trial where he was accused of murder, together with unknown defendants. He was found guilty and an appeal court would subsequently confirm the verdict, albeit with the youth as the sole culprit. Yet he showed no signs of having been in a fight, was small whereas Pasolini was strong and fit, and residents of a nearby shanty settlement had heard a row that involved more than two voices. The appeal court's verdict was greeted with scepticism. Pasolini's episode in *Le streghe* finishes with the words "Being dead or being alive is the same thing".

Change in Garbatella

"All Garbatella shimmered in the sunshine," wrote Pasolini in *Una vita violenta* (A violent life), his novel of 1959 and the second of his works about Rome's underclass. Pasolini knew the district well, as he did many working-class districts of the city, from Pietralata, then in the northeastern outskirts, to Trastevere, just over the Tiber from the historic centre, as well as Monteverde, the district behind Trastevere, Testaccio, inside and close to the Aurelian walls at Porta San Paolo, and San Paolo itself. It was to Al Biondo Tevere, a trattoria on Via Ostiense, not far from the San Paolo basilica and near the junction with Via delle Sette Chiese, which leads uphill to Garbatella, that Pasolini took the 17-year-old youth for dinner before driving to Ostia.

Pasolini had been an active member of the PCI, but the party expelled him on the grounds of moral turpitude and political unworthiness after he was found guilty in 1950, together with two teenage boys, of obscenity in a public place. Nevertheless, he continued to be a staunch man of the left, voted for party and remained close to it. Veteran card-carrying PCI members in Garbatella would remember his visits to the Villetta on Via Passino, the meeting place of the party's Garbatella branch. The district remained a leftwing stronghold for decades after the war. Enrica Zarfati, a long-time Garbatella resident and the last surviving Roman Jew who had experienced the horror of concentration camps, died in 2016 at the age of 94. Libero Natalini died aged 87 in 2003, having joined the underground PCI in 1934, fought against German troops in the defence of Rome in September 1943, and been involved in the resistance as a member of the Gruppi di Azione Patriottica (GAP). Natalini's boyhood home, where Giacomo Matteotti, a friend of his father, often went for dinner, was in one of Garbatella's earliest buildings. Maria Teresa Regard, who died aged 76 in 2000, was another partisan who fought at Porta San Paolo in September 1943. While fighting with the GAP, she met Franco Calamandrei, a post-war journalist and PCI senator, who would become her husband. She would live at the northern end of Garbatella on Circonvallazione Ostiense.

INTO A NEW MILLENNIUM

The collapse of Italy's political parties in the wake of the *tangentopoli* institutionalised corruption scandal in 1992 helped dim the light of the idealism, commitment and political activism that came from older members of Garbatella's PCI. Moreover, many of those with first-hand knowledge of the evils of nazi-fascism had by the 1990s passed to *miglior vita*. In addition, tenants' right-to-buy brought a shift in the class make-up of Garbatella's residents. However, the presence of many university students was probably a factor in changing the district's character. New businesses rejuvenated an ageing quarter. Every street would seem to have one wine bar, trattoria, restaurant, café, pizzeria or pub, and every piazza several, and bars and pubs would stay open late to cater for night owls. Established in 1992, with 35,000 students in 2022 and occupying a long stretch of Via Ostiense—effectively the western boundary for Garbatella—between the abandoned site of the former wholesale food market and the San Paolo basilica, Roma Tre University had outstripped Rome's second university, Tor Vergata, founded ten years earlier. (It still lagged far behind La Sapienza, founded in 1303, where more than 100,000 students were enrolled in 2022.) It was unsurprising that by the third decade of the twenty-first century the once drab area near the gasometer and the Centrale Montemartini archaeological museum on Via Ostiense had become a lively nocturnal gathering place for young people, drawn by new trattorias and bars that rivalled Testaccio.

In October 2003, Roma Tre's rector had greeted Carlo Azeglio Ciampi, Italy's head of state, when he inaugurated Garbatella's Palladium theatre, which the university had restored after years of decay, abandonment and use as a porn-movie cinema, and saved from the threat of imminent transformation into a bingo hall. As well as being part of the university and serving the department of music and theatre, with its programme of concerts and stage and cinema shows for a wider public, the Palladium "strengthens the university's integration with local society," said the rector. Ten years after the Palladium's inauguration, and again with the university's involvement, Garbatella's public baths were resurrected in a stylish restoration to become the district's community library and cultural centre.

In a letter recalling the laying of the district's foundation stone, Paolo Orlando wrote that he expected that its population would grow to 50,000, and by the end of the 1920s it had almost reached the halfway point. Garbatella's residents would number about 45,000 in the second decade of the twenty-first century, but the district had been completed before the second world war and its population had already reached the post-war level with completion. Garbatella did not and could not play a part in dealing with Rome's post-war need for more homes.

EUR—a residential and business district

The EUR district would satisfy the housing needs of some well-off Romans, albeit they would have to wait until the late 1950s before moving in. Abandoned in the year that it was due to host the World Fair of 1942, the district was neglected for a further seven years after the war. By the time the government turned its attention to the site, it had been damaged by vandalism and looting and been partly occupied by homeless people. A new zoning plan was drawn up between 1952 and 1954 in which, unlike the project for the World Fair, residential building had a central place. With its green spaces, broad avenues, an artificial lake set in a park and large areas of higher ground, EUR offered an attractive district to Rome's expanding affluent social elite. Part of the core of EUR in which offices would also be built was allocated to apartment blocks of three to six storeys. The broad strip that separates the two carriageways of Via Cristoforo Colombo on the hill to the south of the lake would be used for gardens and as a site for a covered sports arena for the Olympic Games in 1960. Built between 1956 and 1959 to a design by Pier Luigi Nervi, a structural engineer, and the architect Marcello Piacentini, the Palazzo dello Sport quickly became an iconic architectural landmark. Otherwise, the hill was principally zoned for villas and small apartment blocks of various types on both its northern and southern slopes.

Four high-rise exceptions would stand out to the west of the sports arena. One is the Fungo (Mushroom), a water tower 50 metres high that sticks up from the top of the hill. It was built around the same time as the arena to supply a system for watering EUR's green spaces. Known for singing leading roles in operas by Verdi and Puccini, and a star at Milan's La Scala in the 1950s and 1960s, the tenor Mario Del Monaco was responsible for the later addition of a panoramic restaurant with a pricey menu at the top of the tower. The water tank around which the restaurant was constructed would still be serving its original purpose in the third decade of the twenty-first century. The other three tall buildings are apartment blocks. Twelve storeys high with deep terraces all around from which geraniums cascade from spring to autumn, one stands not far from the Fungo but on the other side of the road. After I spent April 1972 in the Residence Garden on Viale dell'Arte, my home until summer 1977 would be a small apartment that had served the bachelor son of the owner of the block's penthouse. With extensive well-kept gardens, pool and tennis court, the block lived up to its name, Eden Park Condominio.

The owner of the small apartment was Marcantonio Bragadin, a descendant of an officer with the same name who, serving the Venetian Republic as the Captain General of Famagusta in Cyprus, led a year-long, unsuccessful defence against the Ottomans, and was brutally murdered when the siege ended. The Bragadin to whom I paid rent was a retired admiral who wrote screenplays and worked on the production of films with military themes. In October 1972, when he sold both apartments, I had a new landlord. Carlo Rustichelli was a noted composer of film music, and among his two hundred or so film scores was that for *Divorzio all'italiana*, an award-winning, slightly bitter comedy starring Marcello Mastroianni. Among the block's other residents were Massimo Ranieri, a young but well-established singer and actor, and a pair of star footballers who played in the Roma football team. Members of the affluent social elite did indeed choose to live in EUR, as did many rightwing voters. In September 1978, a year after I left the small apartment, a bomb containing three kilograms of TNT exploded at the base of the Fungo, wrecking a café that had been a notorious meeting place for Rome's neo-fascists.

EUR was built quickly, given that the construction industry was busy in many other parts of the capital. By March 1961, within a decade of beginning their sale, the administrative authority had sold all the plots zoned as residential, and building on many of them had been completed. And by 1961 construction was well advanced on numerous office blocks and getting underway on others. Three 70-metre towers were erected on the northern side of the lake for the ministry of finance between 1958 and 1962, while nearby, closing the lake's eastern end, an 86-metre building with twenty-two floors known as the Palazzo di Vetro or Palazzo ENI was being built as head offices for the state-owned oil, gas, chemicals and engineering conglomerate. Work had begun 500 metres away on headquarters for Alitalia, Italy's state-controlled airline. The elegant 72-metre building had twenty-one floors and was completed in 1965. The head offices of the Istituto Mobiliare Italiano (IMI, a Treasury-owned financial institution) neighboured Alitalia's offices to the north on Viale dell'Arte and had been completed two years earlier. Across the road, the ministry of merchant marine was completed two years later.

Meanwhile, construction was going ahead rapidly to the west of Via Cristoforo Colombo. The ministry of foreign trade and the foreign trade institute were built between 1959 and 1962, close to the bulky headquarters of Christian Democracy and to Palazzo Italia, a tower block 71 metres high occupying the west side of Piazza Marconi. Both were completed in 1960. During the middle years of the sixties, INPS built a tower block behind the iconic Palazzo INPS that had added style to E42 nearly thirty years before. Confindustria, Italy's industrialists' confederation, moved in 1972 to a six-storey glass curtain-walled building at the extreme west of the district and close to the Palazzo della Civiltà del Lavoro. Just three important sites were then incomplete. One was the Palazzo delle Poste for the ministry of posts and tele-communications, a dark, brooding high-rise block looming over the lake, and a sharp contrast to the luminous group that the finance ministry occupied on the other side of Via Cristoforo Colombo. The Palazzo delle Poste was completed in 1976. The second site was a patch of rough open ground where, through the 1970s until its transformation into a car park, youngsters played soccer. At a crossroads, diagonally across from the Palazzo delle Poste and facing the finance ministry, between 2008 and 2016 the car park would become the Nuvola, a controversial new conference centre designed by Massimiliano Fuksas.

The third site was at the far end of the lake from the Palazzo ENI. In May 1972 there was a partly completed skeleton of a building on what was prime EUR real estate, overlooking the lake and its park where avenues of Japanese cherry trees had not long finished blooming. Vertical columns supported nine floors of reinforced concrete designed for plumbing to a large number of bathrooms. This was meant to be the Hotel du Lac, an upmarket hotel. The project had been approved in the 1960s, but there was no movement on the site during the five years I lived in EUR. Work had begun but had been suspended, one of the few schemes in EUR that didn't go to plan. Instead it was completed as head offices for Banco di Roma in 1984, reportedly because the bank took possession of the land and unfinished building after foreclosing on a loan to the developer that had turned sour.

EUR is a part of the city I know well. I returned there in April 2022 to look carefully rather than cursorily at buildings that I had visited during the previous fifty years, some of them on many occasions. I stopped in front of the entrance to Palazzo INA at 20 Piazza Kennedy, the building once occupied by the Cassa per il Mezzogiorno. Established as an autonomous agency in 1950 with the aim of closing the yawning economic gap that separated southern Italy from the far wealthier northern part of the country, the Cassa wielded enormous economic and political clout. Through a murky window I could see, around the main courtyard, some of the rose-coloured columns of granite from Baveno that had caught my eye in April 1972. Weeds grew on a ramp to a lower courtyard. The building seemed to have been empty for many years. A sign above the main entrance said that the offices were to let.

Thanks to the Cassa, over a period of forty years Italy's southern regions and two main islands were provided with 16,000 kilometres of roads, 23,000 kilometres of aqueducts, 40,000 kilometres of electrical power lines, 1,600 schools and 160 hospitals. The Cassa's achievements in building this infrastructure were considerable and prevented the gap between north and south from widening as the economic miracle brought increasing well-being to the Bel Paese, above all to the north. Its staff in the 1950s and early 1960s was composed principally of engineers, architects, surveyors, agronomists and economists. Then politicians decided to broaden the Cassa's role, turning its focus away from the provision of basic infrastructure to the industrialisation of the south through capital grants, subsidised loans, tax breaks and employment subsidies, thereby helping to thicken Italy's undergrowth of political clientelism.

Towards the end of 1984, I returned as a journalist to interview the Cassa's chairman for a feature article on a major water management system in Basilicata, Italy's instep region. The article appeared in the *Financial Times* in January 1985. Two months later the chairman was escorted from his office and taken to Milan where prosecutors were investigating cases of extortion involving construction firms and the national roads authority of which he had been general manager. Thirty years later he was living in Lugano and reported to have substantial assets in Switzerland, as well as in Paraguay and Brazil.

Writing for the *Financial Times* and *The Economist* took me to Confindustria's offices to interview chairmen, directors general and heads of research, for the association's annual meetings and for occasional seminars on the Italian economy. IMI's offices were another regular calling point when researching articles for the *Financial Times* and *The Banker*, the paper's monthly magazine for the banking industry. As a medium- and long-term credit institution, IMI was responsible for managing government funds aimed at promoting industrial and technological research and development. Writing on energy matters for the *Financial Times* and its cluster of energy publications required regular visits to Palazzo ENI and to Unione Petrolifera, the oil companies' association, which had offices in a small low-rise block opposite the elegant rationalist-style building housing EUR's administrative authority. I went to the tower blocks of the ministry of finance to learn about taxes and tax evasion, and to the ministry of foreign trade to interview the minister and obtain trade statistics. Researching pieces on pensions brought trips to the offices of INPS.

While still working in management consultancy, I spent a period in the Torre Alitalia, learning how the national airline sometimes made profits by recognising the liabilities of advance ticket sales as revenues. An assignment at Alluminio Italia, an aluminium group owned by EFIM, required talking to managers at its offices in Palazzo Italia on Piazza Marconi. I interviewed Rolando Valiani, EFIM's chairman, for a piece that appeared in the *Financial Times* in April 1990, my first experience of an interview cut short because the interviewee didn't like the questions. Valiani probably knew he was sitting on a corporate, financial and political time-bomb. *Tangentopoli* broke open less than two years later in Milan. Prosecutors got around to EFIM in 1994, having already uncovered and begun the trial of those involved in what was described as the "mother of all bribes" paid by ENI, whose chairman had received almost 5 billion lire (about £2 million at 1994 exchange rates) of the 153 billion lire total of backhanders. In accepting 34 million lire (about £14,000) for family reasons, Valiani committed a venial sin, not a mortal one.

In the same issue in April 1990 as my feature on EFIM, a colleague on the newspaper described ENI's chairman as a "safe" pair of hands. And the issue carried a piece based on an interview I had at the grim, dark tower block in EUR with Oscar Mammì, then minister of posts and telecommunications. In July that year the infamous Mammì Law would legalise Silvio Berlusconi's illegally acquired media muscle. Less than three years after Mammì's defective and partial law was enacted, it attracted the attention of anti-corruption prosecutors in Milan. Their suspicions had been aroused by a lucrative consultancy contract that Berlusconi's Fininvest company had given to a member of Mammì's staff after he left the ministry.

I often went to the head offices of Banco di Roma (state-controlled and one of Italy's biggest banks) after they moved in 1984 from Via del Corso to what was once meant to be a smart hotel at the western end of the lake in EUR. I visited less after its management changed following the bank's takeover by a group headed by the former Rome savings bank. During the years from 1984 to the mid 1990s, I had spoken regularly to the general manager of the savings bank, but relations turned chilly after two articles in *The Economist* in 1997. The first was headlined "Simply Staggering" and brought a letter to the editor from London lawyers acting on behalf of Banca di Roma (as the Banco had become). The second was headlined "Joyless" and began: "Italian finance is always a good bet for sheer outrageousness. Even so, the recapitalisation of Italy's second largest bank explores new limits."

Passing the building by the lake would bring back memories, among them memories of the general manager, guilty of contributing to 2003's fraudulent bankruptcy of Cirio (a food firm) and sentenced to four years in jail, and of conspiracy in the bankruptcy of Parmalat (also in 2003 and also a food firm), which drew a prison sentence of four and a half years. The verdicts were confirmed and sentences handed down by the supreme court, Italy's final court of appeal, the first in 2017 when the former general manager was 82, and the second two years later. And passing that office block brings back memories of a three-day trip to Budapest at the end of October 1986. With the banking system mostly in public hands and apparently not interested in maximising profits, the 1980s were good years for friends of senior management at Italian banks, a group that included journalists and their wives. Privatisations in the 1990s that followed the *tangentopoli* scandal and 1992's financial crisis were accompanied by a tightening of belts.

EUR—an uncertain future

The Capitalia banking group, which brought together the former Banco di Roma, the savings bank and several others, was acquired by Unicredit, a large Milanese bank in 2007. Rationalisation of branch networks and bank offices followed, and there were rumours in 2014 of the closure of the former head offices in EUR. The announcement that the building overlooking the lake was up for sale arrived three years later, and in 2019 it entered the portfolio of Prelios, a real estate services company. Described by Prelios as iconic offices with a unique panoramic view, the 48,000 square metres of office space was to be subjected to a major innovative renovation to fully upgrade both the building and the gardens in which it stands. I walked past it on several occasions in the spring and summer of 2022, but the building was enveloped in silence and there was no sign of activity. It reminded me of the Hotel du Lac in the years I lived nearby, albeit two years later there seemed to be signs of life at the site.

Yet the empty building by the lake and the Palazzo INA, the offices once occupied by the Cassa per il Mezzogiorno, were far from unusual. Colliers International, a major estate agent, had placed a discreet sign at one corner of Palazzo Italia to say it was letting offices in the building. A block on nearby Via Chopin that had housed offices of the state pensions agency carried a sign from agent CBRE (Coldwell Banker Richard Ellis) to say that office space was being let in Chopin 12. CBRE was also agent for lettings in what had been offices occupied by the health ministry. Until *tangentopoli* brought its dissolution at the beginning of 1994, Christian Democracy was the country's largest political party, and no government was formed after 1946 without it being the dominant member. Several signs offering offices and retail space to let were attached to glass panels around a ground-floor portico of what had been the party's headquarters on Piazza Sturzo. A sign saying that Regus was marketing furnished offices, meeting rooms and virtual offices seemed to have been placed there several years before. One of the blocks where IMI's bankers once worked had been renamed Spaces, another business that rents out co-working areas and shared and flexible offices.

Palazzo INA and Palazzo ENI were the first acquisitions of a closed property fund established by the doctors' and dentists' pension scheme in 2007. Its accounts at year-end 2021 showed that Palazzo INA had a book value of 134 million euros (including the cost of improvement work) and the 40,500 square metres of office space was producing nothing by way of rent. On the other hand, the lease of the 37,200 square metres of Palazzo ENI with its book value of 218 million euros had between five and seven years to run and was generating income of just under 300 euros a square metre. Around 2005, I had visited ENI's extensive and expanding office district at San Donato Milanese to the south of the Lombard capital. Seventeen years later, I wondered how much space in Palazzo ENI was empty and what would happen when the lease in Rome expired.

The Torri Ligini tower blocks once occupied by the ministry of finance stand about 200 metres from Palazzo ENI and provide a warning. For many years after the ministry left them they were empty shells, skeletons of buildings offering a dismal example of urban abandonment. After various ideas were floated and sank, the Treasury-controlled Cassa Depositi e Prestiti bank acquired the buildings in autumn 2016 and three years later announced that they would be completely renovated. In autumn 2020, property agents Jones Lang LaSalle were given the mandate for letting the three tower blocks and two four-storey buildings on the site. In a publicity note, they drew attention to the breath-taking views, the care given to the interior design and green spaces "to contribute to staff well-being and the stimulation of creative energy".

* * *

When I walked past in autumn 2022 the project seemed stalled, but work appeared to be moving slowly ahead two years later. Whatever the speed of progress, the Cassa Depositi e Prestiti must surely have been hoping that the lettings market for office space in EUR would be more buoyant when the rebuilt Torri Ligini and their two small neighbours were ready for tenants than it was in the aftermath of the Covid-19 pandemic. Digitalisation and working from home had radically changed employment, working methods and the need for offices since EUR was reshaped in the 1950s and 1960s from being the site of a world fair into a modern, decentralised business district. The late 1960s and early 1970s represented a high point for that small part of Rome with its surface area of around five square kilometres. Perhaps the decline began in the 1980s when Alitalia, already showing signs that would lead to four decades of struggle to keep airborne, sold its elegant and iconic tower block to IBM. The computer giant's restructuring project for the building turned into a major engineering job after the discovery of asbestos, inadequate insulation and structural instability. IBM's fortunes turned sour around the end of the 1980s and the building was taken over in 1996 by INAIL, the national insurance scheme against workplace injuries.

Everywhere there would be wholly or partly empty buildings, large ones, medium ones and small ones. The compact, unobtrusive block where Unione Petrolifera, the oil companies' association, had had its offices also housed NATO's Defense College. The military had moved to Rome from Paris in 1966 when the French president General Charles de Gaulle withdrew France from the organisation's integrated military command. In 1999, the college moved again, a few kilometres from EUR to the Italian army's command, training and barracks complex at Cecchignola. For many years the empty building had been wrapped in netting, another reminder of EUR's past and its need to find a new role for the future.

How the architects and engineers who sit in the offices of Rome's urban planning and implementation department, housed in the rationalist-style block that was designed to cater for the eating needs of visitors to E42, must wish for an all-embracing project to regenerate the district. The establishment of Rome's third university rejuvenated Garbatella, Ostiense and San Paolo, but EUR's tower blocks seem unsuited for a university, even if a fourth state university were to be considered necessary. Yet perhaps the opening of the Nuvola conference centre will encourage international conference planners to consider Rome, and EUR in particular, as the destination for their events. However, even if that should happen, much of the old office space will likely continue to be short of employees looking at screens and tapping keyboards. Politicians and planners will need imagination and fortune on their side in order to regenerate EUR as a thriving district for the twenty-first century.

Sixty and seventy years earlier, in the 1950s and 1960s, buildings were going up everywhere outside Rome's historic centre. Cement-mixers were at work, lorryloads of reinforcing bars, bricks and tiles were being delivered, drains were being laid, water and electricity were being connected, asphalting was underway to cover the earth, dust and builders' rubble of unmade streets, and scaffolding was being erected and taken down. The city probably seemed little other than a checkerboard of building sites, with EUR probably the biggest site of all.

Underground railways

During the closing decades of the twentieth century and the opening decades of the twenty-first, public transport ranked with waste collection at the top of the challenges facing Rome's administrators, and at the top of sources of public complaint. I came to know the Azienda Tramvie e Autobus del Comune (ATAC, the city's bus company) in summer 1974 when I undertook a consultancy assignment to evaluate bus overhaul strategies, forming a positive opinion of managerial and technical competence while doing so. (ATAC was then responsible only for bus and tram services and not for the city's short section of underground railway.) However, political and personnel issues were handicaps to efficiency. A radical strategy I thought worth investigation was that of abandoning overhauls, reducing the time to scrapping, and keeping workshops operating only for normal maintenance and repairs. This would have led to a lower average age of bus fleet and to lower costs thanks to the closure of most of the workshops. This was politically unacceptable. The fleet numbered then around 2,000, as it would fifty years later.

Although buses are central to Rome's public transport system, attention has increasingly focused on the need for efficient, environmentally clean, potentially rapid and high-capacity vehicles, and hence on underground railways. At the census of 1971, Rome had a population of 2.8 million, an increase of about a quarter on 1961, albeit this represented the end to growth. The population would fluctuate little around an average of 2.7 million in the four censuses held between 1991 and 2021. However, two and a half decades of immediate post-war population growth far outstripped capacity to build underground railways. The authorities and construction firms always lagged, unable to match the housing that was springing up with suitable extensions to the network.

Work had resumed on the city's first line in 1948. Part of the project for E42, the railway was meant to join the centre of Rome to the new district where the World Fair was to be held. A photograph taken in March 1940 shows construction of EUR's western underground station at an advanced stage. The line began at the Termini railway station and ran beneath Via Cavour to the Colosseum and then, still underground, on past the Circus Maximus to Piramide. There it surfaced to follow the path of the railway from Porta San Paolo to Ostia as far as Magliana, where it disappeared underground again and continued to EUR. Magliana was the junction where trains heading for the coast continued on the surface. Some underground sections between Termini and Piramide had been completed before war interrupted work, and were used as air-raid shelters.

The 10 kilometres of line from Termini to EUR was inaugurated in 1955. Extensions followed. The first, in the early 1970s, involved the construction of a station at Laurentina, at the end of a single track beyond EUR. A project doubling that track was inaugurated in 1990, at the same time as an extension beyond Termini to the east, ending at Rebibbia, about a kilometre from the capital's main jail. A branch to the north from the station at Piazza Bologna to Viale Jonio was opened in 2015, taking the total length of the line to 23 kilometres. Despite this being Rome's first underground railway, it was called Metro B (MB).

Work began in 1963 on Metro A, the second line, which runs from the southeast of the city to the northwest, passing beneath Termini and tourist magnets in the historic centre such as Piazza Barberini, the station closest to the Trevi Fountain, and Piazza di Spagna, by the Spanish Steps and close to the fashion district. The first section from Cinecittà, where film studios are located, to Ottaviano, a station within walking distance of the Vatican, opened in 1980, and an extension followed later that year to Anagnina, a station near Rome's ring road. The line was extended beyond Ottaviano in 1999, taking its length to 18 kilometres.

The third line, Metro C, repurposed a long section of suburban surface track that had served an early twentieth-century regional light railway to Frosinone, about 80 kilometres southeast of Rome. Work began in 2006 and the first section, in the suburbs, began operating eight years later. The second section, which takes the line to San Giovanni, opened in 2018. As Rome prepared for 2025's Jubilee, the city's authorities announced that the section between San Giovanni and the Colosseum, which will include the station at Porta Metronia, would open in time for the event. Work was underway on a station at Piazza Venezia which was due to open in 2033 and the line will extend beyond the Tiber to Piazza Mazzini and Farnesina, with openings planned for 2035.

On completion of the extensions to the line, Metro C will extend 28 kilometres and Rome's three Metro lines will together have a total length of about 70 kilometres. With a population of about one-half of Rome, Milan had a rapid transit metro system of five lines in 2024 and a total of 104 kilometres. And Brescia, Lombardy's second city, with a population one-twelfth that of Rome, put 14 kilometres of fully automated metro line into operation in 2013.

Answering critics who complain about the slow progress, the city's administrators point to how planners and builders in Rome have faced and continue to face subterranean difficulties both immediately under the surface and deeper down. Safeguarding archaeological relics is paramount, construction work ceasing and archaeologists moving in when these are found. One episode of Federico Fellini's 1972 autobiographical film *Roma* includes a visit to an underground construction site where work was underway on Metro A. The civil engineer accompanying the production crew that was filming explained how the ground beneath Rome was unpredictable and that "an important relic is found every hundred metres". Another factor that has penalised the building of Rome's underground railway system is Italian and Roman officialdom. "The bureaucracy is even more unpredictable than the ground," said the engineer. He added, "The red tape between us and the city authorities is as long as the whole of the metro line." Similar complaints would be made half a century later.

Offices, apartment blocks and even underground railway lines: the four decades that followed the second world war provided a bonanza for building firms and businesses reliant on the construction industry. As for manufacturing, matters continued much as they were during the fascist *ventennio*. Rome's economy would depend little on what was made in the city. With the northern boundary for eligibility for regional development aid running about 25 kilometres south of Rome, through the town of Pomezia, which lies on Via Pontina to the Circeo, Gaeta and Naples, there was no incentive to manufacture in or immediately around the city. Yet even in areas where manufacturing was encouraged through state aid, businesses faced existential challenges as the twentieth century ended.

Industry in retreat

Standing close to Via Pontina, just south of Pomezia, a factory that once belonged to a well-known British firm that made lighting equipment and systems for theatres, film sets and television and film studios has lain empty for many years. Sun, wind and rain have cancelled the name Strand Lighting on an outside wall. The business became part of Rank, the leading British film production company, in 1968, and I visited the factory in 1986, the year Rank Strand bought an Italian competitor called Quartzcolor. The factory where spotlights were made may have belonged to Quartzcolor and arrived with the acquisition, or it may have been an investment by Rank Strand, but whichever the case, it had benefited from capital grants, subsidised loans, tax breaks and payroll subsidies made available by the Italian government through the Cassa per il Mezzogiorno.

For the many thousands of Romans who drive along Via Pontina—regiments of daily commuters into and out of the city all the year, and summer armies of seaside enthusiasts heading to and returning from the coast and the long sandy beaches at Lavinio or Nettuno, or further down at towns like Sabaudia, San Felice Circeo or Sperlonga—the building where theatre and studio lights were once made flashes by in an instant of anonymity, a quality that marks a fair number of vacant industrial and commercial buildings that flank the road. When passing in the first decades of the twenty-first century, I always glanced its way, but Strand Lighting's building, where I spent part of a morning, had yet to be revitalised by a new owner.

The transfer of the production of goods from Italy to countries where costs are lower—the globalisation that began in the 1990s—led to deindustrialisation and manufacturing losses at home, and transformed busy factories into silent and lifeless post-industrial hulks, with broken windows, rusting gates, graffiti-covered walls, and weeds growing tall and thick in car parks and loading bays. Empty buildings like those around Pomezia would litter business parks on the outskirts of towns and cities throughout southern Italy, relics of a long-abandoned industrial development policy.

In a district of Pomezia known as Castel Romano, a few kilometres north of the town's centre, two massive box-like buildings stand out from the countryside by the Via Pontina. Part of a studio complex, with sound stages and a backlot of 150 hectares for outside sets, they were built in the 1960s for the Italian-American film producer Dino De Laurentiis and benefited from state aid. In competition with Cinecittà, the publicly owned studios that lie well within Rome's city boundaries on the Via Tuscolana, Dinocittà arrived too late to enjoy the 1950s cinema boom of Hollywood on the Tiber and the *dolce vita* years it spawned, and by the 1990s the studio complex had closed. However, unlike the empty factory that once belonged to Strand Lighting, Dinocittà was offered another life when a group of Italian businessmen acquired it at the end of 2001. Reports that the studios would be resurrected as a major centre for film production raised hopes that the glitter would again sparkle. Yet Dinocittà's future would be rather more prosaic, holding none of the glamour that goes with film stars, Oscar nominations and award ceremonies, film premieres and red carpets, and that future lay several years ahead.

Opened in 2014, as Rome's answer to Paris's Disneyland, Cinecittà World would simply be an amusement park, albeit one whose name laid claim to a cultural heritage. Speaking in spring 2022 about reopening after the Covid-19 pandemic, the park's chief executive described a three-year-old Volarium ride—a small theatre that travels 10 metres above the ground on an aerodynamic platform with special effects provided by a simulator—as a cinema experience unique in Italy. However, while major figures of movie-making once worked there, and despite the cinema being part of the amusement park's appeal, in truth little remains of those few years of cinematographic glory other than cans of celluloid in film archives, Cinecittà World's small tour of sets, and memories of an increasingly distant past. It's a long way from being a theme park of the world of cinema. One of the two huge buildings in which films were shot on sound stages would house Inferno, a roller-coaster, and the other would be a theatre with a daily show offering Italian songs, described as "The Best of Made in Italy". Cinecittà World's beauty and dance competitions and Halloween specials, and corporate events like the presentation of new cars and training and team-building sessions, would hardly match the glitz and gloss of film-making.

Factories in towns like Pomezia and Anagni, near the Autostrada del Sole that links Rome to Naples, are the nearest that old-fashioned industries, such as metal carpentry, chemicals, pharmaceuticals, clothing manufacture and food processing, approached the Italian capital, and this mostly thanks to decades of southern development incentives. Rome's economy has long been firmly rooted in the Vatican and the Roman Catholic Church, Italian government ministries employing large numbers of civil servants, and other state bodies with big payrolls, such as universities, the national broadcasting corporation, the law courts and various regulatory authorities, albeit with a substantial leavening from a tertiary sector of service industries, led by hospitality and leisure, and a broad base of artisanal activities.

However, even some of those artisans have moved their firms away from Rome itself. Cereria Di Giorgio, which makes paraffin wax candles, is one of these. Before it transferred production to a new factory in Pomezia in 1964, the firm made candles at a site near the very heart of the old city, on Via della Lungara in Trastevere. By the 2020s, the firm was in the hands of the fourth generation of the Roman family that founded it in 1908. Alessia Di Giorgio, great-granddaughter of the firm's founder, noted that the building in Trastevere shared walls with the Regina Coeli prison, a seventeenth-century convent that became a prison after religious orders were suppressed in 1873 by the recently founded Italian state. The candlemaker's move was partly motivated by the development incentives available in Pomezia but mainly by the family's decision to diversify its range of products, a decision that called for more space.

In its small workshop on Via della Lungara, only a kilometre from Saint Peter's basilica, Cereria Di Giorgio was for many years the official candle-supplier to the pope, *Fornitore Pontificio*. That stamp of papal approval probably helped as a marketing device because, as visitors to Rome soon discover, there seems to be a church on nearly every piazza and on many streets in the centre. The index in the Touring Club Italiano's guide to the city lists about three hundred basilicas and churches. Santa Maria in Trastevere, whose facade is graced by a thirteenth-century mosaic, is the best known church in Trastevere, but a further dozen are packed into a narrow wedge between the Tiber and the Janiculum Hill. In the many gloomy Roman churches, with votive candles flickering on stands by side chapels and near entrance doors, large altar candles lit for Mass, and the tall paschal candles burning around Easter, Cereria Di Giorgio had, and still has, an important local market. "For over fifty years we only produced liturgical candles for churches. We decided that we needed to expand our range of products to include coloured and decorative candles," said Alessia Di Giorgio.

Certainly the slender margins on liturgical candles must have been an incentive to target a wider and richer market. The stubby candles for Mass, 7 centimetres in diameter and 20 centimetres high, cost less than three euros in 2022, while tall altar candles 60 centimetres high and 2 centimetres in diameter cost about two euros. And the small votive candles in thin metal cups, called tealights as they are also used as pot warmers, are truly minor items in the income and expenditure statements of the churches, where they are lit and usually paid for by the faithful. Most of those who take tealights from the trays beneath the stands probably put at least fifty cents (half a euro) in the coin-box for every candle they take. Yet Cereria Di Giorgio's price list showed that a packet of eighty tealights, each lasting five hours, costs a little more than eight euros, about ten cents for one. "Churches have found that replacing wax with electricity is bad for balance sheets. Church-goers prefer to light votive candles. The act of lighting the candle, the flame, its thin wisp of smoke and the characteristic smell of burning wax carry more meaning than switching on an electric lightbulb," explained Ms Di Giorgio. Her firm finally abandoned its old site, used as a shop until 2018, shortly before opening a new outlet on Viale Trastevere where its non-liturgical candles are sold. "Via della Lungara is just another narrow street off the road that runs beside the Tiber. It's not a place that attracts shoppers, and people visiting the prison have other matters to think about than buying candles," she said.

Despite the absence of incentives, despite the geographical handicap that firms faced in distance from major markets, and despite the disadvantage of not having a deep local pool of skilled workers like that on which businesses in northern Italy could draw, Rome nevertheless ranked third after Milan and Turin in the 1990s in terms of industrial jobs. This was due in good part to a flourishing cluster of electronics, aerospace, defence and high-technology firms along Via Tiburtina, near the ring road. Researching articles for industry surveys for the *Financial Times* took me there on several occasions during the second half of the 1980s and the 1990s. These years and those that followed in the opening decades of the twenty-first century brought numerous changes of ownership, corporate reorganisations and name changes for the big companies to whose management I spoke and whose factories I visited. And they also brought a significant fall in employment. By 2020 the number of people working in firms in the cluster had fallen to around 2,500, about one-sixth of the peak.

Inevitably, the eighty years that followed the second world war brought major changes to Rome's economy. Always far fewer than in northern Italy, the number of manufacturing jobs fell, and digitalisation and changes to working practices meant smaller payrolls in Rome's bureaucracy. Fortune in the shape of history, church and culture favoured the Roman economy with a compensatory boost from another direction than offices and factories. Tourism came to the rescue.

VI

VISITORS

I repair to Rome, I am content

William Shakespeare, *Titus Andronicus*

Hospitality and leisure. What lies behind those three words? Coaches and coach drivers. Taxis and taxi drivers. Seats on trains, planes, underground trains, buses, ships, trams and ferries. Shops for tourist tat. High-end clothing outlets. Luxury jewellers. Hotels. Desk staff. Chambermaids. Maintenance and technical staff. Administrative personnel. Restaurants and cafés. Waiters, cooks and cleaning staff. And, of course, tourists, people attending sporting events and conferences, and men and women on business trips. Without considering satellite businesses such as industrial laundries, direct employment in hotels, restaurants and cafés in Rome provided work for about 150,000 men and women in 2024. By the 2020s, hospitality and leisure had become central to the economic health of the Italian capital. During the closing decade of the twentieth century and opening decades of the twenty-first, as employment fell elsewhere in the economy, the hospitality and leisure sector flourished and took up some of the slack. Behind the boom was a combination of factors: European airline deregulation, which began in 1986 with the Single European Act and which was completed six years later; an increasing share of disposable incomes spent on travel by Western consumers; large new markets in Asia; and the arrival of low-cost airlines, with Ryanair and easyJet the first to take on Alitalia, Italy's incumbent flag carrier, and to help bring about its bankruptcy and closure.

Raw figures

Statistics tell part of the story of the avalanche of visitors that has struck the Italian capital. The democratisation of travel, and particularly air travel, has shown itself in the numbers of people arriving and departing each year at Rome's main airport at Fiumicino. Some 43.5 million passengers passed through it in 2019, the year before the Covid-19 pandemic, against 23.6 million in 1999 and 17.3 million in 1990. The total of arrivals and departures at Fiumicino amounted to only 10.8 million passengers in 1980 and just 6.4 million ten years before that.

The airport had two modest terminals at the beginning of the 1970s, one for domestic flights, the other for international. That decade brought little change, and an atmosphere of sleepy provincialism continued to hang over the Aeroporto Leonardo Da Vinci at Fiumicino through the 1980s. (Italian airports are usually given names, often of national heroes.) Sleepy provincialism is now a distant memory. Major developments and expansion projects to cope with steeply rising passenger numbers have been unceasing since the 1990s.

The development of international tourism in Rome in five and a half decades ending in 2006 was the subject of research by Davide Fardelli, Tommaso Proganò and Francesco Maria Sanna of Sapienza University ("L'evoluzione del turismo internazionale a Roma: alcune evidenze empiriche"). A line on a graph in their paper clearly illustrates the Eternal City's increasing attractiveness as a holiday destination for foreigners. In 1951, when the second world war was in the recent past, memories of it were vivid, and recovery was the priority, not foreign holidays, just half a million people visited, probably most of them on business of one kind or another. Ten years later the figure was still below 1 million, and a further ten years passed before it doubled again, to 2 million in 1972. Pilgrims for the Holy Year Jubilee of Renewal and Reconciliation declared by Pope Paul VI for 1975 brought a spike in Italians visiting Rome, although this was accompanied by a sharp fall in visitors from abroad. Apart from a blip above the 2 million mark in 1977, the number of foreign visitors stuck at less than 2 million until 1990, when a step change occurred. In contrast to 1960 when Rome hosted the Olympic Games and visitor numbers (Italian and foreign) didn't increase noticeably, football's World Cup in summer 1990 brought a jump in foreign visitors. In the final, held at Rome's Stadio Olimpico, West Germany defeated the defending champions, Argentina. The defeated semi-finalists were Italy and England. The capital was a magnet for fans.

The three academics summarised the four decades preceding the Italia 90 football jamboree: "With the exception of a few years, from 1950 to 1990 the growth in the number of visitors was similar for Italians and foreigners." Then foreigners began arriving in numbers that far outstripped Italians. And air travellers quickly overcame fears after Arab terrorists in America hijacked aircraft on 11 September 2001 to use them for striking buildings in New York and Washington. Two years were sufficient to compensate for the downturn, and the number of foreign visitors arriving in Rome rapidly returned to almost exponential growth, wrote the academics.

There was no let-up. Rome continued to draw people. Four million foreigners arrived in the city in 2005, together with a little under 3 million Italians. Within a decade the number of foreigners had doubled to 8 million while Italian visitors to Rome amounted to 5.5 million. In 2019, the year before Covid-19 turned the world upside down and reshaped human behaviour (albeit only temporarily), the numbers were 10.3 million and 9 million respectively. And despite having suffered during the pandemic years 2020 and 2021, the Eternal City's hospitality and leisure sector quickly recovered. From a total of almost 19.5 million visitors in 2019, it catered for almost 15 million in 2022, and in 2023 it faced an invasion of 21 million, an increase of 8 per cent on 2019.

An analysis for 2022 showed that the United States, home to almost 1.5 million visitors to Rome, accounted for the largest number by far of foreigners arriving in the Eternal City. Britain accounted for nearly 500,000 and Germany a little over 400,000. France and Spain followed with 340,00 and 330,000 respectively. More than 100,000 arrived from each of Japan, China, Brazil and Argentina. However, the three Rome academics drew attention to a noticeable Ryanair effect that began a decade and a half earlier, particularly and unsurprisingly for the Irish Republic. They noted that, proportionately, small and well-connected European countries like Denmark and Sweden topped the foreign-visitor table.

While some foreigners arrived by high-speed train and others by road, perhaps having visited northern cities and Florence on their way to Rome, most probably arrived in Italy through Fiumicino airport, no longer a substandard gateway to a major European capital. And what they found in terms of accommodation when they reached the city itself was a wide choice. Although Covid-19 forced about one hotel in seven to close, by 2022 their number had returned to a record high. And while the figures for alternative accommodation like holiday homes, bed and breakfast, room-lets and serviced apartments show that this part of the hospitality sector was hit harder by the pandemic than hotels, with the total falling to 12,700 in 2022, from almost 19,000 in 2020, nevertheless even this was significantly higher than in 2018. Romans who began offering alternative accommodation in 2019 had badly timed their entry to the market.

The annual report on tourism in 2022, published in 2023 by the city authorities, shows that three-star hotels were the most numerous, with 400 in business during the year. There were 307 four-star establishments, 183 two-star and 51 five-star. The figures help explain why Rome loves its American visitors. They spend. One in five of them chooses a five-star hotel while staying in the city, more than twice the ratio of Britons. Germans are more frugal, only one in sixteen opting for five-star hospitality. And whereas more than half of Italian visitors to Rome choose alternative accommodation rather than hotels, only one in five of foreign visitors does. Yet whether Italian or foreign, the average length of stay is similar, around two nights for Italians and two and a half nights for foreigners.

Arrivals and departures by train

The force of rapidly rising passenger numbers brought about improvements and enlargements to Rome's Fiumicino airport. A similar force had done so several decades earlier to the Termini main railway station, whose grandiose fascist expansion plans had only recently left the drawing board when work ceased because of the war. Conditions and expectations were different in the post-war climate when construction of the new station restarted. Cost, functionality, and harmony with what was already built and with post-fascist architectural ideas were the criteria for completing the reconstruction of Stazione Termini. A national competition was held in 1947 to determine the new station's shape.

Externally, what people see in the twenty-first century is the station that was inaugurated in December 1950. The facade is striking. More than 120 metres long and 12 metres high, a cantilevered roof in reinforced concrete provides a large canopy extending 19 metres beyond a vast glass-panelled entrance. Supported by thirty-three reinforced concrete pillars clad in red marble, the roof sweeps upwards over the atrium and ticket hall, and then down over an airy concourse 14 metres high at the head of the twenty-two platforms within the station's covered perimeter. Italy's state railway company carried out a total internal renovation in the late 1990s, completed in time for the Millennium's Great Jubilee Holy Year of 2000. The station needed refurbishment. The dim squalor of the space below ground and the passageways leading to the Metro underground railway entrance was transformed into a well-lit shopping mall. Similar alterations to Stazione Termini's atrium and concourse turned the station into a place that no longer needed to be transited rapidly and watchfully.

The enormous increase in the number of people visiting Rome was helped by a revolution in railway travel around the same time as that in air travel. Examples of how the future of European travel would soon look had been offered by France in the 1980s and Spain in the 1990s. Less than one-half of people who travelled between Paris and Lyons used trains in 1981 against just over one-fifth who flew between the two cities. Three years later, a year after the inauguration of the full length of a high-speed line, trains attracted three-quarters of travellers and the percentage of people flying had been reduced by two-thirds. The story was similar in Spain after high-speed trains began running between Madrid and Seville in 1992. Yet Italy had been ahead of both in 1977 when the state railways inaugurated Europe's first section of high-speed track on the line from Rome to Florence, 140 kilometres between the capital and Città della Pieve in Umbria.

Having led the way, Italy slowed and its development of high-speed railways only began to gather pace in the 2000s, with the completion of sections of track between Milan and Bologna in December 2008, between Bologna and Florence a year later, a short section of track in Rome also in 2009, and tunnels and a new station underground in Bologna in 2013. The effects were quickly seen. Between December 2008 and January 2009, the share of travellers using the train between Rome and Milan increased from less than one-third to almost one-half, while those who flew fell from over one-half to under 40 per cent.

By the 2020s, more than two-thirds of people travelling between Rome and Milan chose to travel in high-speed trains. The fastest train in the 1970s took five and a half hours. The shortest journey times were under three hours in 2024, with as many as seven trains an hour between Italy's political and administrative capital and its financial and business capital. Venice would be served with two direct high-speed trains every hour from Rome and journey times of around four hours. Many trains heading north from Rome would stop at Florence, facilitating journeys of tourists on a rapid twenty-first-century Grand Tour visiting the Bel Paese's three best-known historical cities for art and architecture, Rome, Florence and Venice. The line connecting Rome to Naples entered service in 2009, and the two cities were then about one hour apart. Tourists struggling with luggage became a common sight at Termini station.

They have a choice. High-speed rail services are provided by the state-owned Ferrovie dello Stato with Frecciarossa (Red Arrow) trains and a private business, Nuovo Trasporto Viaggiatori (NTV), whose deep maroon trains are called Italo. Talking in October 2008 about plans to launch Italo's services in 2012, Luca di Montezemolo, NTV's chairman, told me that he and his associates in the company were sure they had a winner. "Italy is a country made for high-speed trains. There is nothing to be gained from investing in airlines," said Montezemolo. Radical changes in Italian domestic airline services would soon confirm his prediction. Having been granted five daily slots for flights from Rome to Milan's Linate city airport in 2013, easyJet, a British low-cost carrier, abandoned the route two and a half years later. Demand for airline travel between Italy's two principal cities had collapsed.

Italo and Frecciarossa trains are sleek and fast, but some well-to-do travellers with distant memories of journeys from Rome to Florence and Milan can remember when travel north from the capital was graced by a far more stylish train. Decades before the streamlined high-speed trains that connected Italian cities in the twenty-first century, the *Settebello* all-first-class train in service between Rome and Milan from 1952 to 1984, with its rounded, bulbous nose, had an appearance that suggested its designers had worked in the aerospace industry and been helped by a wind tunnel. Observation compartments at the front, beneath a driver's cab that protruded a little above, and at the rear of the train each seated eleven passengers, allowing them to see what train drivers saw along the track ahead and to look back as the track disappeared behind.

The *Settebello* represented a post-war peak of Italian railway optimism, a result of the early boom years of Italy's post-war economic miracle. Alongside the rebuilding of its inventory of rolling stock after the heavy losses sustained during the second world war, the Ferrovie dello Stato state railways decided to build a small fleet of luxury trains. They planned initially that eight trains would be made, but this number was revised downwards due to cost. The trains were to be a showcase for the best of Italian style, design and engineering, and a flagship for the state railways, whose board of directors turned to leading architects, industrial designers and engineers to achieve their aim. The skilled workmen building the first train thought that it was unbeatable and nicknamed it the *Settebello*, after the seven of coins, a winning card in a game called *scopa*. And the name was taken up officially.

The *Settebello*'s compartments discreetly spoke luxury. They combined light grey livery with pale green trim, elegant internal decor, comfortable seating and a generously spacious layout. Indeed, train timetables for 1973 described train 802, which left Rome at just after ten in the morning and arrived in Milan at just before four in the afternoon, a journey time of about six hours, not only as the *Settebello* but also as *lusso* (luxurious) and *superrapido* (super-quick). Luxurious was a fair description, but super-quick was an exaggeration. Even so, the *Settebello* and its daily service of two trains each way was fast for its time. The trains could carry 190 passengers—the dining car seated 56—and offered great comfort at high cost when travelling between Rome and Florence and the north. How pleasant to lunch while watching the passing countryside or to dine while the lights of towns and stations along the line flashed by. Being seated at a table set with crisp white linen and sparkling glassware, and choosing from a menu of good standard dishes cooked to order in a galley—pasta followed by a main course and dessert, washed down with a half-bottle of decent wine—was an agreeable way to eat while on the move.

All restaurant cars had gone from Italy's railway network by 2010, but the *Settebello* and its luxurious dining car had stopped running long before. Looking back from the mid 2020s and truly *superrapido* journeys from Rome to Milan with wi-fi internet connections freely available throughout the trains, and telephone and laptop charging points by every seat, the *Settebello* represented a gentler era of relaxed, low-pressure travel. With smartphones switched on, glued to ears or lying on seat-back trays alongside laptop computers, and travellers' fingers tip-tapping on keypads or keyboards, Frecciarossa and Italo carriages often seem like the offices to be found in the two cities at the ends of the high-speed line. The small Tandy 200, the first journalist's laptop, appeared in 1985 and mobile phones began bringing their revolution to life and work a decade later. The years when piles of magazines, newspapers and books were carried onto trains to accompany long journeys, and conversations were struck up with fellow travellers, became memories of leisurely travel long past. Certainly the new world of laptops, internet connections and smartphones would offer no time for real dining. Indeed, it would barely offer time to grab snacks.

For businessmen, bankers, management consultants, journalists, politicians, top civil servants and senior diplomats travelling with their expenses reimbursed, and for those with means to pay their own way, the *Settebello*, even more than other trains of the Trans-Europe Express network between major European cities, which were made up of first-class carriages only, conveyed a cachet of exclusivity. And for Italy, the *Settebello* was not simply a luxury train, and an expensive way to travel from Rome to Florence and northern Italy. Like the uniforms worn by Alitalia's female cabin crew until its final years of decline to demise, the train was a flag carrier for Italian style and design, for the best of Italy, and a symbol of a nation that had put a war, loss and defeat behind it. The workers who built the *Settebello* had rightly named it a winner.

Tennessee Williams, Gore Vidal and Ralph Ellison stayed a while

Some foreign visitors to Rome in the 2020s arrive having travelled in the first-class or club-class sections of aircraft or seated in the spacious executive and business carriages of Frecciarossa or Italo trains. But far more arrive on flights of packed aircraft belonging to low-cost carriers or jammed into the cramped economy sections of the old flag carriers such as Air France and

British Airways. And large numbers arrive in the crowded but more spacious and comfortable Frecciarossa Standard and Italo Smart-class railway carriages. The few foreign visitors who arrived in the post-war 1940s mostly did so by road or by rail, often in old, slow and uncomfortable trains that had survived the war. Americans began their journeys in transatlantic liners.

This is how Samuel Barber, an American composer of classical music, travelled in the late 1940s. In 1946, thanks to a fellowship from the John Simon Guggenheim Foundation, Barber was able to resume the regular trips to Europe that he had begun in 1928. Renewals of the fellowship in 1947 and 1949, and invitations to supervise residents at the American Academy in Rome, took him there for the spring of 1948 and the autumn of 1949. His return to America following three months in Rome was reported by the *New York Times* in December 1949.

Barber was no stranger to the Eternal City, nor to the American Academy with its large building, the Villa Aurelia, which was built around 1650 for Cardinal Girolamo Farnese. Its setting, in four and a half hectares of garden on the Janiculum Hill above Trastevere, seems ideal for inspiring creative work. In 1935 Barber had been awarded the Prix de Rome for being the most promising American music student at the time, and the prize gave him full lodging and a regular stipend for two years. Two Pulitzer Travel scholarships allowed him to extend his stay. The young composer flourished. Among the works that Barber composed during his pre-war period at the American Academy in Rome were the Symphony in One Move-ment and String Quartet in B Minor. Both were premiered there. A meeting in 1935 with Arturo Toscanini, a legendary orchestral conductor, led to what would be Barber's best-known composition. The *Adagio for Strings* is an arrangement for string orchestra of the quartet's adagio. Played publicly for the first time in 1938 by the NBC Symphony Orchestra under Toscanini, it found a global audience at the funeral of President John F. Kennedy in 1963.

Barber was instrumental in bringing together two celebrated American post-war visitors to the Italian capital. Tennessee Williams and Gore Vidal met early in 1948 at the composer's home on the Janiculum Hill. With *A Streetcar Named Desire*, which had opened on Broadway in New York in December 1947, Williams consolidated the fame and critical and commercial success that he had found with his play *The Glass Menagerie* in 1944. Williams was 36 years old when he and the 22-year-old Vidal, already known as a writer, were introduced. Williams had bought a Jeep from a homeward-bound American serviceman, and the two writers shared a springtime trip to the Amalfi Coast south of Naples soon after they met.

Whereas American writers such as F. Scott Fitzgerald, Ernest Hemingway and Gertrude Stein—members of the first world war's Lost Generation—had descended on Paris and the French Riviera in the 1920s, Rome and Italy were the destinations of many American writers in the late 1940s and the 1950s. Hollywood on the Tiber probably played a part in this shift of focus for some of them. Ralph Ellison was not one of these.

A New Yorker by adoption, Ellison was 39 when he made his name as a writer with the publication of *Invisible Man* in 1952. The book has been described as one of the most important American novels of the twentieth century. Following the award of the Prix de Rome and a fellowship at the American Academy, Ellison began two years at the Villa Aurelia in October 1955. Letters to friends show that his reaction to the Eternal City was complex and contradictory. Against the creative tension in New York—"more and better rendered music" and "more interesting writing"—he found Rome rather provincial. Moreover, Ellison didn't like the food and found other American Academy fellows stand-offish. He was Black and perhaps racism was a factor. Indeed, Ellison admitted to being homesick for Harlem. He wrote that he had been reluctant to go to Rome, but had he not done so he would "have missed one of the major human experiences". As for writing, he made little progress on his second novel.

Even so, Rome helped him plough another cultural field. Jed Perl, an author and art critic, notes that for a brief period in the late 1940s Ellison was an aspiring professional photographer. Perl describes Ellison's black-and-white studies of street life in Harlem as striking. Sara Marzioli, an academic at the University of Nebraska Omaha, has studied Ellison's Roman photographic work. She believes that the photos he took while at the American Academy are a means through which the writer reflected on the entanglement of history with fiction. Marzioli points to the centrality of humans in historical spaces, the appropriation of monuments by ordinary people, in Ellison's photos of Rome in the mid 1950s.

Indeed, among Ellison's photos listed by the Library of Congress, which holds the writer's papers, are those of a man holding a camera on Via delle Carrozze (a street running from Piazza di Spagna to Via del Corso), of people sitting on the bases of columns at Via della Conciliazione, and of a man assembling a pile of lumber and baskets at Campo dei Fiori (the site of public executions and now described by Rome's city authorities as "a typical scene of old Rome"). As well as Saint Peter's basilica and views from the Janiculum Hill, Ellison also photographed a poster that advertised the film *Poveri ma belli* (Poor but handsome), filmed in Rome and Ostia, and released in 1957. According to Perl, "For Ellison photography may have been a way of sketching, ruminating, fooling around, working off steam, procrastinating before confronting the main event, which was composing an American story that kept decomposing."

In contrast, Rome not only provided a long-term base for Tennessee Williams but was a city where he felt at home. Italy's recovery from the second world war was underway when he arrived, but the economic miracle had yet to begin. He would experience Rome through the years of Hollywood on the Tiber and the *dolce vita*. America was militarily and economically the dominant global power, but its social and cultural norms were a straitjacket for some of those who lived there. Williams immediately felt at ease in the Italian capital and in tune with the people he met. Indeed, after crossing the Italian border on arriving from France he had found his "health and life seemed magically restored". Despite periods of writer's block, living in Rome helped release Williams's creativity into works like *Cat on a Hot Tin Roof* and *Baby Doll*. His novel of 1950, *The Roman Spring of Mrs Stone*, was a memento of his early years in a city that he described as "the capitol of my heart". The US dollar was strong and the Italian lira weak. A good life could be led without economic stress.

Something of what Tennessee Williams saw or described is perhaps what some visitors to Rome search for in the twenty-first century. People-watching from a pavement table of a café on Via Veneto or Piazza del Popolo, or soaking up the atmosphere of the late afternoon in March, which began *The Roman Spring of Mrs Stone*, might satisfy some: "Domes of ancient churches, swelling above the angular roofs like the breasts of recumbent giant women, still bathed in golden light, and so did the very height of that immense cascade of stone stairs that descended from the Trinita di Monte to the Piazza di Spagna."

Gore Vidal wrote prolifically, his work ranging from screenplays, non-fiction books and essays on many subjects to historical and modern novels. He became a public intellectual in America, and he was a far longer-term visitor to Rome than Williams. For around a quarter of a century, from the mid 1960s to the early 1990s, his Roman home was the top floor of the building where Feltrinelli's flagship Rome bookshop occupies the ground floor on Largo di Torre Argentina. Unsurprisingly, Vidal was one of the figures of Hollywood on the Tiber, albeit towards the end of that fragment of modern Roman history.

His script was the basis of the screenplay for William Wyler's film *Ben Hur*, which was shot at Cinecittà studios in 1958. Vidal met Federico Fellini while they were both working there, and he would appear as himself in Fellini's film *Roma* in 1972. Vidal also wrote a screenplay for *Caligula*, Tinto Brass's controversial and sexually explicit film about the Roman emperor who reigned between 37 and 41 CE. Vidal had the credentials for writing about Rome, the city where he spent a large part of his life. *Julian*, one of his most successful books, is a deeply researched novel based on the life of the last non-Christian ruler of the Roman empire. In a note at the beginning of the book, published in 1964, Vidal thanked the American Academy in Rome for the use of its library. Vidal drew inspiration from the city where he lived. From the terrace of his apartment he looked over the ruins of temples built between the fourth and first centuries BCE.

Williams also drew inspiration from living in the city. "Rome is full of the sound of running water, near or distant, loud or barely distinguishable; running water and stone steps are almost as much the signature of the city as the cream-colored domes against the blue sky," he wrote. Hearing fountains and the *fontanelle* or *nasoni* spouts of drinking water would have been easier in the 1950s when the number of cars and commercial vehicles, measured in tens of thousands against around two million in the 2010s, would have brought a much lower level of ambient noise.

Fountains and pines

Thirty years before Williams captured the Eternal City in words, so in music did the composer Ottorino Respighi, who taught composition at the Santa Cecilia Conservatory. For the *Grove Concise Dictionary of Music*, Respighi is "best known as the composer of highly coloured orchestral pieces". None are better known than his trilogy of symphonic poems: *Fountains of Rome*, *Pines of Rome* and *Roman Festivals*. Respighi wrote on his score of *Fountains of Rome*: "In this symphonic poem the composer has endeavoured to give expression to the sentiments and visions suggested to him by four of Rome's fountains, contemplated at the hour in which their character is most in harmony with the surrounding landscape, or their beauty appears most impressive to the observer." That the work was completed just three years after the composer's arrival in Rome, when he was still looking around with the fresh eyesight and enquiring mind of a visitor or tourist, suggests that fountains were for him one of the features that characterised the city.

Respighi began at dawn at the Valle Giulia on the edge of the gardens of Villa Borghese where the first fountain that Respighi celebrates in his music is one of a pair made in 1911, the year of the half-centenary of Italian reunification. With the sun breaking through a cool dawn mist, the mood of the music looks back, reflecting on and longing for the past, albeit for a not-so-distant time when flocks of sheep grazed fields that reached the Roman walls. Time of day and place take Respighi's music for the second of his subjects far from the pastoral theme of daybreak in the Valle Giulia, to Piazza Barberini and the Triton Fountain in bright midday sunlight. For his third subject, the Trevi Fountain in the afternoon, Respighi imagined, "The solemn theme, passing from woodwinds to brass, assumes a triumphal aspect. Fanfares echo: pulled by sea-horses and followed by tritons and mermaids, Neptune's chariot passes across the glowing expanse of water." Respighi closes his symphonic poem at sunset beside the late-sixteenth-century fountain in front of the Villa Medici, not far from the top of the Spanish Steps. The composer described the time of day as nostalgic. "The air is full of tolling bells, murmuring birds, rustling leaves. Then all becomes calm in the silence of the night."

Just as the centenary of the first performance of Respighi's *Fountains of Rome* brought renewed interest in the composer's work, so in 2024 did the centenary of the first performance of *Pines of Rome*, which had taken place in December 1924. When Respighi and his wife moved to a villa at number 37 Via della Camilluccia on the northern hills just outside the city in 1930, they called their home "I Pini" (The Pines). And perhaps then, before sprawling post-war construction caused the villa to be renumbered 591, many pines stood out above the countryside, parkland and gardens of the district's villas. In the 2020s, a pair of tall, scrawny umbrella pines stands near the villa's locked green gates. But Respighi's inspiration for his symphonic poem, written before the move to Via della Camilluccia, had come from elsewhere in the Eternal City.

The music begins brightly in the Villa Borghese gardens where children are playing in a grove of pine trees. Respighi sees them in music as they "dance ring-a-ring of roses, play at military marches and battles, shriek like Swifts in the evening, and scatter away". Imagining pines near a catacomb, the second movement begins slowly. "Then suddenly the scene changes and we see the shadow of pines by the entrance to a catacomb: a sorrowful chanting rises from below, spreads solemnly like a hymn and vanishes mysteriously." The site of the third movement is the Janiculum Hill where Garibaldi and his soldiers defended a revolutionary Roman republic against French troops intent on restoring papal power. Respighi imagined the air quivering, the pines of the Janiculum silhouetted in a full moon, and a nightingale singing. In the fourth movement, the composer takes the orchestra and the listener along the Via Appia with a march. For Respighi, a morning mist lies across a countryside watched over by pine trees, and steps of marchers can be heard, vague but unceasing. Then comes a vision of ancient glories. "Trumpets sound, a republican army breaks into view in the sun's daybreak splendour, along the sacred way to a triumphal ascent of the Capitoline Hill." Alas, the sentiments and images that came to Respighi's mind when composing *Fountains of Rome* would be unlikely to come to the minds of visitors in the 2020s whose Rome is that of mass tourism with its packed streets and piazzas.

Equally, visitors to the Eternal City a century after the composer wrote the *Pines of Rome* would have difficulty in seeing or imagining what Respighi saw in his mind's eye when he scored the music. Together with its fountains, the Eternal City's pine trees gave Respighi colourful and evocative material to write the compositions for which he is best known. More properly called the stone pine, the umbrella pine is a familiar tree in southwest Europe. According to the *European Atlas of Forest Tree Species*, published by the European Commission's Joint Research Centre, the stone pine is one of the most characteristic trees of the Mediterranean flora and occupies a broad range of climate and soil conditions. With its preference for sandy soils, the tree is used for consolidating dunes. Grown for timber, resin, bark, pine cones and particularly pine nuts, its economically valuable edible seed, the stone pine is a multi-purpose species.

As extreme summer weather and forest fires become more frequent, so the threat to the flora of the Mediterranean basin increases. Reassuringly, the *European Atlas* considers that, thanks to its thick bark, high crown and absence of low branches, the umbrella pine is considerably less fire sensitive than other Mediterranean pines. However, even stone pines burn well, as the massive fire in the Pineta di Castel Fusano, near the coast at Ostia, showed in 2000 when about 300 hectares of pine woods and Mediterranean maquis were devastated by the blaze. And since 2014 Rome's pines have faced another threat, from an insect known as the pine tortoise scale. Describing pines as iconic trees in Italy, the European Food Safety Authority said in 2022 that the insect was having a serious economic, environmental and social impact in the south and was "contributing to the severe decline in the health and some mortality of stone pines, particularly in Naples and Rome".

A small news item appeared in the Rome pages of *Corriere della Sera* in May 2023. The article was headlined "Tens of pines to go in Villa Borghese". Trees due to be cut down in the near future had been marked with red crosses. A whole row of pines had been attacked and weakened by pine tortoise scale and were at risk of toppling. These were some of the pines that Respighi celebrated in the first movement of his symphonic poem. The chairman of the agronomists' association said that 95 per cent of Rome's 120,000 stone pines had been attacked by the pest, causing heavily infested trees to suffer severe needle loss and dieback. The city authorities had put in hand a therapeutic plan, but the outcome depended on their capacity to administer the chemical treatment and on the efficacy of the treatment itself. The pest's high female fecundity, measured in the large number of eggs laid, coupled to the arrival of three generations of pine tortoise scale each year, presented a major challenge that could only be met through constant vigilance and effective action.

Whatever their problems, the trees in the centenary year of Respighi's symphonic poem mostly continued to be a fine sight, as indeed they were intended to be when they were planted. The district that Mussolini's regime had planned to be the World Fair of 1942, the Esposizione Universale di Roma (EUR), carried heavy symbolism and so did the highway passing through it. The umbrella pines in EUR and beside the road were part of the symbolism. From its beginning, fascism laid claim to ancient Roman roots and the pine was part of its story. Giulia Caneva, professor of environmental botany at Roma Tre University, notes that ancient Rome was full of pine trees both because they were suitable for local soil and because they symbolised resilience and life. For the fascist regime, pine trees provided a visible message that the regime was joined to and drew inspiration from the greatness of its distant Roman predecessor.

Visitors seeking evidence of the greatness of ancient Rome can still find it in many parts of the city's outskirts, perhaps more agreeably than in the historic centre. As much as anywhere, that greatness is evident beyond the Aurelian Walls in the countryside of the Appia Antica Archaeological Park. Just as Respighi imagined the legions of marching soldiers tramping along the Via Appia between columns of pines as dawn approaches, so perhaps can modern-day visitors if they go early in the day and walk on more distant sections of the flagstones that have paved the way since around 300 BCE. Pine trees still stand there. A note from the ministry of culture which oversees the park reported in summer 2018 that work had begun on pollarding 120 of the pines flanking the ancient road. "The trees, which by now are an integral part of the landscape of the Via Appia, enjoy good health overall and only three have been cut down because they were completely dry and were a hazard," said the ministry. Whether pines or fountains, both are part of the city's image for many visitors as well as Romans.

Water spouting, spraying, splashing, spurting, falling, cascading or simply dribbling from fountains provides some of the memories that tourists take away from Rome. Towards the end of the eighteenth century Goethe expressed his admiration for those who had built the aqueducts to supply water to the city in almost five hundred years of Roman civil and hydraulic engineering that ended around 230 CE. For Pliny the Elder, who lived in the first century CE, anyone seeing Rome's water system would think that the whole terrestrial orb offered nothing more marvellous. In his 1966 book *The Fountains of Rome*, H.V. Morton noted that eleven aqueducts were supplying around 1,200 fountains when the Visigoths sacked the city in 410 CE. Vandals followed Visigoths with another sacking of the city in 455, but the action that brought an end to the wealth of water that had amazed and enchanted visitors was the aqueducts' destruction by Goths in 537. Pope Martin V's arrival in Rome in 1420 following his election as pope by the Council of Constance marked the beginning of a new era. Rome's Renaissance was about to start and Romans would not wait long before water again began flowing.

The photogenic fountains that draw visitors belong mainly to the late sixteenth century and the seventeenth century. Like most visitors, when I arrived in Rome I enjoyed exploring and discovering the city, its narrow streets, its basilicas and churches, the catacombs along the Via Appia, ancient monuments, trattorias and ice cream parlours. Discovering Rome also meant visiting some of the city's fountains, watching the play of water on stone, and admiring the imagination of those who designed them, the skill of those who made them and the foresight of those who had ensured that the city had water not only for drinking but also for decoration. By autumn 1972, the project that had taken me to Rome seemed to be ending, and I would be returning in December to an office in Marylebone, London. What better way to remember the Eternal City than by revisiting some of its fountains with a camera?

Many Romans were away at the beginning of November 1972, taking a few days of annual leave in addition to the national holiday that falls on the first of the month, All Saints' Day. But I stayed in Rome and fourteen postcard-size black-and-white photographs would be reminders of the day I strolled around the centre from one fountain to another. Five show details of the Fountain of the Four Rivers on Piazza Navona, on which Gian Lorenzo Bernini and his team of masons worked from 1648 to 1651, but there's only one of the Paul V Fountain on the

Janiculum that Goethe had admired, two of the fantastical Trevi Fountain completed in 1762, two of the Barcaccia, two of Bernini's Triton Fountain on Piazza Barberini from 1643, and two of the Fountain of the Four Tortoises.

Made out of travertine like the Trevi Fountain, the Barcaccia at the foot of the Spanish Steps, designed by father and son, Pietro and Gian Lorenzo Bernini, was completed in 1629. If statistics were to be compiled of visitors to Rome's fountains, the Barcaccia's location, not only a few paces from the Spanish Steps but at an entry point to the fashion district, would probably ensure it a place among the three most visited.

Unlike the Piazza Navona, Piazza di Trevi, Piazza di Spagna and Piazza Barberini, Piazza Mattei and its Fountain of the Four Tortoises is away from the crowded streets that channel tourists between major sites. Yet H.V. Morton thought this was the city's loveliest fountain. There's nothing majestic about the piazza where it stands, a small, gloomy space behind the ghetto. Four bronze youths lean against the stem of the marble fountain, pushing tortoises one-handed over the edge of the bowl that overhangs them. A strong jet of water spurts from the centre of the bowl, and jets of water leave the mouths of putti beneath the bowl and the mouths of fishes on which the youths are sitting, the water collected in four basins at the corners of the fountain's base. According to legend, a love story lay behind the fountain, whose beauty so enchanted a maiden who lived in the piazza that her heart was won by the young man through whose efforts it arrived suddenly one night in 1584.

What was striking on the day I visited those fountains was the city's emptiness. Almost out of sight, one car and two motor scooters appear at the edge of the photographs of the fountain on Piazza Mattei. When I returned fifty years later, half a dozen motor scooters occupied the side of the road where the two motor scooters had been, and there were three cars, two of them in front of the fountain. Even more striking was the absence of people. My photographs of the Trevi Fountain showed a sharp split between shade and bright sunshine—fine weather that a few decades later would have drawn an enormous number of visitors every day, and far more on national holidays. Instead, a view looking across the fountain showed three people sitting or leaning on a wall on the other side and one person walking behind it. Passing the Trevi Fountain soon after restrictions introduced during the Covid pandemic were lifted, I found the surrounding pavements thick with people.

One Saturday in July 2023, the front page of the Life and Arts section of the *Financial Times* newspaper carried a half-page picture of the Piazza di Spagna on the first of May, the Barcaccia fountain barely visible among the hordes thronging the piazza and spreading down Via dei Condotti. They had little room to move, a jostling football crowd, perhaps tens of thousands. The title of the essay that the photograph illustrated, and whose subject was the impact of mass tourism, was: "Wish You Weren't Here". I took one of my two photographs from close to where the photographer of the *Financial Times* would stand. It showed one car arriving from Via dei Condotti on the other side of the piazza, two cars passing in the direction of Piazza del Popolo, and a total of eight people, four of them beside the fountain. The second photograph, looking across the fountain towards Piazza del Popolo, showed no cars and no people.

Can visitors in the twenty-first century capture some of the atmosphere that I enjoyed in the early 1970s or that Tennessee Williams found in Rome in the late 1940s and the 1950s? Long queues to visit the Pantheon, the Colosseum, Saint Peter's basilica and the Vatican Museums and Sistine Chapel, all of them among the top attractions listed in guidebooks and on internet websites, are Rome's evidence of the radically different nature of tourism brought by the democratising force of mass travel. It is hard to see that force being reversed soon.

Indeed, the number of visitors in 2025 was expected to set yet another record. The year will be a Jubilee, wrote Pope Francis in February 2022, and will signal renewal, hope and faith following the doubt and suffering caused by the Covid-19 pandemic. Perhaps the possibilities offered by modern travel have encouraged the promulgation of Jubilees. After four Jubilees in each of the centuries from 1400 to 1799, there were only two in the nineteenth century but seven in the twentieth. The twenty-first century had opened with Pope John Paul II's second Jubilee—his first was in 1983—and Pope Francis presided over the century's second on the theme of mercy in 2015. According to forecasts made in 2024, Rome would welcome between 32 million and 40 million visitors in 2025. Whether or not pilgrims can find uplifting experiences while jostled by massive crowds is open to question.

The tourist flood that often seems to submerge the city in the twenty-first century is a world away from what pilgrims found half a century before. The total number of visitors to Rome in 1975, the Jubilee Year of Renewal and Reconciliation, was less than 5 million. After Pope Paul VI died on 6 August 1978, there were no long queues of the faithful in Saint Peter's Square wanting to pay their respects as the dead pope's body lay in the basilica, albeit there would be more following the death of his successor, Pope John Paul I, of a heart attack in his sleep less than two months later. His papacy had lasted just 33 days. According to a Vatican communiqué concerning his death, the pope's face had blanched on being told about the murder earlier that late-September evening of a young Roman communist outside the Italian Communist Party's Appia Nuova branch by terrorists of the neo-fascist Nuclei Armati Rivoluzionari (NAR, Armed Revolutionary Units).

Pope Paul VI's long papacy, which had begun in June 1963, ended three months after he delivered the funeral eulogy for a politician to whom he had been close. Aldo Moro, a former

prime minister, had been murdered in Rome by leftwing terrorists of the Red Brigades in May 1978. There seems more than a
trace of unintended irony in Pope Paul VI's announcement of the
Jubilee Year of Renewal and Reconciliation in an apostolic letter
on 23 May 1974. Just five days later, neo-fascist terrorists of the
Ordine Nuovo (ON, New Order) set off a bomb during a trade
union gathering in a square in Brescia. The bomb killed eight
and wounded one hundred. However, neo-fascist terrorists
weren't new to this form of outrage. They had been threatening,
injuring and killing their fellow citizens with bombs since April
1969. The Years of Lead were underway.

VII

POLITICAL TERRORISM FROM LEFT
AND RIGHT

Here is a mourning Rome, a dangerous Rome, no Rome of safety

William Shakespeare, *Julius Caesar*

Southbound traffic on the Autostrada del Sole between Rome
and Naples was light that morning early in April 1978 when I
was driving to a business park a little west of a town called
Frosinone, about 80 kilometres from the capital. Part of an
assignment on which I was working involved a firm with a factory there. I had passed the exit for Anagni and a Lepetit pharmaceuticals plant and a long flat, straight stretch of road lay
ahead. As it rose uphill out of the valley, and just around a curve
to the right, a baton-waving Carabiniere military policeman
pointed me towards the slip road into the La Macchia Ovest
service area. Not waving batons but holding machine pistols,
several other military policemen were standing beyond the
baton-waver. And others in the service area also carried their
Beretta M12 weapons at the ready when I got out of my car to
open its boot.

La Macchia Ovest seemed like the set for a shoot-out in a gangster movie. With so much firepower loaded and primed for action, it was no place for rash behaviour or sudden movements. Six years later, when I was preparing a feature on Beretta for the *Guardian* newspaper, a spokesman for the Carabinieri would tell me, "Frequent gun handling gives Carabinieri a close relationship with their weapons. Carabinieri's pistols are in regular use, like reporters' typewriters." Hardly words of reassurance for the nervous. At just under 4 kilos loaded and 42 centimetres long when its slim metal stock is folded, the Beretta machine pistol is light and handy. Used for working at close quarters, the M12 fires 9-millimetre ammunition from a magazine of up to forty rounds and can empty a full large magazine in less than five seconds. It has negligible recoil, an effective range of about 150 metres, and has been described as a masterpiece of engineering and manufacturing, and a gold standard for sub-machine guns. The gun began entering service with Italy's various police forces in 1961, is widely used by police forces and armies throughout the world, and was a favourite weapon of Viet Cong liberation fighters.

The Aldo Moro affair

Italy's Brigate Rosse (Red Brigades) leftwing terrorist group had included a Beretta M12 in the armaments they deployed on Via Fani in the north of Rome a few weeks before my encounter with the military policemen at the service area on the Autostrada del Sole. Sealing off Rome with roadblocks would have called for almost impossibly large resources, and setting up random checks well after the kidnapping of Aldo Moro, a leading Christian Democracy politician, seems a waste of them, so perhaps the authorities had been tipped off that members of the Red Brigades were on the move south along the motorway to Naples, maybe while transporting their prisoner away from the city. Certainly the reverberations of the bloody episode on Via Fani were being felt as strongly in early April as they were on 16 March.

Shortly before half past nine that Thursday morning in March, the RAI state broadcaster's second radio channel had interrupted its programme to announce that the chairman of Christian Democracy had been kidnapped and his team of bodyguards killed. A news crew from the broadcaster's first television channel was soon at Via Fani, and a journalist was describing the scene to viewers, instructing the cameraman to point the camera at bullet holes in a car's door. "Look at them, shots clearly fired by a machine gun ... and there's the body of another policeman ... and another to the right ... I was accidentally treading on cartridge cases ... the blood ... the blood on the ground, an automatic pistol, so ... four bodies, four bodies ... here, at ten o'clock in the morning on Via Fani." At ten minutes past ten, a member of the Red Brigades telephoned the Ansa news agency with a brief message to say that they had kidnapped Moro and "eliminated his bodyguards", and that a communiqué would follow.

A news crew from the state broadcaster's second television channel was also quickly at the scene, with a journalist interviewing an eyewitness who had got out of bed when she heard the noise in the street below and bullets striking her bathroom. She described the terrorists as very calm and unhurried. One of the many voices she heard was that of a young woman, although she couldn't tell whether the voice was that of a passer-by or a member of the terrorist squad. Among the voices, which were those of young people, she distinctly heard the voice of an older man saying "Leave me alone". And she saw Moro being held by the arm and led to the car in which the terrorists took him away. The politician didn't appear to be hurt. The cars carrying Moro and his bodyguards had been ambushed at two minutes past nine, and the bloody attack was over and the terrorists were leaving the scene with their hostage at five minutes past nine. Via

Fani had been the scene of one of the most dramatic events of the *anni di piombo*, the Years of Lead, for just three minutes.

Replacing a plaque put there many years before, an unmissable memorial—a semicircle of white stone divided down the centre by a slim, fractured and truncated obelisk of dark grey stone—was unveiled where Via Fani crosses Via Stresa on 16 March 2018. On the left of the white stone are the names of the three policemen and two Carabinieri military policemen who were murdered, four of them dying at the crossroads, the fifth at the nearby Gemelli hospital a few hours after being shot. An inscription on the right quadrant says that the memorial is there to remind people of the five men who were brutally killed in a terrorist attack while courageously showing loyalty to the state and sacrificing their lives to protect democratic institutions.

Celestina alla Camilluccia, across the street from the memorial, partly hidden by shrubs and with one side lying along Via Stresa, is a typical trattoria that offers numerous types of pizza baked in a wood-fired oven and a full menu of Italian specialities. According to its brochure in 2022, the trattoria's diners eat well, drink better and laugh a lot, and there is a garden of Mediterranean maquis, "a little Eden for those who want to eat outside". The district around Celestina alla Camillucia, the Trionfale–Camilluccia hilly northern suburbs, was developed in the 1950s and 1960s, and Via Fani is one of several similar, quiet residential streets. In the 2020s, the quiet is broken by the occasional passing of a route 990 bus travelling between the city centre at Lungotevere Marzio, a boulevard beside the Tiber, and the Monte Mario railway station on the line to Viterbo, and by queues of peak-hour traffic using the street as a rat run to avoid jams elsewhere.

It was onto Via Fani that a large dark blue Fiat 130 official car carrying Aldo Moro turned at just after nine o'clock that morning in March 1978. Its driver and one bodyguard from the

Carabinieri had collected Moro from his apartment on Via del Forte Trionfale a few minutes earlier, and their car was followed closely by another carrying three policemen. As the two-car convoy reached the junction on Via Trionfale where Via Fani begins, a lookout posted by the Red Brigades gave a signal at which two cars the terrorists had stolen set off to position themselves for action, one car carrying false diplomatic licence plates in front of Moro's car, the other behind the car carrying the three policemen. A trap was being prepared. Moro had come about 1,400 metres from his home and had only another 400 metres of freedom as his car travelled downhill between three- and four-storey blocks set back from the street within small gardens. With their wide terraces, these were apartments of comfortably-off, middle-class families. Moro often passed there to reach the church of Santa Chiara, a place for prayer at the beginning of his working day that he usually visited on his way to the centre.

The trap shut suddenly when the leading car, of what Moro's bodyguards were probably unaware had become a four-car convoy, braked sharply and came to a halt at the junction where Via Fani and Via Stresa cross. The Red Brigades had two other cars waiting. Also waiting was a group of four men disguised as civil aircrew who had been hiding behind bushes that shielded a café called Olivetti, which was closed that day. Moro and his party of drivers and bodyguards had been ambushed. As the cars shuddered to a halt, with the car carrying the three policemen shunting into the one in which Moro was travelling, the four men stepped out quickly onto the pavement and then onto the road. Weapons ready, two of them fired at close range at the driver and bodyguard in Moro's car and two at the three policemen in the car behind. Investigations showed that the terrorists fired a total of ninety-one shots, of which forty-five hit their targets. Moro was unhurt despite the intensity of fire focused on his car.

Joined by the final car of the convoy, which had sealed the rear of the trap, the terrorists had three cars at the crossroads for their getaway. They drove north, uphill along Via Stresa, which was one-way in that section, and effectively doubled back parallel to Via Fani. Via Stresa ends at Piazza Monte Gaudio, a junction on Via Trionfale and about 200 metres from the top of Via Fani where the Red Brigades had begun their action. The closing moments of Moro's abduction had been noticed, and a witness followed the convoy along Via Stresa and down Via Trionfale towards Rome's centre for about 300 metres. However, he failed to see the terrorists' cars turn off to the right along Via Pennestri and into a sequence of strategic changes of direction in a complex network of streets to the north and west of the Vatican, with cars being abandoned, members leaving the group and new vehicles being used. The trail had been lost well before Moro, then hidden in a chest, was transferred to a Citroën Ami 8 station wagon in the underground car park of a supermarket about four kilometres from the apartment that would be his prison for the next fifty-five days.

Having decided in 1976 to kidnap a leading Christian Democracy politician, the following year the Red Brigades bought an apartment at number 8 Via Camillo Montalcini in the name of a woman member. This was to be a base for an operation in whose initial planning they considered three targets: Giulio Andreotti, Amintore Fanfani and Aldo Moro. Andreotti had been prime minister for a little over a year and a half at the time of Moro's kidnapping, and both Fanfani and Moro had held the post, the latter having preceded Andreotti. Interviewed for a television programme in 1990, one of the terrorists said they abandoned an operation involving Andreotti because this would have required resources beyond those on which the Red Brigades could draw. Moro was a softer target. The Santa Chiara church that he attended regularly on his way to the centre was reconnoitred as a potential location for the kidnapping but discarded because the piazza in which the church stands was an area where they risked encountering police patrols. Although that site was an operational dead end, reconnaissance there revealed that Moro's car had not been bullet-proofed.

As the crow flies, Via Camillo Montalcini is about twelve kilometres from the junction of Via Fani and Via Stresa. It is in the Portuense district of southwest Rome, although residents often say they live in Villa Bonelli, which sounds smarter. It was there that the terrorists took Moro in the Citroën. Despite being near the last stop and turnaround of two bus routes, this was a quiet, residential area with little traffic. Set above and back from the pavement, the four-storey block with its deep-terraced apartments stands across the road from a public park and a nineteenth-century villa that takes the name of its second owner. Michelangelo Bonelli had bought the property in 1925 when the villa and its park, on a hill high above the Tiber, were surrounded by countryside. People arriving on foot from Villa Bonelli station on the railway line to Fiumicino airport face a steep uphill walk of several hundred metres but, pausing to look back, they can enjoy a sweeping cityscape as it opens up across EUR and Rome's southern suburbs to the Alban Hills in the distance.

Rome's city authorities purchased Villa Bonelli in the 1980s, designating it as offices for the XI municipality, and the gardens service placed a notice of the park's rules at the gate on Via Camillo Montalcini. Bicycles and motorcycles are forbidden and so are ball games, though boys living nearby widely disregard that rule. During afternoons when school is over and at weekends, they take over a flat space just inside the railings, and the street echoes with their shouts and the sound of footballs being kicked. Locked securely in the apartment, Moro would have known nothing of the park across the street, and of the view it offered over the city where he had been involved in politics since 1946 and been professor of criminal law at the university since 1963. Perhaps even in 1978, young football players shouted to each other as they kicked a ball around, fifty metres away from where Moro was a prisoner, but if they did, their shouts would have gone unheard by him.

* * *

Two days after Moro's abduction, a journalist working for a Rome newspaper received a telephone call to say that there was an orange envelope on top of a passport-photo booth in a pedestrian underpass in the centre of Rome. The envelope contained the first of nine communiqués issued by the Red Brigades. (A tenth was shown to be false.) It began: "On Thursday 16 March, an armed squad of the Red Brigades captured Aldo Moro, chairman of Christian Democracy, and placed him in a people's prison." For the Red Brigades, Moro was the political godfather and most conscientious executor of directives issued by imperialist headquarters. They described Europe as having been transformed from liberal nation states into imperialist states of multinationals aimed at annihilating the proletarian revolution. The communist vanguard had identified Christian Democracy as the proletariat's most ferocious enemy. Aldo Moro would be put on trial in his people's prison.

The second communiqué arrived a week later. Headed "The trial of Aldo Moro", the document listed the various political appointments that he had held, beginning with that of minister of justice in 1955. His government roles had included those of minister of education and foreign minister as well as two spells as prime minister, one of which lasted four and a half years. He also spent five years out of government but running the dominant Christian Democracy as party secretary. Even after his kidnapping he was being spoken of as a future head of state, an institutional role that encompasses the posts of head of the magistracy and head of the armed forces. According to the Red Brigades, Moro's political career showed that he had become the point man for Italy's bourgeoisie in constructing an imperialist state, and on this and other matters he was being examined by the people's court to ascertain his direct responsibilities.

A third communiqué was found on 29 March. The envelope also contained a letter from Moro, addressed to the internal affairs minister, which mentioned an exchange of prisoners. But, in a unanimous decision, his party's leaders rejected this. Just over two weeks had passed when, on 15 April following a telephone call to the Milan offices of *la Repubblica* newspaper, a fifth communiqué was found in a rubbish bin on Via dell'Annunciata, a street in central Milan, close to the offices of *Corriere della Sera*, Italy's newspaper of record, and not far from the city's main police station and the office block housing bureaux of the foreign press. The people's court had reviewed thirty years of the Christian Democracy regime, said the communiqué, the interrogation of Aldo Moro had ended, he had been found guilty and sentenced to death. The fevered atmosphere of Italian politics since 16 March, and the media's reporting of the Moro case, became more fevered.

The drama of Moro's kidnapping and imprisonment heightened with two events that occurred only three days after the Red Brigades' fifth communiqué. Police discovered a hideout in the north of Rome where they found a civil aircrew uniform that had been used as disguise on Via Fani and the real number plates of the car that had carried diplomatic plates for the ambush. And a communiqué arrived which falsely claimed that Moro had been executed by means of suicide and that his body was in a mountain lake. Some years later the author of this communiqué was identified as a noted Roman forger with ties to organised crime, the neo-fascists and Italy's secret services. (He would be murdered in mysterious circumstances in 1984.) For one former member of the Red Brigades, the communiqué was clearly false and the work of the government and the police to send a message that no negotiations were possible and that the state was washing its hands of Moro.

Of numerous letters the kidnapped politician wrote, over a dozen were to colleagues, and in them he increasingly underlined the gravity of his situation. In a letter addressed to Benigno Zaccagnini, the party's secretary, and other senior party figures, which was found on 4 April, Moro returned to the issue of the responsibility of Christian Democracy leaders that he had raised in the letter to the home affairs minister found on 29 March. Moro noted that he had been reluctant to take on the party presidency. When he next wrote to Zaccagnini, the letter found on 20 April, he asked why personal friends and the party's rank and file had failed to raise their voices on his behalf. As for Christian Democracy's leadership, "Is it possible that all of you agree in wanting my death for reasons of state?" Moro did not forgive or justify any of them. A batch of nine letters found on 28–9 April, included one to Giulio Andreotti asking that God would enlighten him, so that he would do what mattered for Moro's family and not what mattered for furthering his own career. The Red Brigades' eighth communiqué, which was found on 24 April, named thirteen "imprisoned Communists" to be freed as the price for Moro's release. In one of his final letters, to the leader of the Christian Democracy parliamentary group, Moro noted that Palestinian prisoners had been released in exchanges. But Christian Democracy's leaders, firmly supported by the Italian Communist Party, had opted for inflexibility. There would be no negotiation, no exchange of prisoners.

"My dearest Noretta, after a moment of very slender optimism, perhaps due to my misunderstanding of what I was being told, I believe we are now at the end," Moro began his last letter to his wife, Eleonora. Full responsibility lay with Christian Democracy for their absurd and unbelievable behaviour, and many friends had failed to speak out, but all that was in the past. As for his family:

For the future, there is an infinite tenderness for you at this moment, the memories of all and each one, an enormous love full of apparently insignificant but in reality precious memories. ... Kiss and caress everyone for me, every cheek, every head. To each one of them, my immense tenderness passes through your hands. ... I will always be with you, my love, for you to hold me close. ... Now, after there seemed a slender hope, suddenly and bewilderingly the order of execution arrives. Dearest Noretta, I am in God's hands and yours. Pray for me, remember me with tenderness, hug the darling little ones, everyone of them. God be with you all.

The Red Brigades' ninth communiqué was found on 5 May. Christian Democracy's leaders had clearly refused the offer of "freedom in exchange for freedom", and the battle that began on 16 March had reached its end in "carrying out the sentence that was passed on Aldo Moro". On 9 May, at about half past twelve, a member of the Red Brigades telephoned a young assistant of Moro at Rome's university, a friend of the politician, asking him to tell Moro's family that his body was in a red Renault 4 car. Its registration plate began with the number 5 and it was parked on Via Caetani. The street's position in central Rome, between the central offices of Christian Democracy on Piazza del Gesù and the headquarters of the Italian Communist Party on Via delle Botteghe Oscure, is often assumed to have been symbolic. Moro had been the architect of a "historic compromise" between Italy's two main (and opposing) political parties, and of the Communist Party's support for the formation of Andreotti's national solidarity government in 1976, despite Andreotti's opposition to the agreement. A large metal plaque is fixed high on the wall above where the Renault 4 was parked. It was placed there by Rome's city authorities a year after Moro's body was found, and forty years later the passage of time had made the words almost illegible.

Moro's family insisted that his wishes should be respected and that there should be no state funeral, no official ceremony, no speeches, no national mourning, and no commemoration medals after his murder. Moro was buried in a private family ceremony in the small cemetery of Torrita Tiberina, about 55 kilometres north of Rome. Even so, and without a coffin holding the body of the dead politician, the government organised a memorial ceremony in the San Giovanni in Laterano basilica, in the presence of leading politicians and of Pope Paul VI, who delivered a eulogy. The pope ended with an appeal to the Almighty: "Lord, hear us! And who can hear our lamentation if not you, O God of life and death. You have not granted our prayer for the life of Aldo Moro, of this good man, gentle, wise, innocent and friend; but you, O Lord, have not abandoned his immortal spirit, marked by a faith in Christ, which is the resurrection and life. For him, for him, hear us, Lord!" In his final letter to his wife, Moro had written, "The pope has done little; perhaps he will regret this." Pope Paul VI died on 6 August 1978, just three months after Moro was murdered.

The Red Brigades in Rome

A timeline of killings, kidnappings and assaults on people and property by extremist leftwing groups shows that they began in the early 1970s in northern Italy. The symbol of the Red Brigades, a five-pointed star, appeared for the first time in Milan in September 1970, and the north would continue to be an important area of operations for them. In the south, however, the Armed Proletarians, about fifty strong, began with a robbery in May 1974 in Naples. They were mainly active there and in Rome during the following three years, but the police had completely dismantled their network by 1977. Four of the fourteen hideouts that the authorities discovered were in Naples and ten in Rome or on the coast near Rome. Among the victims they claimed in Rome were a supreme court judge, kidnapped and released in May 1975; another supreme court judge, wounded in January 1976; a policeman murdered in December that year; and another policeman, murdered in March 1977.

About then the Red Brigades focused their attention on the capital. They were responsible for knee-capping a senior civil servant of the ministry of justice in February 1977, and in June that year, after commuting a death sentence, they knee-capped the editor of the RAI state television's first channel TG1 news service. Also in June 1977, Red Brigade members targeted the head of the economics faculty at Rome's university. The following month they wounded a member of Christian Democracy's organisation and in November their target was a Christian Democracy regional councillor. Yet even before their bloody action on Via Fani, the Red Brigades had made a big leap in their targeting in Rome. On 14 February 1978, they murdered Riccardo Palma, a magistrate who headed a department in the prisons service at the ministry of justice and whom they held responsible for new rules for treating inmates of high-security prisons. That was incorrect. Palma had been responsible for ensuring that building work in prisons was carried out within budgeted times and costs, and to contractual standards. "They killed him because he was a soft target ... because he was a symbol," said Palma's son. The Czechoslovakian Skorpion machine pistol that was used to murder Palma near his home, a few hundred metres from Rome's Policlinico main hospital, would be used three months later to murder Moro.

Why did Rome become the centre of operations for the Red Brigades? In an interview in 1990, one of the terrorist group's founders said, "We formed this basic idea that if we really wanted to strike at the heart of the state, then we had to go to Rome, because Rome offered important places and people as targets." Moro's kidnapping and killing had been preceded by Riccardo Palma's murder. Later in the year, the Red Brigades would murder another magistrate in the Italian capital.

Girolamo Tartaglione was the victim. At around two o'clock in the afternoon of 10 October 1978 he was returning to his apartment on Viale delle Milizie in the Prati district. Passing a porter's lodge, Tartaglione walked along a passageway and into a spacious courtyard around which a complex of six-storey apartment blocks for state employees had been built in the early twentieth century. Half a dozen doorways provide entry to the various blocks and to their staircases and lifts. Tartaglione turned left and made his way to the third doorway. He was without bodyguards when two terrorists approached him near the entrance and shot him in the head. Three other terrorists were keeping watch, ready to help the killers' getaway if needed. A small metal plaque on the wall to the right of the doorway was placed there on 10 October 2020 by the Lazio regional authorities, Rome's city authorities, the condominium and the national magistrates' association. The plaque tells visitors that it was placed in memory of the magistrate murdered by terrorists because he was a "man of the State and respectful of its Constitution".

Commemorating their dead colleague, the magistrates' association noted that he was internationally recognised as an expert on criminal law, on criminology and, above all, on prisons and imprisonment. He had contributed to a law on prison reform enacted in 1975. As head of the department of prison affairs at the ministry of justice he had worked for "the humanisation of punishment and improvement in conditions" and had organised a framework of assistance for prisoners and their families, particularly for the children of prisoners. His senior position in the justice system and his work on prison reform had made him a target for the Red Brigades, and they mentioned this in the communiqué they issued after the murder. However, Tartaglione had spoken against releasing an imprisoned terrorist whose name had been on a list of those whose release the Red Brigades had sought in exchange for freeing Aldo Moro, and this may have been a factor. "Men and women of this nation do not forget his sacrifice and gratefully receive and respect his legacy," says the plaque on the wall at the place where he was shot. But as the plaque was unveiled, was that so? After such a long passage of time, like others during the Years of Lead, his killing had almost inevitably become little more than a matter of increasingly distant history for many Italians.

* * *

The three years from 1978 to 1980 represented the Red Brigades' peak of attacks on people belonging to Italian state organisations in the capital. After the murders they committed in Rome in 1978, they returned to action on 3 May 1979 by storming Christian Democracy's regional headquarters on Piazza Nicosia in the heart of the historic centre. The thirteen terrorists involved split into three groups, with two groups entering the building and the third remaining on watch outside. This third group was brought into action by the arrival of three policemen in an unmarked patrol car while the other two groups were inside the building, placing explosive charges and gathering confidential documents. Those outside included one who took part in the Red Brigades' ambush on Via Fani and used a Kalashnikov at Piazza Nicosia, and the woman whose name was used to purchase the apartment on Via Camillo Montalcini, who was armed with a Beretta M12. One policeman died immediately, a second died a few days later, and the third was seriously wounded.

Piazza Nicosia is a few steps from Lungotevere Marzio, a boulevard beside the Tiber, and only a five-minute walk, down Vicolo della Campana, past La Campana, Rome's oldest trattoria, and along Via della Scrofa to Palazzo Madama, where the Senate sat and still sits. Little wonder that the first item on the senators' agenda that day was the Red Brigades' assault on Christian Democracy's offices. As Amintore Fanfani, the speaker, rose to his feet, the assembled senators all rose with him. "Honourable colleagues, again—and I feel mortified to say: again—we meet to offer words of homage and gratitude to officers of the police force, one of whom died and the others were wounded in a new attack on the democratic order of the State, which happened this morning only a short distance from the Senate."

Speaking at length, Virginio Rognoni, the home affairs minister, gave the senators a detailed account of what had happened in Christian Democracy's five-storey building and the piazza outside. The offices had been guarded day and night, and a patrol car had been assigned to check regularly that all was in order. The attack was made when a parliamentary election campaign was starting and, as well as painting a five-pointed red star and the letters BR on walls by the stairs, one of the terrorists had written: "We will transform electoral fraud into a class war." However, only two of the four explosive charges the terrorists attached to radiators had exploded. For Rognoni, serious crimes like the one that morning showed clearly the perverse advantage that terrorists obtained from surprise. He noted that the terrorists enjoyed the possibility of choosing the times, places and methods of their attacks, and that the number of their potential and vulnerable objectives was large.

"Given its punitive character, the pitiless ferocity with which young people used arms against the police and those who opposed them, and the brazen arrogance in the choice of an objective of considerable political significance, in peak-hour traffic, in a well-known place in the historic, administrative and commercial centre of Rome, the attack in Piazza Nicosia seems to me even more abhorrent," said Rognoni. He added, "We certainly shouldn't delude ourselves that such bloody events cannot happen in who knows which cities, which streets, against which buildings and against whom." Indeed, the Red Brigades would be responsible for three more murders of state officials in the Italian capital during the next twelve months.

The first was the shooting on Lungotevere Arnaldo da Brescia in July 1979 of the Carabinieri lieutenant colonel responsible for organising bodyguards for magistrates working in Rome. The Red Brigades aimed at an even higher echelon of the state hierarchy in February 1980 when they murdered Vittorio Bachelet, a law professor at Rome's Sapienza University, who held the office of deputy chairman of the Consiglio Superiore della Magistratura (CSM, the magistracy's governing body). During his deputy chairmanship, an executive role that began in December 1976, Bachelet had led the magistracy's commemorations of four of its members who were murdered by extremist leftwing groups. Bachelet had just finished giving a lecture at the university when he was shot at point-blank range on the steps of the political science faculty. One of the two killers, who were able to escape in the confusion, was the woman who had fired the Beretta M12 in Piazza Nicosia.

One morning just over a month after Bachelet was killed, Girolamo Minervini left his home in an apartment block on Via della Balduina, about two kilometres north of Vatican. Like much of Rome's semi-centre, it is a district of blocks of apartments built for middle-class families during the 1950s and 1960s. That day, 18 March 1980, was Minervini's second day as head of the department of penal institutions at the ministry of justice, and it began with a walk to a nearby stop to catch a bus to the ministry. He had turned down an allocation of bodyguards because he considered such precautions were useless, and he didn't "intend that three or four young men should be massacred". He had told his son on the evening before taking up his new job that in war generals shouldn't refuse to go where soldiers get killed. Minervini had given his son details of an insurance policy and his wife's pension rights. Minervini's name was on a list of targets drawn up by the Red Brigades, and he was sure that in taking up his new job he was accepting a death sentence.

Yet the Red Brigades' plan to murder Minervini had been ready well before he was offered and began that job, and terrorists had been tailing him for several days before the killing. The magistrate took a bus that went downhill along Via della Balduina. After crossing Piazzale degli Eroi, it turned left onto Via Andrea Doria and right shortly afterwards at traffic lights onto Via Ruggero di Lauria. As the bus turned, passengers standing at the front were able to see the huge dome of Saint Peter's basilica as it came into view, looming above the building at the end of the street. The dome would not have been visible to Minervini at the back of the crowded bus. Standing near him were three terrorists and, as the doors of the bus opened, one of them drew a pistol fitted with a silencer and fired it. Passengers rushed for the doors and, firing randomly, the killer wounded three as he and his accomplices escaped.

In a brief message to the Ansa news agency and *la Repubblica* newspaper the terrorists said, "We have executed Girolamo Minervini. A communiqué follows. The Red Brigades." Citizens of the surrounding Trionfale district would place a small tablet on a wall beside the bus stop on Via Ruggero di Lauria. It reads: "Girolamo Minervini, magistrate. He was working for a magistracy in defence of free institutions. Enemies of democracy barbarously assassinated him. 18 March 1980." The CSM decided unanimously in June 2020 that extracts from the magistrate's personal file held in their personnel and professional assessment archives should be made public, together with papers concerning the trials of his murderers. Two years later, profiles of nineteen magistrates murdered during the course of duty were available on the CSM's institutional website. A dozen were of magistrates killed by the Mafia, seven were of victims of terrorism during the Years of Lead, four of these murdered in Rome.

More blood was shed in Rome as 1980 ended. Terrorists of the Red Brigades killed the head of medical services at the

Regina Coeli prison on 1 December and a Carabinieri general, the deputy head of prison security, in the evening of the last day of the month as he was returning from church with his wife. On 12 December, the Red Brigades had kidnapped Giovanni D'Urso, a magistrate who headed the prison service at the ministry of justice, announcing on 4 January that they had sentenced him to death. A revolt by prisoners in two high-security prisons on 28 December (the immediate cause of the general's murder) heightened tension, but prosecutors in Rome responded early in January 1981 by laying charges of aiding and abetting the kidnapping against sixty-five prisoners, and issuing warrants against them. Early in the morning on 15 January, D'Urso was found alive, tied up in a small car left in Via Portico d'Ottavia in the old ghetto and not far from the ministry of justice. Yet again, Red Brigade terrorists had shown they could move with ease around the city. Had the magistrate been murdered, the prisoners would have faced charges of aiding and abetting a murder.

Historians and commentators say that the Years of Lead ended in the early 1980s, some putting the year at 1982, and although leftwing terrorism was absent from Rome after the killings and the kidnapping in December 1980, the capital was the scene of two outlying murders by a surviving fringe of the Red Brigades. The first was in February 1984 when the victim was an American diplomat, the director general of the Multilateral Force and Observers established to oversee 1978's Camp David Accords between Egypt and Israel, which were sponsored by America. Leamon Ray Hunt was returning home and waiting for the gate of his villa in the EUR district to open when his bullet-proofed car was attacked. No rounds penetrated the coachwork, but the rear window was breached by a terrorist who had jumped onto the boot and fired at close range from there. The large Sant'Eugenio hospital was only 300 metres away, but the head wounds that Hunt received were such that he died an hour later. Responsibility was claimed by the Red Brigades—Combatant Communist Party. Just over a year later, in March 1985, the same group would claim responsibility for the murder of Ezio Tarantelli, an economics professor at Rome's Sapienza University, where he was shot with a machine pistol after giving a lecture.

Extreme-left terror in the north

With the kidnapping and fifty-five-day imprisonment of Aldo Moro and his murder, and the killing of five bodyguards during the ambush of the politician's car on Via Fani, and the murders of magistrates and senior military officers, Rome was perhaps the place where the leftwing terrorism had its greatest impact and obtained its widest coverage by the media. However, the murders, kidnappings and woundings by leftwing extremists were most numerous in northern Italy. The first murder had been in Genoa towards the end of March 1971 when, aiming to obtain funds for their operations, terrorists calling themselves XXII October Group shot and killed an employee of the city's social housing authority who was carrying wage packets for distribution to staff. Genoa was also the city where the first magistrate was murdered. Francesco Coco was killed, together with his two Carabinieri bodyguards, by the Red Brigades in June 1976. By then, they had kidnapped a number of people in northern Italy, all subsequently released; the victims between 1972 and 1975 had included managers at two carmakers (Alfa Romeo in Milan and Fiat in Turin), a trade union leader in Turin, a magistrate in Genoa, and the managing director of a major winemaker in the province of Asti, about 50 kilometres southeast of Turin.

Although the founding leaders of the Red Brigades had already been caught and brought to trial in Turin, the closing years of the 1970s and the year 1980 were the bloodiest. And one of the most dramatic and sensational occurred during the trial.

Nearly fifty terrorists of the Red Brigades had been gathered behind the steel bars of pens in the city's court and a similarly impressive number of lawyers belonging to the Turin bar association engaged in their defence were present as the trial got underway in May 1976 with great difficulty and in the face of enormous obstacles. Tension still ran high when, on the afternoon of 28 April 1977, the bar association's chairman was gunned down in the entrance lobby as he was returning to his chambers. Hearing the word "Avvocato", the lawyer had turned and, as he did so, the killer shot him. The second half of that year was notable for the Red Brigades' campaign of terror against journalists, with woundings in Genoa, Milan, Padua and Turin, as well as in Rome, and the murder in Turin of a leading columnist of *La Stampa*, a newspaper owned by the Agnelli family, whose principal assets in an extensive business empire included the carmakers Fiat and Ferrari.

After being busy in Rome in 1978, and before killing Bachelet and Minervini, the Red Brigades focused on the north. In 1980 their victims included a leftwing trade unionist, and a Carabinieri colonel and his driver in Genoa, three policemen in Milan, and the manager of an industrial plant at Mestre near Venice. By then, however, the Red Brigades had been joined by another extreme leftwing group, Prima Linea (Front Line), whose first actions were against the industrialists' association in Monza, north of Milan, and in the city itself, against the *Corriere della Sera* newspaper, both in December 1976. Members of Front Line carried out bank robberies to finance their terrorism, as well as the murders of two prosecutors who worked in Milan's court. On the morning of 29 January 1979, Emilio Alessandrini had just taken his 9-year-old son to school and was stopped in his car at a busy junction about a kilometre and a half from the court when two of Front Line's killers, backed up by a third man, shot him. Newsreel footage showed the dead magistrate slumped over the steering wheel of his orange-red Renault 5, bullet holes clearly visible in the car's door.

With the killing of Alessandrini, the number of magistrates murdered by terrorists since 1976 rose to six, yet those working on major cases involving extremist political bands continued to travel in ordinary family cars, on public transport or on foot, and without police protection. The year that Alessandrini was shot was the year that sales of bullet-proofed cars in Italy began to take off, and they reached about 3,000 the following year. Protecting passenger space all around with sheets of manganese steel and carbon fibre material, replacing standard windows and wind-screens with 21-millimetre toughened glass or special crystal glass, installing anti-incendiary protection at front and rear, strengthening brakes and suspension, and fitting larger wheels with run-flat safety tyres added between 200 and 300 kilos to the weights of large saloon cars. Such modifications also tripled prices. However, major firms thought the cost was worthwhile for many board directors and top managers, and so did the state, although magistrates in the front line of defending Italian democ-racy mostly went unprotected during the Years of Lead. Guido Galli was one of those unprotected, paying with his life on 19 March 1980, shot by Front Line terrorists in the corridor out-side lecture theatre 309 at Milan's state university where he was due to teach. Six months before he was killed, Galli had com-pleted a 311-page indictment of a leading leftwing terrorist.

A month and a half before they murdered Galli, terrorists belonging to Front Line killed the production manager of the Icmesa chemicals factory in Seveso, about 15 kilometres north-west of Monza. A cloud of highly toxic dioxin had accidentally been released by the factory in July 1976, contaminating a large area in that part of the Milanese industrial hinterland, and the terrorists held the manager responsible. Industrial managers, trade unionists, lawyers, civil servants, journalists, policemen, factory guards, factory chargehands, students, politicians, doctors and magistrates became items in a long inventory of intimidation, knee-cappings, kidnappings and murders. From Piedmont and Liguria in the west through Lombardy to the Veneto in the east, the campaign of leftwing terror scarred northern Italy during the 1970s, and terrorist outrages blighted the beginning of the 1980s. "Do you remember evenings around the end of the 1970s, how streets were deserted after offices closed?" asked a Milanese friend and colleague from that period as, late one evening towards the end of the 1990s, he was driving me to my hotel after dinner at a trattoria near Milan's Stazione Genova railway terminus. The Years of Lead were in the past and forgotten by many, and once again streets in the centre of the city were busy with people enjoying their free time.

That extreme leftwing groups were able to murder and injure as they did, and to create a climate of tension and fear, was due to several factors. According to Giancarlo Caselli, a judge in Turin who tried cases involving terrorists of both the Red Brigades and Front Line, the authorities knew little or nothing about leftwing extremism when it began, and they needed time to understand its roots, aims and methods of operation, and to identify those who were active terrorists and those who provided support. For Caselli, terrorist groups can easily become effective. All they need is a mixture of fanaticism, ideology, the organisational capability to exploit opportunities offered by big cities, and the ability to create and maintain links with civil society. Even with small numbers, such groups can strike hard. "What made the Red Brigades dangerous, not militarily but politically, was their ability to establish links with sections of civil society and with intellectuals," he said.

Caselli's analysis reminds me of an occasion when I was being driven in a taxi from Turin's Caselle airport one morning in the late 1970s or early 1980s. Stuck in traffic near the centre of the city, I asked the driver the reason. There was a court hearing in one of the trials, and prisoners, who had the right to be present at hearings, were arriving. Tight security measures were unsurprising. In June 1978, when the assize court delivered its verdict in the first Red Brigades' case, sixteen of the forty-six on trial who were being held in Turin's prison attended the hearing. In December 1983, at the end of the assize court's trial of Front Line terrorists, in which one hundred and thirty-four stood accused, sixty-seven were taken to the court from Turin's prison and a further fourteen were brought from five other prisons in northern Italy, including five from the prison in Bergamo to the east of Milan. Traffic congestion was inevitable. Adding to his explanation of the reason for the traffic jam hindering my journey, the taxi driver, a man in his fifties, told me, "They [the terrorists] have a reason for what they do. Work at the Fiat factory in the 1950s and 1960s was like slavery."

In September 1972, magistrates had discovered a list of two hundred policemen who were on Fiat's payroll to gather information about its workers and thereby allow the carmaker to create files on workers' political leanings and affiliations. As well as being fostered in staff common rooms of universities and in student circles, leftwing terrorism had wide and deep roots on the shop floors of factories and in the canteens of organisations involved in public services. Student unrest in Italy in 1968 had been followed in 1969 by a "hot autumn" during which worker dissatisfaction that had been brewing for years boiled over and made itself felt through strikes and demonstrations. Writing for the *Guardian* newspaper about my visit in November 1980 to Zagato, a coachwork stylist and bodywork maker on the outskirts of Milan, to learn about how they made cars bullet-proof, I noted that trade union leaders in Milan had said that extreme leftwing cells were active at Alfa Romeo, the Falck steelworks, Italtel (Italy's largest maker of telecommunications equipment) and Ercole Marelli, a leading manufacturer of electrical equipment.

POLITICAL TERRORISM FROM LEFT AND RIGHT

Terror from the extreme right

While groups on the far left of the political spectrum initially enjoyed the support of many working-class people as well as students, groups on the extreme right could count on help from parts of the Italian secret services, the armed forces and the magistracy, aided and abetted by America's CIA. And that help long preceded the social and industrial unrest of the closing years of the 1960s. Blame for initiating the Years of Lead lies squarely with terrorists of the far right and their political and institutional enablers. Fascism had never been beaten out of society or uprooted from it. Italy's constitution prohibits fascism, but courts encountered difficulties with anti-fascist laws, and demonstrations supporting fascism effectively went unchallenged, as they still do. Interviewed for a television series about the Years of Lead, a magistrate said, "In trying to win power, rightwing terrorists were responsible for about 85 per cent of all the terrorism in Italy between 1969 and 1975. That was their declared aim." Indeed, in December 1970, Junio Valerio Borghese, who had been an officer in the forces of Mussolini's rump republic at Salò, led a failed coup, an event whose threat to democracy was played down by the authorities. But Italy's extreme right had already begun striking random terror among their fellow citizens.

Bombs placed by rightwing terrorists exploded at the Stazione Centrale main railway station and at a conference centre in Milan in April 1969, twenty people being injured in the explosion at the conference centre. There were more bombs from the extreme right four months later in Turin, Milan and Rome. Far worse happened on 12 December that year when a bomb exploded at a branch of the Banca Nazionale dell'Agricoltura on Piazza della Fontana in central Milan. Seventeen people were killed and almost a hundred were wounded. On the same day eighteen people were wounded in the explosion of three bombs in Rome.

An unexploded bomb was found in Piazza della Scala in Milan, and others were found outside courts in Turin, Milan and Rome. The crimes were committed by a group called Ordine Nuovo (ON, New Order). The same group was responsible for a bomb that exploded during a demonstration on Piazza della Loggia in Brescia on 28 May 1974. That bomb killed eight and wounded one hundred among a large gathering of trade unionists who were protesting against extremist violence and neo-fascism.

Reporting in May 2024 on a ceremony commemorating the fiftieth anniversary of the neo-fascist outrage in Brescia, the *Corriere della Sera* noted this was not a collective commemoration. Senior governmental figures were absent. This was an event for the rightwing government to avoid or minimise. Italy's head of state was present, but the government sent just one junior minister as its representative. President Sergio Mattarella was unsparing in his comments about the *terrorismo nero* behind the bomb. The murderers' intention was clear: "to punish and terrorise those who protested against neo-fascism and in favour of democracy". And Mattarella underlined that the anti-fascist resistance movement of the second world war was a progenitor of the democratic post-war Italian republic.

Mattarella gave his address in the city's Teatro Grande, and a public figure attending the event was heard to say that if somebody were to shout "Viva l'Italia anti-fascista" in Brescia, he or she would not be apprehended by the police. Six months earlier, at the opening of the La Scala opera season in Milan, a member of the audience had shouted these words and later been stopped and questioned by the police. The guest of honour was Ignazio Benito Maria La Russa, the president of the Senate, second only to Mattarella in the hierarchy of Italy's state offices. La Russa had followed his father, a local boss of Mussolini's Fascist Party in Sicily and a senator for the neo-fascist Movimento Sociale Italiano between 1972 and 1992, into extreme rightwing politics. Ignazio

La Russa began his political career in the party's Fronte della Gioventù (FdG, young people's section) in Milan in the early 1970s and was a co-founder of the Brothers of Italy political party.

A little more than two months after setting off the bomb on Piazza della Loggia, New Order neo-fascists focused their attention on railway passengers, targeting the Rome-to-Munich Italicus express with a bomb that exploded as the train was nearing the exit of a 19-kilometre tunnel on the Florence-to-Bologna railway line. Twelve passengers were killed and forty-eight injured in the explosion. Fortune was kind. The number of killed and wounded would have been far higher had the bomb exploded while the train was still deep inside the tunnel. That was a minor affair compared with what would follow six years later, on 2 August 1980, with the triggering of a bomb in a crowded waiting room beside platform number one at Bologna's main railway station. Almost two hundred people were wounded and eighty-five were killed, among them Angela Fresu, the youngest at just 3 years old, and Antonio Montanari, the oldest at 86, who are remembered on a large stone tablet on a wall outside the station, along with the other victims, young, middle-aged and elderly.

In that single act of barbarity, neo-fascist terrorists killed more people than the Red Brigades killed in total throughout all the Years of Lead. On platform number one, a dark metal plaque notes that the spot has been recorded in a UNESCO programme encouraging peace and non-violence. According to the tablet outside the station, those who died at Bologna Centrale were "victims of fascist terrorism".

The murder of Vittorio Occorsio

Although using explosives for the mass murder or attempted mass murder of random victims was a usual modus operandi, Italy's extreme right terrorists also targeted individuals. Two of the most egregious cases took place in Rome, where they murdered magistrates who were investigating and prosecuting neofascist criminals. Vittorio Occorsio was the first to die, shot on 10 July 1976 soon after leaving home in his car to drive to the criminal court where he was due to be on call as duty magistrate that day, a Saturday. An eight-page tribute published by the CSM, the magistracy's governing body, noted that it would have been Occorsio's last day at work before going on holiday and that, despite graffiti threatening him, he had been without bodyguards for more than a month.

Via Mogadiscio, where Occorsio lived, is a quiet residential street in what is known as Rome's Quartiere Africano (African district) because the streets are named after places in what had been Italy's African colonial empire. Occorsio's home was near the junction with Via del Giuba. As he drove downhill along the narrow one-way street, a high block of apartments without terraces loomed claustrophobically on his left. There was a stop sign at the junction immediately ahead and an arrow pointing to the right because Via del Giuba, like Via Mogadiscio, was a one-way street. A four-storey building from the early decades of the twentieth century was across the road and stood out from more recent apartment blocks. Two gunmen waiting for Occorsio at the junction went into action when he stopped. His car was struck by two bursts of machine pistol fire, the first against the windscreen, the second from close range when the magistrate was desperately trying to escape his killers. Investigators found thirty cartridge cases at the scene. The murderers left leaflets on Occorsio's body that were headed with the symbol of a double-headed axe and the words Movimento Politico Ordine Nuovo (New Order Political Movement). The leaflets carried a subheading: "Bourgeois justice stops at life imprisonment, revolutionary justice goes further".

Occorsio's murder eliminated the magistrate whose investigation and prosecution of members of the extreme right in Rome over more than a decade had given him unequalled experience and knowledge of "black terrorism". He had moved to the prosecution service in the capital in 1964 to head a small group of magistrates dealing with cases of slander and criminal defamation, and remained there until he was murdered. A case arising from an article published in 1967 by *L'Espresso*, a weekly news magazine, had taken Occorsio into the dark nexus of extreme rightwing politics, army generals and secret services. A plan had been drawn up in March 1964 by General Giovanni De Lorenzo, the head of the Carabinieri, together with the Carabinieri generals commanding the divisions in Milan, Rome and Naples, to seize local headquarters of the police, trade unions and political parties, and to take control of the offices and transmissions of the state broadcasting corporation. Senior conservative politicians were complicit in *Piano Solo*, which was to be activated should the Italian Communist Party and its allies seem likely to take power. De Lorenzo, who had become head of the Italian army in 1966, sued *L'Espresso* when it published its story.

The general had been given the task of running Italy's military secret services in 1955, a job he kept for seven years as he worked his way up the army's chain of command. It was the exposure of the service's secret files, well over 100,000 on members of Italy's institutions and political parties, and admission by the defence minister of deviant military secret services, which led to the removal of De Lorenzo from the army's top post in 1967. De Lorenzo was elected to parliament as a member of the Monarchist Party in 1968, but switched allegiance in 1971 to the Movimento Sociale Italiano (MSI, Italian Social Movement). The neo-fascist party was founded in 1946 by men who had joined Mussolini in the Repubblica Sociale Italiana (RSI, Italian Social Republic), which the Duce had established at Salò, after Italy signed an armistice with the Allies in September 1943.

Occorsio had been on duty on 12 December 1969, when explosions killed and wounded clients and staff at the Piazza della

Fontana branch of the Banca Nazionale dell'Agricoltura in Milan and wounded sixteen people in Rome. He decided that the series of four explosions, three of them in the capital, was effectively part of a single criminal scheme and that this should be investigated by magistrates in Rome. It was Occorsio's responsibility to set investigations in motion and lead them. While the police and the home affairs ministry quickly blamed anarchists, he believed that the explosions were not their work. For Occorsio, something more complex and murkier lay behind the bombs. Although Occorsio asked in September 1970 that a noted anarchist should be sent for trial, the list of people that his investigations had identified included rightwing extremists, among them a leading member of the MSI and founder of Avanguardia Nazionale (AN, National Vanguard), a fascist and anti-communist movement even further to the right. However, the court in Rome decided that the crime did not fall within its jurisdiction and the trial was transferred to Milan, and from Milan to Catanzaro in Calabria. After numerous trials, appeals and retrials, the supreme court ruled in 2005 that the explosion in the Banca Nazionale dell'Agricoltura had been caused by New Order (ON), but no individual was found guilty of committing the crime or of aiding and abetting it.

From investigating and prosecuting a case of criminal defamation, in which Occorsio had asked the court to discharge the defendants as not guilty, the magistrate found himself investigating and prosecuting darker and more dangerous matters. In March 1971 he issued arrest warrants for thirty-nine people belonging to ON, the indictment alleging the re-establishment of a fascist party in violation of a law enacted in 1952 that criminalised the encouragement and support of a political party of that colour. According to the magistracy's governing body, Occorsio became the most vulnerable and isolated member of Rome's prosecution service. The trial began in June 1973 and ended on 21 November that year with guilty verdicts for thirty of the accused. Two days later, the internal affairs ministry published a decree banning New Order. However, that was the end neither of the new fascists nor of Occorsio's interest in what the extreme right was doing. Discovering that former ON members had continued to associate and recruit new members, he began formal investigations into 120 of them in mid 1975. Occorsio had also uncovered links between neo-fascists, deviant Freemasons and organised crime. He was preparing indictments when he was murdered.

Thanks to an observant young bystander who was interested in motorcycles, Occorsio's two killers were soon identified. The first was caught in October 1976, less than four months after the murder, and the second in February 1977. The trial and appeals were held quickly and life sentences were confirmed in March 1980 by the supreme court. However, only the executors of the crime were punished. The CSM notes that after twenty years and eleven trials none of those suspected of aiding and abetting the magistrate's murder were found guilty. Thirty-five years after the killing, a small stone tablet was unveiled on the wall of an apartment block at the junction of Via Mogadiscio and Via del Giuba. The inscription reads: "In this place the prosecutor Vittorio Occorsio (1929–1976), courageous defender of democratic institutions, gold medal for civic valour, was victim of a terrorist attack."

The murder of Mario Amato

Early in the morning of 23 June 1980, Mario Amato left the apartment on Via Monte Rocchetta where he lived with his wife and two small children, and walked the short distance downhill to Viale Jonio. At a stop near the end of the street Amato planned to take a bus to the large court complex on Piazzale Clodio where he worked. His own car was being repaired and he had asked for a service car, but the working hours during which they were available did not fit his early start to the day. Amato didn't notice as a young man behind him drew near. When he reached the bus stop, the man took out a 38-calibre gun and fired a single shot to Amato's head. Mario Amato was the last magistrate to be murdered by Italian political terrorists. In a telephone call soon after the murder a terrorist said, "This is the NAR. We have killed Amato, the magistrate. You can find a leaflet in the telephone box on Via Carlo Felice." Sergio Amato, the magistrate's son who was 6 years old at the time, broke the news of their father's murder to his sister. Three terrorists would be found guilty of the crime and sentenced to imprisonment for life, the sentence confirmed by the supreme court in December 1987. Ten years after the crime, one of the killers would remember, "It wasn't a particularly difficult operation ... in fact it was even easier than we thought it would be."

In March 1980, three months before he was murdered, Amato told the CSM, the magistracy's governing body, about the lack of resources allocated to investigating, capturing and prosecuting terrorists associated with the Nuclei Armati Rivoluzionari (NAR, Armed Revolutionary Units) and the apparent lack of interest of Rome's chief prosecutor in investigations and trials. Despite evidence and accusations concerning serious crimes, the chief prosecutor did not care. They were crimes involving not only individuals but whole sections of society, said Amato, emphasising that "rightwing terrorism comes from the middle and upper ranks of the bourgeoisie. The terrorists are sons of professional people, of colleagues, businessmen and so on, people who react in many ways." These weren't children of trade unionists, of factory workers, of hospital orderlies or of clerks, but children of the well-to-do and well-connected who could and did pull strings. They were children who lived in the city's smartest districts and attended the capital's best high schools.

When Amato was transferred to Rome in June 1977, the chief prosecutor assigned him all Occorsio's work, and by March 1980 he was responsible for 600 criminal cases, among them every case regarding rightwing terrorism. Amato's was a one-man effort, with no help from superiors or colleagues. Organisation was wholly absent and management of Rome's prosecution service was "letting in water in every part". Amato drew the CSM's attention to how, between the beginning of 1979 and March 1980, the capital had been the target of four attempted but failed bomb attacks by rightwing terrorists. One target had been the Campidoglio, Rome's city hall; another the Regina Coeli prison in the centre of the city, off a boulevard beside the Tiber. He reminded council members that its own offices, a couple of hundred metres from Stazione Termini, Rome's main railway station, had also been targeted. "The attack failed only because the timer didn't work. We don't yet know whether this was due to incorrect connections or to a malfunction, but the fact remains that this attack employed 55 sticks of dynamite which, had they exploded in busy Piazza dell'Indipendenza, would have caused mass slaughter."

Amato was swamped by a tide of personal attacks in the press and by lawyers connected to the extreme right of society that he was investigating. He had found himself "having to investigate a very difficult ambience, that of the Roman right" and was accused of exaggeration and invention. He said that the risk of personalising trials would be reduced if a colleague were assigned to work alongside him on these cases. Instead, colleagues kept their distance, and he was left isolated and alone and having to deal with what the chief prosecutor considered Amato's problem rather than the problem of the prosecution service. The CSM would begin disciplinary action against two magistrates. One involved the chief prosecutor and aimed at removing him from Rome, but this was forestalled by the magistrate's own request to move elsewhere. The other concerned a senior colleague, an examining magistrate ten years older than Amato, whose conduct was even more deplorable than that of the chief prosecutor. Antonio Alibrandi was called to answer for it at a disciplinary tribunal in 1981.

As well as the statements Amato made at two hearings the previous year, the second only ten days before he was murdered, the CSM noted that the tribunal had taken into consideration a document that Amato had written to it and that had been found by his wife among his papers. The CSM considered its contents to be reliable. Given to the magistracy's governing body in October 1980, the document described the episodes that led to the disciplinary hearing. It deserved the maximum credibility, the tribunal said, and Alibrandi's attempts to discredit it with insinuations about its origins "were without any foundation". For the tribunal, the document offered authentic testimony in a simple narrative that seemed inspired neither by feelings of hatred nor of accusatory intent but by Amato's wish to work in peace and to be respected for what he was doing. Amato was one of a small group of magistrates who had happened to find themselves dealing with political terrorism and political terrorists, and these magistrates deserved the maximum consideration and respect, particularly from colleagues, said the tribunal.

Issuing its judgment in September 1982, the CSM's disciplinary tribunal said, "Alibrandi attempted on several occasions to push Amato into adopting a more favourable attitude towards 27 people charged with reconstituting the Fascist Party." There was clear evidence that Alibrandi refused to accept a court summons as a witness in a case involving his son. Moreover, in finding against Alibrandi, the tribunal also noted, "It is proven without doubt that Alibrandi interfered with the search of offices of the Fronte della Gioventù for which police had a warrant." Alibrandi's interference in a case that involved his son, Alessandro, and the use of intimidation that amounted to aggression were "certainly not appropriate to his position as a magistrate". The tribunal ruled that Alibrandi should be reprimanded, albeit, after amnesty legislation in 1986, this was reduced on appeal in 1990 to admonishment.

After joining the Fronte della Gioventù (FdG, young people's section) of the MSI, which his father supported, Alessandro Alibrandi soon engaged deeply with his father's politics, embracing violence and becoming involved at the age of 16 in his first armed clash with the police in March 1977. Later in the year he was one of a group that murdered a Communist during a demonstration in the Balduina district of the city, and around the same time he became a founding member of the NAR. By March 1980, when Amato issued a warrant for his arrest, he had participated in robberies, arson, woundings and murder. Avoiding capture, Alibrandi stayed briefly in London before travelling to Lebanon in November 1980. After returning to Italy in June the following year, Alibrandi was soon back to his life of neo-fascist crime. But it was cut short on 5 December during a shoot-out with police at Labaro, just outside the GRA ring road to the north of Rome. A policeman also died.

In Britain, perverting or interfering with the course of justice, as Antonio Alibrandi did, is a criminal offence. Under Section 51 of the Criminal Justice and Public Order Act of 1994 a Crown Court may impose a sentence of up to five years' imprisonment and/or a fine. It's hard to believe that Bar Disciplinary Tribunals in Britain would have decided other than to disbar a barrister guilty of interfering with justice or that Britain's Judicial Conduct Investigations Office would have simply rapped an offending judge's or prosecutor's knuckles. More likely he or she would have been immediately suspended from duties, investigated, placed on trial and, if found guilty, subject to the appropriate penalties and expelled.

When Antonio Alibrandi died in September 2018 at the age of 91, a Brothers of Italy councillor on Rome's city council asked for two minutes' silence to be observed for the dead man in recognition of his four years as a councillor between 1993 and 1997 in the ranks of the MSI. In an appreciation of Alibrandi, the *Secolo d'Italia* newspaper, one-time party organ of the MSI, which shares the address of the Brothers of Italy political party, described him as not simply a man of the right, but "of the extreme right". Little wonder that faced with a neo-fascist adversary at a more senior level in the magistracy of the Rome court, the 42-year-old Mario Amato was worried about having to tackle singlehandedly neo-fascist crime in the capital.

Remembering Mario Amato

Viale Jonio is on the wrong side of the tracks and the wrong side of the river Aniene. Tufello, Monte Sacro and Val Melaina, the area through which the road runs, rank low in residential desirability. (They are not mentioned in the one thousand pages of the Touring Club Italiano's guide to Rome.) The road, a busy dual carriageway with plane trees growing along its central reservation, is a scruffy end-of-the-line for Rome's Metro B underground railway, which has served locals since 2015. The station is just 700 metres from a four-storey apartment block at number 272 Viale Jonio, where a white stone memorial, its base protected by a low steel chain, stands on the pavement outside.

When I went there on a warm November morning, a pot of autumn-blooming cyclamen was on the ground by the memorial and about twenty small pale lilac-coloured flowers were taking a touch of beauty to an unattractive spot that the *terrorismo nero* of neo-fascists had stained with bloody ugliness. Someone had remembered the man who was murdered there. An inscription on the memorial reads: "To the magistrate Mario Amato, killed here 23 June 1980, victim of terrorism".

In a paper published in *Questione Giustizia* in 2019, Giancarlo Scarpari wrote that even magistrates who served as judges in fascist special tribunals were amnestied after the war. Few magistrates had joined the resistance. Post-war continuity was such that one-time judicial functionaries of Mussolini's regime were called to try cases of fascist crime. Born in 1940, Scarpari entered the magistracy when change was underway. Magistratura Democratica, an association of progressive, liberal and mostly young magistrates, was founded in 1964 to safeguard social rights, challenge encrusted and discredited values, and modernise Italy's judicial culture.

Certainly the professional environment in which Antonio Alibrandi began his career as a magistrate in the 1950s was one that was favourable to newcomers whose politics were conservative or further to the right. President of Rome's assize court in the early 1970s, Orlando Falco had been required, as all would-be magistrates were from 1938, to show his Fascist Party membership card and to make a declaration that he was an Aryan male. Between October 1944 and December 1947 a vetting commission investigated Falco's work under the fascist regime. Two nephews of Falco were involved in Rome's extreme right, one with New Order and the other with National Vanguard, in the period when Vittorio Occorsio was investigating and prosecuting members of those organisations. The culture of the magistracy was changing, but those at the top of Rome's judicial hierarchy were overwhelmingly fascist appointees.

Falco, who died in 1994, had retired in 1982 to Switzerland, where his financial assets amounted to between five and six million Swiss francs. He also had around two and a half billion lire in cash and securities in Italy. According to a judgment of a court in Milan in 2000, "There can be no doubt about the strangeness of a retired magistrate possessing enormous wealth about whose origin nothing is known." Falco's wealth came to light in the second half of the 1990s when prosecutors in Milan were investigating cases of judicial corruption in the Italian capital. Fascism or neo-fascism, judicial corruption and egregious cases of politically inspired false arrest and judicial cover-up: the closing decades of the twentieth century were an inglorious period for the courts in Rome.

Piazza di Trevi with its milling crowds of tourists, there to see the fantastical baroque fountain and perhaps, if they can get close enough, to toss a coin into the water and wish to return one day to the Eternal City, seems a world away from Via Monte Rocchetta and Viale Jonio. The Trevi Fountain is in Rome's historic centre, near Via del Corso and the prime minister's offices in Palazzo Chigi, and not far from the Quirinal Palace, the residence of Italy's head of state and once the home of popes. Seven kilometres away, the district in which Via Monte Rocchetta and Viale Jonio lie offers no attractions, little history and even less charm. Yet at the beginning of May 2022, Sergio Mattarella, Italy's president in his institutional role as the non-executive president of the CSM, created a link that ties the flamboyant and playful fountain to the plain and sombre spot where, because his job was to investigate and prosecute terrorists, Mario Amato was murdered. In the spacious and airy penthouse of an eighteenth-century building that faces the fountain, Mattarella had inaugurated the Scuola Superiore della Magistratura "Mario Amato", an institute for the professional development of magistrates dedicated to Amato's memory.

Courts had found that the beneficial owner of the apartment was Ernesto Diotallevi, a man shown to have had deep relationships from the early 1980s with Sicily's Cosa Nostra and with Rome's Banda della Magliana, the capital's organised crime mob. With its windows opening onto one of the most evocative corners of Rome, the apartment had been a symbol of the power and invincibility of organised crime. Writing in a volume published to mark the inauguration of the magistracy's institute, Giovanni Salvi, chief prosecutor in the supreme court, noted that

Diotallevi had been involved in summer 1982 in the mysterious disappearance of Roberto Calvi. Known as God's Banker, Calvi, who was chairman of Banco Ambrosiano, reappeared dead in London, his body left hanging under Blackfriars Bridge. The bank's collapse, wrote Salvi, would be one of the threads woven into the evidence that courts heard in the lengthy process of confiscation of the top-floor apartment that finally ended on 30 December 2020.

In his investigations, Mario Amato uncovered links between rightwing terrorists and the Banda della Magliana, and he was discovering others in the tangled and murky undergrowth of finance and the state. Ten days before his murder, Amato had told a hearing of the CSM that he was arriving at an overall picture of the NAR which involved a level of responsibility far above the level of those committing the crimes. The secrets of the deviant P2 masonic lodge, with its penetration of the magistracy, politics, the armed forces, industry and finance, and its close ties to the extreme right, would only begin emerging in March 1981. "Amato was assassinated on 23 June 1980 by terrorists belonging to the NAR, the same who would later be found guilty of the bombing in Bologna on 2 August 1980. Amato's prediction was based on deep knowledge of the criminal world," said Salvi at the inauguration ceremony.

On 6 April 2022, an assize court in Bologna convicted a fifth member of the NAR for the explosion at the railway station and found that the crime had been organised by senior figures of the P2 lodge who enjoyed the protection of members of Italy's secret services. More than forty years had passed since Mario Amato was gunned down on Viale Jonio in a dull part of northeast Rome. He had foreseen that terrible crimes were about to be committed.

Perhaps, around the time that Mario Amato was murdered, some Italians could imagine a future in which neo-fascism would become acceptable. Few would have foreseen, however, an electorate that would vote in 2022 in such numbers as to propel the Brothers of Italy into the dominant role in a populist and nationalist coalition government on the far right of the political spectrum. That such a party, whose origins lie at the end of a line running back through the People of Freedom, the National Alliance and the Italian Social Movement to Mussolini's last redoubt in Salò, would ever be Italy's principal party of government was inconceivable. Even after Silvio Berlusconi formed a government in June 2001 and cleared the way by drawing ministers from its ranks, the odds seemed heavily weighted against a neo-fascist party being anything other than a minor feature on Italy's political landscape. Against the odds however, a hundred years after Mussolini's thugs murdered Giacomo Matteotti and eighty years after nazi-fascists were ousted from Rome, the second highest of Italy's offices of state and the office of prime minister were occupied by politicians who cut their political teeth in the young people's section of a party established by fascists involved in the Duce's Salò republic.

Yet deeds count more than labels. Flexing its muscles during its first two years of power, the government led by the Brothers of Italy displayed a liking for authoritarianism and an intolerance of dissent. Its enthusiasm for changing Italy's republican constitution, drawn up between 1946 and 1948 by politicians who had known the shame of fascism and pain of war, worried liberals and progressives. (The drafters of the constitution inserted checks and balances to prevent the arrival of another Mussolini.) Moreover, the government showed a readiness to treat the magistracy as an adversary. Some feared that its keenness to trim the magistracy's independence was a first step along a path to turn magistrates into government functionaries and to subordinate the administration of justice to ministerial whims.

By a bus stop in sight of the dome of Saint Peter's basilica, a tablet on a wall notes that Girolamo Minervini was working for a magistracy in defence of free institutions. He had been shot while standing at the back of a crowded bus. At the spot in Rome's Quartiere Africano where Vittorio Occorsio was murdered, a tablet tells passers-by that the prosecutor was a courageous defender of democratic institutions. Within walking distance of the place where Minervini died, a plaque remembering Girolamo Tartaglione's murder claims that the nation does not forget his sacrifice and respects his legacy. Such words rang hollow in 2024. If Mario Amato had lived he would have been almost 85 when the Brothers of Italy formed a government. Instead he died at the age of 42, shot on a street in Rome's northern suburbs by a neo-fascist terrorist.

AFTERWORD

STEPS ACROSS THE PAST

The sun of Rome is set. Our day is gone

William Shakespeare, *Julius Caesar*

Early one day at the beginning of February 2022, under a blue
sky and with little more than an occasional puff of breeze that
barely moved two flags which drooped against flagpoles outside
the environment ministry, the kind of weather that shows most
places to the best, I began a walk that would take me to Cinecittà
and back, stopping on the way there and on return at the church
of Santa Maria in Palmis. Five minutes after leaving home I had
passed three apartment blocks and the offices of PwC, an accoun-
tancy and consultancy firm, crossed the main road from Rome
to Ostia, and was walking through a patch of open land into the
Appia Antica park. Overnight ground frost still sparkled on
blades of grass, and the soil had softened and glistened where the
sun reached. There were few people around, but sisters of a religious order, a group of women in white dresses and black cardi-
gans, walked ahead of me and crossed the Appia Antica in front
of the church. They didn't enter and continued towards the San
Sebastiano basilica.

The gate into the Parco della Caffarella is about a kilometre from Santa Maria in Palmis, along a narrow metalled road, much of it kept in shade by walls, bushes and tall trees. China's permanent mission to the United Nations Food and Agriculture Organization is neighboured by the abandoned gardens of empty villas, perhaps built illegally but not amnestied by three laws passed between 1985 and 2003. The Quo Vadis Club is across the road and a tennis court was in use, the noise of balls being struck breaking the silence.

A line of trees on the eastern side of the park is visible from the top floors of buildings behind the park's western side. The trees stand in front of what appears in the middle distance to be an unrelieved but irregular and fractured strip of apartment blocks along and behind Via Latina and other roads forming part of the park's eastern boundary. However, the broad deep valley lying between the two sides remains hidden, and it was into the valley that I walked. This large open space and the slopes surrounding it had been hotly contested in the latter part of the twentieth century. Although the city authorities had zoned the area as a public park in 1965, it became an urban no man's land, dangerous and degraded, a place where prostitutes plied their trade and a site for dumping construction waste, of which Rome was producing great quantities as developers, exploiting political and bureaucratic lethargy, indifference and complicity, illicitly built apartment block after apartment block. Land on both sides of what would be the Caffarella park was cemented over.

Extending almost to the Aurelian Walls, and stopped short by the tracks of the Rome-to-Pisa railway line, the Caffarella park had been in developers' crosshairs ever since they began their construction onslaught on that southern wedge of the city in the mid 1950s. Partly used as a waste dump, it had also been extensively parcelled out by stake-your-claim allotment gardeners. However, the high risk that this green space faced of total and rapid transformation into permanent urbanisation with concrete and asphalt was stymied by a campaign of young people living in apartments along the Via Latina and streets nearby. They knew what happened after the city authorities made their first ruling of expropriation of land in the Caffarella valley in 1972; the regional administrative tribunal reversed the ruling, and its decision was then upheld by the council of state. And, as the seventies became the eighties, builders increasingly found the valley a convenient dump for construction waste, more land was grabbed for allotments, and five mushroom farms were established whose spent soil added further contamination to groundwater and to the small river Almone. Twentieth-century Romans made an open drain of a river that ancient Romans had considered sacred and used for purification rites linked to the cult of Cybele, the goddess of motherhood and fertility.

However, the young people's efforts in gathering signatures for petitions, garnering press support and lodging complaints with prosecutors obtained results. Courts began ordering land to be seized. A petition carrying 13,000 signatures, presented to parliament in 1988, led to 26 billion lire being allocated for expropriation of the Caffarella. In the same year, the regional government of Lazio passed a law setting up the Appia Antica park of which the Caffarella was part. Only a twentieth of the whole park, an area of around 4,600 hectares, would be publicly owned, the rest remaining in the hands of old aristocratic Roman families, other private owners and businesses. But designation as a park gave the land within its boundaries legal protection against development and erected a defensive barrier around the Caffarella park's 190 hectares, whose green integrity had been threatened by a rampant, speculative spree of illegal use and construction from the mid 1950s to the 1980s.

Walking across the broad, flat meadow through which the Almone flows—the short grass a surprisingly fresh green, trees hiding the apartment blocks that pack the space beyond the park—it was hard to believe that there were streams of fume-emitting cars, buses and lorries and an unyielding denseness of buildings only a few minutes' walk away. Not a whisper of urban sound slipped into the valley: no rumble of tyres on asphalt or cobbles, no noise of engines, no rattle of coachwork or thump of suspension as vehicles hit bumps and potholes, no roar of motor-cycles accelerating away from traffic lights, no wailing of ambu-lance and police sirens. These were uncrowded minutes, stress-free for me as for a flock of about two hundred sheep, grazing undisturbed before the arrival of walkers accompanied by dogs that had been let off their leads. Yet after about half an hour I was out of the park and, while not back in the throbbing thick of the city, walking along Via Latina towards Via Appia Nuova. There's a dip in the final stretch before the two roads meet, a shallow valley where wicked spirits were thought to have roamed until a statue of the Virgin Mary caused them to vanish, and that stretch is called Via dei Cessati Spiriti.

Something more influential than a statue of the Virgin Mary would be needed to deal with the traffic on the Appia Nuova. After passing the airport at Ciampino, by then almost merged with the Appia Antica after running close to it for several kilo-metres, this major artery leads to Castel Gandolfo, where the pope has a summer palace, and then on to the Tyrrhenian coast at Terracina. It's a key commuter route, an important dual car-riageway link between Rome's centre and the Grande Raccordo Anulare ring road, and it carries a large volume of traffic. Travelling along it by car is unpleasant, walking beside it worse. I wondered how the Chattanooga Saloon, across the Appia Nuova from the end of Via dei Cessati Spiriti, was doing with its Mexican offerings of *guacamole tipico*, *burritos*, *tacos* and *chips croccanti di mais*. Certainly, the pizzeria just along the road, whose dull crimson wall directly abuts the carriageway that takes traffic away from the centre, had the appearance of a place whose owners had long given up hope of making a success of their business. And those who had sold cement barbecue stands had reached a similar conclusion, their outside display overgrown with weeds and tall grass.

Yet the atmosphere that pervades the road onto which I turned when leaving the Appia Nuova suggests this never had enjoyed better times. The area around Via Anicio Paolino seems a place where the wicked spirits may have moved: land marked with single-storey or low-rise residential buildings behind high walls that have coachwork repairers, car workshops, and sundry trades like scrap metal recovery, glaziers and printers as neighbours. A statue of the Virgin Mary had been placed on a pedestal at a street corner in 1988, the second part of a Marian year that finished on the Feast of the Assumption in August, an inscription "Ave Maria, prega per noi" (Hail Mary, pray for us) on the column. Perhaps this statue also keeps wicked spirits away. A lone workman was moving around a building site, partly hidden behind corrugated metal panels above which the upper part of the skeleton of a two-storey apartment block protruded.

The walk to Cinecittà was mostly an exploration of a Rome previously unknown to me, of parts of the city never visited during the years I'd lived there. The Torre del Fiscale tower that came into view after about a kilometre was another tick on a list of new places. A notice fixed to chain-link fencing warned me to watch out for falling masonry. Made of stone and bricks, the 30-metre-high tower was built in the thirteenth century at the meeting point of the Aqua Marcia and Aqua Claudia aqueducts. Fortified against attacks, the tower was meant to allow observation over the surrounding countryside and deter the theft of crops or worse. At the tower's base, an arch under one of the two aqueducts took me onto a narrow dirt footpath, a well-kept olive grove on one side. This was at the southern edge of the Parco di

Torre Fiscale. After a few hundred metres the footpath dog-legged into a tunnel under the old Rome–Formia–Naples railway line and, soon after, followed beside an older, nineteenth-century railway, the line from Rome to Naples via Cassino. Hard going even in dry weather with firm ground under the feet, the foot-path's steep and uneven slopes would be a treacherous, muddy obstacle course after rain.

Tall arches of the Aqua Felix aqueduct appeared ahead as I climbed the last few metres. I walked through them on the foot-path, but it seemed an affront to history that a railway cutting had been dug to allow lines to pass beneath it. Nearing the top of the slope and framed in the arches, a short section of the soaring supports of the Aqua Claudia, or Claudian Aqueduct, came into view, its columns of peperino and tufa stone blocks stacked about 20 metres high offering an example of the engineering skills of the Romans who oversaw the work around the middle of the first century. And once beyond the Felix Aqueduct I faced an even more awe-inspiring sight, an unbroken length of almost a mile of the Claudian Aqueduct that stood out from a vast meadow, the grass a vivid green, the scene completely still: no people, no flocks of sheep, no packs of stray dogs, no solitary dogs, a place carrying a silent weight of the past. Six of the eleven aqueducts that were built to supply ancient Rome crossed this area in the south of the city, which would become the Parco degli Acquedotti. With the park split by the Rome–Cassino–Naples railway line, only the eastern side is easily reached by people living in buildings on nearby streets, and it was into this side of the park that I walked.

I followed the Felix Aqueduct, passing the parish church of San Policarpo, built between 1964 and 1967 when the district, then at the city's edge, was being developed and the large number of homeless people who had built a shanty settlement in the arches beneath the aqueduct was evidence of a torn social fabric. The second world war had brought a stream of refugees, fleeing along Via Casilina from the fighting that pitted German soldiers against Allied forces between Rome and Naples, and some who had used the arches to create makeshift homes would still be living in them when I moved to Rome in 1972. Dotted here and there with umbrella pines and tall, dense mimosa bushes—scented masses of bright yellow lit by sunshine—the green space, from which the *baraccati* shanty-dwellers were long gone, breathed well-being and order. After leaving the park and following a short stretch of Via Lemonia, I turned onto Circonvallazione Tuscolana and the final kilometre before Cinecittà. Lining a handful of tree-shaded streets, well-maintained four-storey blocks of apartments with broad balconies and set within small tidy gardens, are typical of many built in Rome's suburbs during the 1960s and 1970s as homes for middle-class families of bank managers, doctors, teachers, lawyers, and senior and middle-level civil servants who filled the ranks of ministries and state organisations. These streets are far more congenial than Via Tuscolana, along which developers strung buildings in the 1950s, squeezing together plain six-storey blocks whose apartments hang around reinforced concrete skeletons, and whose entrances open directly onto pavements.

Behind a high wall at the end of Circonvallazione Tuscolana, their entrance on Via Tuscolana, are the Scuola Nazionale di Cinema (National Film School) and the Cineteca Nazionale (National Film Archive), limbs of the Centro Sperimentale di Cinematografia, which, like Cinecittà itself, was founded in 1935. Cinema provides the state's strongest weapon, Mussolini had said when establishing the L'Unione Cinematografica Educativa (LUCE, educational film union) in 1924, two years after marching on Rome and seizing power. A crucial cog in the fascist propaganda machine, the Istituto Luce made newsreels to boost the Duce and his regime. A bare-chested Mussolini, filmed at a grain harvest, made an unforgettable figure when, having helped to load a threshing machine, jaw jutting and fist pumping, he proclaimed, "Oggi è una giornata di sole. Oggi è una giornata fascista." (Today the sun's shining. Today's a fascist day.) The roles of Cinecittà and the Istituto Luce would be similar in the third decade of the twenty-first century, the former responsible for running studios where films are made, the latter tasked with what politicians call the institutional and cultural side of the business.

Controlled by a film and audiovisual department at the press and propaganda ministry, Cinecittà was expected to provide what the fascist regime thought was needed to make Rome the capital of the European film industry. The studios opened in 1937 on 14 hectares of land with five of fourteen planned sound stages, and 45 hectares ready for expansion. (A further 540 hectares were acquired in 1943, but the total area of the site was reduced to 150 hectares in 1949.) Italy entered the war in June 1940 and left in September 1943, signing an armistice after the Allies had taken Sicily and advanced onto the mainland. In January 1944, when Allied forces were held up at Cassino, 140 kilometres southeast of the capital, the studios were bombed mistakenly by the United States Army Air Forces during a raid against the nearby Centocelle military airport in support of Allied landings at Anzio. Sound stages were damaged and film production halted. German forces would use buildings for storage. They would be requisitioned by the Allied Control Commission when the Allies took Rome in June 1944. Equipment had been looted and what remained was taken away by retreating German forces.

That was all far in the past when I stood at the end of Circonvallazione Tuscolana by a wall hiding the Centro Sperimentale di Cinematografia. In front of the wall, a poster behind a panel of glass in a metal frame caught my eye. Neither the poster nor its frame carried a date, but the faded colours of the poster, set against a north-facing wall, possibly to protect it from direct sunlight, suggested it had been there for several years. Headed with the title "Luoghi e personaggi della memoria—cinema" (Places and personalities from the past—cinema), it showed images of an original poster for the film *Quo Vadis*, the emperor Nero playing a harp while Rome burned in the background, the names Robert Taylor and Deborah Kerr in large print below, and two stills from the film beneath the poster advertising it. And beside the three images were explanatory notes in Italian and English about the film and its significance for Cinecittà. I had begun my morning at Santa Maria in Palmis (the church of Quo Vadis) and here in front of me, near where my walk to the studios would finish, and bookending that walk with what seemed suitable symmetry, was a reminder of the film that took Hollywood to the Tiber.

Small, discreet, almost hidden, the poster was part of a campaign the ministry of culture launched in 2007 to tell people about cinema's role in Italy's national cultural heritage. The campaign was pegged to Rome's international film festival in October the following year and enjoyed support from the city authorities, the poster carrying Rome's crowned shield badge with the letters SPQR diagonally from top left to bottom right, and Comune di Roma beneath the shield. This commemoration of the film *Quo Vadis* was placed at the corner of the Circonvallazione Tuscolana when Walter Veltroni, leftwing politician and keen cineaste, was mayor of Rome. He had been minister of culture between 1996 and 1998. According to the English explanatory note:

The first great American colossal shot in post-war years in Rome at the Cinecittà studios was *Quo Vadis*, a 1951 costume drama directed by Mervyn LeRoy (San Francisco 1900—Los Angeles 1987). The film, adapted from the novel of the same name by Henryk Sienkiewicz, a Polish writer and Nobel prize-winner for literature, is set in Imperial Rome at the time of Nero (played by an excellent Peter Ustinov). The city was completely reconstructed at Cinecittà. Indeed, this film marked, after the difficult war years, the full resumption of work at the studios on Via Tuscolana and one of their happiest and most creative periods. Aiming for a magnificence never seen before, the American studio Metro Goldwyn Mayer invested about seven million dollars to make the film, a record for the cinema at the time. Over one hundred huge sets were built and 32,000 costumes made to the designs of Herschel McCoy. Roughly 20,000 extras, 63 lions, seven bulls and 450 horses were involved in filming. Among the main interpreters, other than Peter Ustinov in the role of Nero, were Robert Taylor (Marco Vinicio, a Roman patrician and hero of the story) and Deborah Kerr (Licia, a foreign maiden with whom Vinicio was in love). The music was by the Hungarian Miklós Rózsa. According to legend, the young Sergio Leone helped in making the scene of Rome's burning, one of the film's key episodes. The film was released in 1951 but was not well received, apart from Peter Ustinov's performance, which won him a Golden Globe award as best supporting actor.

I turned the corner onto Via Tuscolana, a major artery like Via Appia Nuova, and was back into noise and air pollution and the bustle of everyday modern Rome. I had been in this part of the city about fifteen years before, visiting the studios to research an article, being taken around the backlot, shown sets that included the one built for Martin Scorsese's 2002 film *Gangs of New York*, and taken onto sound stage number five where Federico Fellini had worked. In 1997, I had written about the studios' privatisation, when state disposals were being driven by a pressing need for fiscal discipline to squeeze the lira into the European Union's single currency. Both the treasury minister Carlo Azeglio Ciampi and Walter Veltroni considered Cinecittà a non-strategic asset and an excessive burden on the public purse. However, when I visited, private-sector control wasn't yielding the results that private-sector businessmen had hoped. And in the years after my visit, the studios incurred heavy losses, were ridden with strikes, and suffered a series of major fires on sets and sound stages and in a warehouse where costumes and scenery were stored.

AFTERWORD

"The re-nationalisation of Cinecittà is a strategic operation to relaunch one of Italy's most important cultural businesses," said Dario Franceschini, the minister for culture, in January 2018. I was reminded of how Italy's loss-making national airline, and its state-owned and heavily loss-making steelmaker, food businesses, telecommunications group and much else had been considered strategic. I visited the ministry of culture's website early in 2022 and found that a cinema and audiovisual department oversaw the phoenix of Via Tuscolana. With an organisational structure of commissions and subcommissions, and the publication of departmental decrees and decisions, the bureaucracy of the ministry's department seemed to offer a different approach to film creation from that of the buccaneering spirits inhabiting and circling Hollywood. Cinecittà had recently been granted a large loan by the Cassa Depositi e Prestiti state bank.

When I reached Cinecittà I had walked about ten kilometres and had been walking for two and a half hours. None of those involved in filming *Quo Vadis* in 1950 would have undertaken such a walk. Indeed, the idea would not have arisen. The three parks I had walked across didn't exist until many years later. How different the Rome of 1950 was from mine that day seventy years later. There were no blocks of apartments behind the Centro Sperimentale di Cinematografia on Circonvallazione Tuscolana or along much of Via Tuscolana. Soon after passing beyond the Aurelian Walls at the Porta di San Giovanni, the drivers of cars carrying leading members of the cast of *Quo Vadis* and major cogs in the film's production from hotels on and around Via Veneto would have faced light traffic, the road in open country for part of the journey. But the 1930s rationalist-style entrance comprising a single-storey central gatehouse flanked by modest two-storey buildings across the road was unchanged.

Rome's second underground railway line began serving Cinecittà in 1980, and stairs down to the station are directly outside the studios, but I decided to retrace the path I'd just taken: Circonvallazione Tuscolana, Via Lemonia, the Acquedotti park, the narrow track of beaten earth through the Parco di Torre Fiscale, Via Anicio Paolino, Via Appia Nuova, Via dei Cessati Spiriti, Via Latina and the Caffarella park. I pulled open the door to the church of Santa Maria in Palmis, entered, sat on a pew, rested for a while, and then stood up to place a few coins in a collection box fixed to a candle-holder and take two votive candles from a tray. I had lit candles for family that morning when setting out for Cinecittà. Now I would light another two.

One was for the writer Irwin Shaw, who experienced the glory years of Rome's *dolce vita* and Hollywood on the Tiber. Playwright, writer of radio serials, screenwriter, novelist, Shaw was also a prolific and skilful writer of short stories, and they rank alongside those of F. Scott Fitzgerald and Ernest Hemingway. "God on Friday Night", perhaps Shaw's shortest, certainly very short but among his best, centres on the Jewish Friday night ritual of lighting candles. Shaw was Jewish, born in South Bronx to Russian immigrant parents, and when writing the story he may have drawn on memories of seeing Shabbat candles placed and lighted in candlesticks, or perhaps in menorahs, by windows of homes in Brooklyn where he grew up, and of prayers said in Yiddish. In an introduction to a collection of his short stories, Shaw wrote in 1978 that, because he was not particularly devout, his chance of salvation lay in a place sometime in the future on a library shelf. Recalling the occasions I met him around the beginning of the 1970s, and his work that I subsequently came to admire, I lit a votive candle. "Non guasta," I thought. It can't hurt.

I held the second candle, remembering the actress Deborah Kerr, star of the film *Quo Vadis*. Towards the end of January in 1972, while living and working in London, I had found myself unexpectedly at a professional and personal crossroads, and received a letter from her in mid-February to say that she had been thinking a lot about me over the previous week. "Oh God! How difficult life can be," she added. Less than a month later, after I told her I would soon be moving to Rome, Kerr wrote, "Peter and I are so happy about your new job ... it sounds absolutely perfect for you, and I do envy you being in Rome in the Spring ... it is the most divine city and Italians are really adorable people." I lit the candle and placed it in the holder. The flame weakened, steadied, then brightened and flickered strongly. I went to Rome for a six-month project and had now lived there for fifty years.

INDEX

251

INDEX

INDEX

INDEX

INDEX

INDEX

INDEX

INDEX

INDEX

INDEX

INDEX

INDEX

INDEX

INDEX

INDEX

INDEX

INDEX

INDEX

INDEX

INDEX

INDEX

INDEX

INDEX

INDEX

INDEX

INDEX